The Colonial Construction of Indian Country

Indigenous Americas
Robert Warrior, Series Editor

Chadwick Allen, *Earthworks Rising: Mound Building in Native Literature and Arts*
Chadwick Allen, *Trans-Indigenous: Methodologies for Global Native Literary Studies*
Raymond D. Austin, *Navajo Courts and Navajo Common Law: A Tradition of Tribal Self-Governance*
Lisa Brooks, *The Common Pot: The Recovery of Native Space in the Northeast*
Kevin Bruyneel, *The Third Space of Sovereignty: The Postcolonial Politics of U.S.–Indigenous Relations*
Eric Cheyfitz, *The Colonial Construction of Indian Country: Native American Literatures and Federal Indian Law*
Glen Sean Coulthard, *Red Skin, White Masks: Rejecting the Colonial Politics of Recognition*
James H. Cox, *The Red Land to the South: American Indian Writers and Indigenous Mexico*
Brendan Hokowhitu and Vijay Devadas, *The Fourth Eye: Māori Media in Aotearoa New Zealand*
Daniel Heath Justice, *Our Fire Survives the Storm: A Cherokee Literary History*
Daniel Heath Justice and Jean M. O'Brien, *Allotment Stories: Indigenous Land Relations under Settler Siege*
Emil' Keme, *Le Maya Q'atzij / Our Maya Word: Poetics of Resistance in Guatemala*
Thomas King, *The Truth About Stories: A Native Narrative*
Valerie Lambert, *Native Agency: Indians in the Bureau of Indian Affairs*
Scott Richard Lyons, *X-Marks: Native Signatures of Assent*
Aileen Moreton-Robinson, *Talkin' Up to the White Woman: Indigenous Women and Feminism*
Aileen Moreton-Robinson, *The White Possessive: Property, Power, and Indigenous Sovereignty*
Jean M. O'Brien, *Firsting and Lasting: Writing Indians out of Existence in New England*
Jamaica Heolimeleikalani Osorio, *Remembering Our Intimacies: Moʻolelo, Aloha ʻĀina, and Ea*
Shiri Pasternak, *Grounded Authority: The Algonquins of Barriere Lake against the State*
Steven Salaita, *Inter/nationalism: Decolonizing Native America and Palestine*
Leanne Betasamosake Simpson, *As We Have Always Done: Indigenous Freedom through Radical Resistance*

(continued on page 237)

THE COLONIAL CONSTRUCTION OF INDIAN COUNTRY

Native American Literatures and
Federal Indian Law

ERIC CHEYFITZ

Indigenous Americas

University of Minnesota Press
Minneapolis
London

The lives of American Indians are interwoven with the federal government. Federal ownership of tribal and individual lands, the expansive array of governmental services, the control and investment of tribal funds, the assumption of criminal jurisdiction—lives of few tribal members are untouched by the Washington bureaucracy of the Interior Department.

Vine Deloria Jr., *American Indians, American Justice*

Here it doesn't matter what was decided in the marble building in town. It doesn't matter what's written on paper. The old people are the ones who know the laws of this place, this world, laws stronger and older than America.

Linda Hogan, *Power*

Settler colonialism is a mode of sustained violence. [. . .] The violence of colonial conquest requires a vast war-making infrastructure and a complex network of institutions for justifying, rationalizing, and extending colonial violence into an occupation. Among the most potent, persistent, and least acknowledged of these is law itself. The violence of colonialism is a violence inaugurated by law.

David Correia, *An Enemy Such As This*

For Darlene Evans, whose critical insight is on every page of this book, as it has been continually on all my work for the past thirty years

The lives of American Indians are interwoven with the federal government. Federal ownership of tribal and individual lands, the expansive array of governmental services, the control and investment of tribal funds, the assumption of criminal jurisdiction—lives of few tribal members are untouched by the Washington bureaucracy of the Interior Department.

—Vine Deloria Jr., *American Indians, American Justice*

Here it doesn't matter what was decided in the marble building in town. It doesn't matter what's written on paper. The old people are the ones who know the laws of this place, this world, laws stronger and older than America.

—Linda Hogan, *Power*

Settler colonialism is a mode of sustained violence. [. . .] The violence of colonial conquest requires a vast war-making infrastructure and a complex network of institutions for justifying, rationalizing, and extending colonial violence into an occupation. Among the most potent, persistent, and least acknowledged of these is law itself. The violence of colonialism is a violence inaugurated by law.

—David Correia, *An Enemy Such As This*

CONTENTS

ACKNOWLEDGMENTS		xi
INTRODUCTION		1
ONE	The Colonial Construction of Indian Country	7
TWO	The Colonization of Native Identity through Biologic	65
THREE	Collaborative Identities	97
FOUR	Settler Colonialism and the Tyranny of Borders	137
FIVE	Trickster Logic: The Transgression of Borders	159
SIX	*Bearheart:* The End of Borders	175
NOTES		199
INDEX		229

ACKNOWLEDGMENTS

I came to the subject of this book because of my collaboration on the Navajo–Hopi land dispute with the Navajo (Diné) women of Big Mountain, (now) Arizona. In particular, my wife, Darlene Evans, and I were invited into the home of Katherine Smith, at home now in the spirit world, a longtime resister to the U.S. government's settlement of the dispute that displaced thousands of Navajos from their traditional lands, causing enduring trauma. Katherine and two of her daughters, Marie Gladue and Mary Katherine Smith, remained on what was left of their land after the Hopi tribal government, in collaboration with the feds, imposed harsh limits on Diné life, taking control of what are known as the Hopi partitioned lands. Katherine, in her traditional attachment to the land (her steadfast caretaking of it for the Holy People, as she phrased it), remains a spiritual, educational, and political inspiration for me, a model of enduring teachings and resistance in the upholding of Diné values against the oppression of settler colonialism.

Following my time at Navajo and stemming from it, I developed the methodological approach that this book represents—reading the intersection of U.S. federal Indian law and Native American literature—in a seminar I gave at the University of Pennsylvania law school. That seminar was enabled by Colin S. Diver, who was then dean of the law school. I want to thank him and the students who took the seminar—I wish I could name them all—for their committed input, which helped move this project forward. Alvaro Reyes, who attended that seminar, and after graduation from Penn law developed strong ties with the Zapatistas, has remained a friend and a supporter of my work, as I have of his. Zapatista theory and practice are an important part of this book.

Serving as an expert witness on the Ward Churchill defense team—along with Michael Yellow Bird and other Native scholars, Native students, and non-Native faculty who turned out to support Ward and more broadly Native studies at the University of Colorado at Boulder—deepened my knowledge of federal Indian law and my commitment to Indigenous studies as both theory and practice.

Over the years, collaborations with colleagues nationally and internationally have informed my work in general and this book specifically. Shari Huhndorf and I have collaborated on several projects, and her friendship, insight, and energy remain inspiring, as does that of N. Bruce

Duthu. Bruce collaborated with Shari and me on the award-winning special edition of *South Atlantic Quarterly*, "Sovereignty, Indigeneity, and the Law," which was initially given as a conference sponsored by Cornell University's American Indian and Indigenous Studies Program (AIISP), my professional and intellectual home. Thanks go to Michael Hardt, the editor of *SAQ*, for publishing the conference papers.

The first version of this book appeared as part 1 of *The Columbia Guide to American Indian Literatures of the United States since 1945*, which Columbia University Press published in 2006. The contributors to that volume—Arnold Krupat, Michael Elliott, Kimberly Blaeser, David Murray, Kendall Johnson, and Shari Huhndorf—have all inspired my work over the years. Arnold Krupat's work, which has significant citation in this book, has been generative in my understanding of Indigenous epistemologies; his friendship, which developed after we knew each other's work, has been a constant.

The imprints of my former graduate students and now colleagues, teaching in the United States and abroad—Mark Rifkin, Kendall Johnson, Alex Harmon, Lena Krian, Daniel Radus, Rebecca Macklin, and Virginia Kennedy—are on this work, as are the imprints of my AIISP colleagues Jolene Rickard, Troy Richardson, Paul Nadasdy, Kurt Jordan, and Urszula Piasta-Mansfield.

Ongoing conversations with my dear friend and colleague Neil Saccamano have not only continually informed my thinking but have also been sustaining over the years since we were in graduate school together in comparative literature at Johns Hopkins.

Conversations with my friend and former student at Georgetown University, Bill McGarvey, have been invaluable in making me think precisely about issues in this book.

My brother, Kirk Cheyfitz, is, simply put, an integral part of the life I live daily, which includes my intellectual life. Where I am, he is; his thinking and questions are interwoven with these pages.

The editors of this book, Jason Weidemann and Robert Warrior, have supported this project from its beginning, and I am grateful to them for taking it on and seeing it through. In addition to his editorial support, Robert Warrior's work, as it has been for so many scholars and students of Indigenous studies, has been important to my own.

As she did for my last book, Ashleigh Imus did the expert copyediting of the manuscript, preparing it for submission. Ann Mason composed the index.

INTRODUCTION

In 2006, Columbia University published *The Columbia Guide to American Indian Literatures of the United States since 1945*, which I edited. The guide encompassed a group of essays that read American Indian literary history from a colonialist point of view, thereby acknowledging in its collective topic that American Indian literatures—fiction, poetry, drama, and nonfiction—represent the effects of ongoing colonialism on American Indians and, crucially, resistance to it. In Chickasaw novelist, poet, and essayist Linda Hogan's novel *Solar Storms*, the Native narrator remarks: "For my people, the problem has always been this: that the only possibility of survival has been resistance."[1] By "resistance," I, following Hogan and a range of Native writers, thinkers, and activists, do not simply mean "reaction," though that is part of the definition, but also the alternative forms of sociality that have historically characterized Indigenous communities across the globe, which I will elaborate in this book. From Scott Momaday's *House Made of Dawn* (1968) to Tommy Orange's *There There* (2018), the focus is clearly on these effects and resistance. This focus goes back to the first U.S. Native novel, *Joaquin Murieta: The Celebrated California Bandit* (1854) by Cherokee author John Rollin Ridge (Yellow Bird). The focus can be read from various perspectives in that novel's immediate successors: *Wynema: A Child of the Forest* (1891) by Muscogee author S. Alice Callahan, *Cogewea: The Half-Blood* (1927) by Okanogan author Mourning Dove (Hum-Ishu-Ma), *Sundown* (1934) by Osage author John Joseph Matthews, and *The Surrounded* (1936) by Salish-Kootenai author D'Arcy McNickle. The progenitor of this literature of resistance is Pequot essayist and activist William Apess, who from the late 1820s to the mid-1830s was an eloquent advocate of Native rights.[2]

Part I of the guide, which I wrote, is a book-length monograph titled *The (Post)colonial Construction of Indian Country: U.S. American Indian Literatures and Federal Indian Law*. The present volume is an update and thus a rewriting in significant part of that work, retitled *The Colonial Construction of Indian Country: Native American Literatures and Federal Indian Law*. I have changed *(Post)colonial* to *Colonial* because in rethinking this project in light of settler colonialism (see chapter 4), I no longer think the *post-* applies, even in its parenthetical form, meant to ironize it in the first place. I also altered the title of the current book so that it does not only reference Native literatures in the United States, although the primary focus of federal Indian law is the over 340 reservations in the lower forty-eight states, the territory legally defined as Indian Country. Now, the book references, crucially, Inuit filmmaker Zacharias Kunuk and Tlingit author Nora Marks Dauenhauer as well as Hawaiian scholar and activist Haunani-Kay Trask, while noting that the 228 Alaska Native villages come under a different legal agenda articulated in the Alaska Native Claims Settlement Act of 1971; and Native Hawaiians, while certainly a colonized population since the 1890s, have not formalized a legal relationship with the federal government. Further, I have included material from Indigenous communities in Mexico and Bolivia that bears on issues of sovereignty and law currently at play in both the United States and Canada, where the work of Yellow Knives Dene scholar Glenn Coulthard is also important. My reference to such examples is expressed in the title by *Native American Literatures* (Indigenous literatures from across the Americas). Although my primary focus is on American Indian literatures of the United States, the importance of this work from Canada and Latin America suggests that the study of Indigenous literatures is a comparative project, as the work of Chadwick Allen has emphasized.[3]

As with the first iteration of this work, this one is not intended to be comprehensive (an impossible task in any event, given the breadth and depth of American Indian literatures and the hundreds of cases of federal Indian law) but exemplary: a method of reading both American Indian literatures and federal Indian law, which argues a necessary conjunction of the two. In arguing for this conjunction, I have organized this book to provide both exemplary close readings of literary texts that critically represent federal Indian law as well as an analysis of the history of federal Indian law that, while not tied explicitly to any literary text, is meant to provide an overall context for American Indian literatures.

Crow–Creek Sioux scholar, novelist, and poet Elizabeth Cook-Lynn insists on the importance of federal Indian law in forming the fundamental context for Native American studies, emphasizing that "the study of [the 'machinations of the government and the courts'] should be at the core of curricular development."[4] Following Cook-Lynn, and emphasizing that treaties between the United States and

Indian nations are the ground of federal Indian law, I want to focus immediately on two essays in Abraham Chapman's 1975 anthology *Literature of the American Indians*. Without commenting on their implications for the field of Native American literatures, Chapman reprints essays by Americanists Constance Rourke ("The Indian Background of American Theatricals") and Lawrence C. Wroth ("The Indian Treaty as Literature") that suggest one form of the intimacy of law and literature.[5] In a book published posthumously in 1942, Rourke remarks that the pre–Revolutionary War treaties negotiated between colonists and Indians "are in truth our first American plays," a collaborative "poetry of a high order."[6] Without crediting it, Rourke seems to be taking off from the Wroth essay published in 1928, which designates "these printed documents as the single original American contribution to the types of literary expression." Wroth sees in the "dramatic form" of the treaty a play of conflicting ways of life between Natives and settlers— what amounts to a classic drama of colonialism.[7]

Both essays point to a rich potential field of study: federal Indian law as a collaborative American literature, in which the term "collaboration" would be understood in the nuanced range of its meanings from cooperation to coercion. Wroth is particularly interested in the treaties between the Six Nations of the Iroquois (Haudenosaunee) Confederacy and the English colonists at a time when the Iroquois held the "balance of power" between the English and the French.[8] That balance ended with the English victory in the French and Indian War in 1763, a necessary prelude to the American Revolution and the subsequent demise of Iroquois power in the context of U.S. expansionist politics, where it had no longer a strategic part to play, although Michael Leroy Oberg notes that in 1794, "at the time the call went out from the American government to invite the Six Nations to a council [at Canandaigua, New York], the United States feared that the Iroquois warriors might join a powerful Indian confederacy north of the Ohio River that had already defeated two American armies."[9]

Wroth sees in the prerevolutionary colonial dramas, where the Iroquois and the settlers have a relative parity of power, nevertheless a "tragedy" of colonial politics, for "it is possible to hold the balance of power and be at the same time the corn between the mill-stones" of European political machinations.[10] In these dramas the meaning of "collaboration" seems to emphasize cooperation. Yet as Wroth suggests, if at this moment cooperation is the explicit meaning, coercion is the word's implicit sense: "The Indian knew his doom was upon him, but he suffered no man to hustle him along the path."[11] As his melodramatic language suggests, for Wroth, the treaty was a classical tragedy, with fate as the principal engine, whereas in a colonial context, we can read it as a documentary drama of cultural conflict, the prelude to genocide and resistance, over land within the context of global European competition for markets.

Wroth calls our attention not only to the content of the law as drama—the Indian treaty as intercultural dialogue (and I should emphasize here that under the U.S. Constitution, the treaty has the status of the supreme law of the land)—but also to the form of the law as the expressive matrix of that content. If for Wroth the content represents a balance of power between the Iroquois and the English, then in the matter of form, the Indians held sway:

> For the Indian of the of the Long House the dance of life went to a rhythm that reached back through centuries of ceremonial observance. Wherefore in the business of treaty-making he forced upon the white people the rigidly formal conference familiar in the day of his fathers and in the old time before the stranger was known in the land. To deal satisfactorily with him in treaty, the English and Dutch, matter-of-fact in affairs of court and camp, were compelled to adapt themselves to a procedure entirely foreign to their instincts and casual practices.[12]

In spite of the ethnocentricities of Wroth's perspective here (his blindness to the ceremonial form of European contracts so that he understands the Indian ceremony as "rigidly formal," in contrast to the "casual practices" of Europeans), he points usefully to these prerevolutionary treaties as mixed, or collaborative, forms, written in English but incorporating Native oral traditions. Such incorporation of or attention to Indian oral forms would diminish as the collaborative treaty-making process became increasingly over time an exercise in European coercion of Indians rather than cooperation between cultures. But the notion of a collaborative, or mixed, writing (a writing in dialogue with oral tradition) points suggestively to the position of Native writing itself in a colonial situation. As Abenaki critic and writer Joseph Bruchac puts it, "Expression of traditional values in the language of the oppressor has been one of the results of introducing a European written language into predominantly oral cultures. As is the case with African literature,

Native American oral traditions and traditional values have breathed new energy into the adopted language."[13] As Native writing has developed from the nineteenth to the twenty-first centuries—from *Wynema*, which is conflicted in its dialogue with Native and Euramerican values, to *There There*—traditional Native values have come to dominate Native literatures.

In focusing on the collaborative drama of treaty making, Wroth inevitably calls our attention to the crucial problem of translation in the field of Native American literatures. At the treaty conferences, "the speeches, of course, were delivered through interpreters, and when the interpreter was a man of imagination, the figurative language of the natives was done justice."[14] The relationship of interpreters to "justice" (rendering accurately the Native diplomatic jargon) is, of course, not simply a formal but also a political matter. The very process of translation reminds us that to gain representation, both literary and political, in the treaty, one had to appear in the form of written English. How many Indians who were thus represented could read the texts that were representing them? Extremely few. Thus, even when the content of these early treaties between the Iroquois and the English refers to a cooperative collaboration based on a balance of power (not the absence of conflict, it is important to emphasize, but its containment), the form of the treaties as written English suggests coercion.

If, as Wroth and Rourke argue, the Indian treaty is the archetypal American literature, then it is precisely because the form and content articulate the colonial situation, where Indian communities are subject to, even as they resist, cultural, social, economic, and political translation. What is true of the form and content of the Indian treaty specifically is true of federal Indian law in general, of which the treaty is both prelude and basis. Within a Western legal framework, Native American tribes rightly claim sovereignty because the treaty by definition recognizes the parties to the contract as independent foreign nations. But increasingly, as we will read in what follows, from the Constitution forward, the U.S. government in acts of Congress and Supreme Court decisions compromised this sovereignty, until in 1871 Congress interdicted any further treaty making with Indian tribes, thus confirming Chief Justice Marshall's oxymoronic definition of the tribes as "domestic dependent nations," formulated in 1831 in *Cherokee Nation v. Georgia*.[15]

This colonial dynamic of translation, represented significantly in the agonistic structure of federal Indian law, has been the major theme of U.S. Native American writing from its appearance in published form in the late eighteenth century to the present. Federal Indian law has thus been the indispensable text and context to an understanding of U.S. Native American oral and written expression.

THE COLONIAL CONSTRUCTION OF INDIAN COUNTRY

American Indians, who are the Native Americans living in the lower forty-eight states, are the largest part of the Native American population in the United States, and the only part governed by federal Indian law in terms of its largest provenance: land. Both Alaska Natives and Native Hawaiians distinguish themselves terminologically from American Indians, where U.S. federal Indian law provides the legal structure for colonialism as it operates in Indian Country, which is both a legal and a colloquial designation for reservation lands and allotments still held in trust by the federal government. Since 1971 Alaska Natives have come under a different legal agenda with the instantiation of the Alaska Native Claims Settlement Act, which created regional and village corporations that hold Alaska Native lands in freehold, as opposed to the "trust" relationship between Indian nations and the federal government, in which the government holds, for the most part, reservation land and some allotments in a trustee relationship with the 347 federally recognized Indian nations in the lower forty-eight states, though twenty of these nations do not have reservations.[1] For the most part, Native Hawaiians have no formal legal relationship with the federal government, so information about this group is not present on the Bureau of Indian Affairs (BIA) website, which suggests an erasure of Native Hawaiians in the colonial history of the United States. However, both Alaska Natives and Native Hawaiians are affected by colonialism,[2] which is a fact across Native America in both the United States and Canada, where it is also structured by Canadian federal Indian law. Joanne Barker elaborates:

> Today some understand "Native American" to include American Indians, Alaskan Natives, and Native Hawaiians, that is, all of the descendants of the original inhabitants of what are now the fifty states. However, many Native Hawaiians reject this inclusion

because they do not want to be placed under the administration of the BIA as "nations within." They prefer to be recognized under the United Nations' classification of Hawai'i as a nation illegally occupied by the United States that qualifies for decolonization.[3]

In a speech given on September 8, 2000, at a ceremony on the 175th anniversary of the BIA, Kevin Gover, a Comanche tribal member issued "a formal apology to Indian people for the historical conduct of this agency," "the first mission" of which, Gover stated, "was to execute the removal of the south-eastern tribal nations. By threat, deceit, and force, these great tribal nations were made to march 1,000 miles to the west, leaving thousands of their old, their young, and their infirm in hasty graves along the Trail of Tears. [. . .] And so today I stand before you," Gover continued, "as the leader of an institution that in the past has committed acts so terrible that they infect, diminish, and destroy the lives of Indian peoples decades later, generations later."[4] Diane Glancy's novel *Pushing the Bear* details through a representation of the voices of the Cherokees on the Trail the human suffering of those who walked the Trail and their consciousness of the laws that removed them there.[5]

Gover references the Trail within a history of the BIA, which it is necessary to outline not only to understand the context and ramifications of his speech but also because key texts in American Indian literature are a direct response to the machinations of the BIA, as I will detail. Indeed, all of American Indian literature, like *Pushing the Bear*, is necessarily written within the boundary of the BIA even as it acts to live beyond that boundary. The Bureau of Indian Affairs was established by President James Madison in 1824 as part of the Department of War. In 1832, Congress authorized the president to appoint a commissioner of Indian Affairs; in 1834, Congress enacted a law to officially organize a Department of Indian Affairs. In 1849, the BIA was transferred from the Department of War to the newly created Department of the Interior. By the 1850s, overseeing Indian reservations had become its principal arena of activity, as it continues to be today.[6] In this context, the term "colonialism" has a broad meaning: control by the federal government over Indian Country, which is centrally defined by the trust relationship. This relationship between the tribes and the federal government is at best a double-edged sword. While ostensibly guaranteeing federal protection of Indian assets, principally land, it also casts these nations legally in the role of subordinate sovereigns ("domestic dependent nations"), an oxymoron I will elaborate in what follows. Thus, Indian nations find this land placed in the hands of a federal bureaucracy overseen by Congress, which has historically grossly mismanaged it—if we understand by mismanagement not simply dereliction of duty through incompetence or venality but enactment of federal policies destructive of Native life, materially and spiritually.

A major aspect of this mismanagement finally came to light on June 10, 1996, in a class-action lawsuit brought in the district court of the District of Columbia by Blackfeet tribal member Elouise Cobell and other Native American representatives against two departments of the United States government, the Department of Interior and the Department of the Treasury, for mismanagement of Indian trust funds created under the General Allotment, or Dawes, Act of 1887—itself an act of federal "mismanagement" performed in the name of "civilizing" the Indians. This act "authorized [the president of the United States], whenever in his opinion any reservation or any part thereof of such Indians is advantageous for agricultural and grazing purposes, to cause said reservation, or any part thereof, to be surveyed, or resurveyed if necessary, and to allot the lands in said reservation in severalty to any Indian located thereon" in parcels ranging from 160 to 40 acres.[7] The result of this act was to reduce Native communal land holdings by 90 million acres through the sale to non-Natives of so-called "surplus" lands left over from the allotments as well as through the sales of Native allotments. The act intensified Native poverty in an attempt to force Indians to assimilate to the Western system of property (individual ownership) for which they were unprepared—hence the many sales of allotments. The fact of the allotment act, then, was the massive impoverishment of Indian communities for the benefit of western development. In pushing Congress to annul the Dawes Act, which it did in 1934 with the Wheeler-Howard Act, known as the Indian Reorganization Act (IRA),[8] John Collier, commissioner of Indian Affairs, sent a memo to Congress that tabulated the Native loss: "Through sales by the Government of the fictitiously designated 'surplus' lands; through sales by allottees after the trust period had ended or had been terminated by administrative act; and through sales by the Government of heirship land, virtually mandatory under the allotment act: Through these three methods, the total of Indian landholdings has been cut from 138,000,000 acres in 1887 to 48,000,000 acres in 1934."[9] Collier noted in the same memo, which was incorporated into the IRA: "The approximately one third of the Indians who as yet are outside the allotment system are not losing their property; and generally they are increasing in industry and are rising, not falling, in the social scale."[10] As Chippewa legal scholar Keith Richotte Jr. notes: "Although many reservations were allotted many were only partially so and some escaped the process altogether."[11] I will have much to say about this situation in what follows.[12] The federal government holds in trust 55.7 million acres of Indian land, 80 percent of which is reservation land; the remainder is in individual trust allotments.[13]

A January 23, 2007, summary of the *Cobell* case by John Ahni Schertow on the *International Cry* website notes that the suit intended

> to force the federal government to account for billions of dollars belonging to approximately 500,000 American Indians and their heirs, and held in trust since the late 19th century.[14]
>
> Through document discovery and courtroom testimony, the case has revealed mismanagement, ineptness, dishonesty and delay by federal officials, leading U.S. District Judge Royce Lamberth to declare their conduct "fiscal and governmental irresponsibility in its purest form."
>
> Then–Secretary of the Interior Bruce Babbitt, Assistant Secretary of the Interior Kevin Gover and Treasury Secretary Robert Rubin were held in contempt of court in February 1999 by Judge Lamberth for their departments' repeated delays in producing documents, destruction of relevant documents and misrepresentations to the court in sworn testimony. [. . .]
>
> In April/May of 2005, a national tribal task force working group formed to provide recommendations to the SCIA [Senate Committee on Indian Affairs] and the House Resources Committee [. . .] including a settlement number of $27.5 billion, to Congress. . . . [In July 2006], [Senator John] McCain, [chair of the SCIA], propose[d] an $8 billion settlement.[15]

Wikipedia summarizes the fate of Judge Lamberth: "On July 11, 2006, the U.S. Court of Appeals for the District of Columbia Circuit, siding with the government, removed Judge Lamberth from the case—finding that Lamberth had lost his objectivity. 'We conclude, reluctantly, that this is one of those rare cases in which reassignment is necessary,' the judges wrote."[16] The Court of Appeals judges acted here on the assumption, in accordance with the agonistic structure of Western law, that there are two sides to every story and that Lamberth had been favoring one with his comments about the "racist and imperialist government that should have been buried a century ago."[17] But his words merely condense the history of U.S. Indian policy—a policy both implementing and rationalizing genocide. There is in fact no question about this history, so there are not two valid sides to this story. Thus, the agonistic format of Western law is inappropriate for framing this case. Rather, if the case had not been presented under the auspices of a colonial body of law, it should have been presented in terms of restorative justice, a traditional, Indigenous mode of customary law wherein those transgressed against meet with the transgressor and negotiate the terms of restitution within which balance can be restored to the community. Legal scholar Brendan Tobin notes "the importance of customary law as an instrument for decolonizing inherited common and civil law regimes."[18] In the *Cobell* case, as is the case with the totality of federal Indian law, restoring balance to the community through restorative justice would mean, as I will argue, complete decolonization—that is, erasure of federal Indian law, which is the very structure of U.S. colonial relations with Native nations.

If the United States had recognized even a modicum of restorative justice for its mismanagement of American Indian resources, then it could at least have accepted the award of $27.5 billion proposed by the Native task force in the *Cobell* case. But as Richotte notes: "Eventually Congress stepped in and, with negotiations among the involved parties, crafted legislation to resolve the issue. Passed in 2010, the Claims Resolution Act set aside $3.4 billion to accomplish a number of goals. [. . .] The final total of the Claims Resolution Act was well short of the over $46 billion that some estimated the federal government owed the plaintiffs."[19] James Warren, in an article written at the time of settlement, notes: "The facts are these: Following the House's approval, the Senate is considering whether to approve a $3.4 billion settlement of a 15-year-old lawsuit, alleging the government illegally withheld more than $150 billion from Indians whose lands were taken in the 1880s to lease to oil, timber, minerals and other companies for a fee."[20] Whatever the actual figure of the money missing from the accounts of hundreds of thousands of American Indians is—$150 billion, $46 billion, $27.5 billion, or the $8 billion suggested by Senator McCain—$3.4 billion represents the typical short-changing that is an endemic part of the history of U.S.–Indian legal settlements, whether in treaties (most of which have been broken at one time or another), court cases, or statutes. The United States, including Alaska and Hawaii, is built on stolen Native land; the worth of that land can only be assessed as being trillions upon trillions of dollars, but the cost in Native lives lost in defending it from invading settlers and the federal government is incalculable.

The Sacred White Turkey, published in 2010 by Lakota novelist Frances Washburn, is centrally involved with the focus of the *Cobell* case: the mismanagement of Indian trust funds (Individual Indian Money Accounts), though in Washburn's novel there is no doubt that the "mismanagement" is embezzlement, which may well have been the case in fact as well as fiction—though this angle, unsurprisingly, was not pursued by the government. The novel, published in the same year as the *Cobell* settlement, never mentions the case. The novel's action takes place thirty-three years before *Cobell* in 1963 on the Pine Ridge Reservation, home of the Oglala Lakota. However, the action of the novel is narrated from the perspective of 2008, near the climax of the case, by one of its two principal narrators, the granddaughter, Stella, of the other principal narrator, Hazel, a skeptical practitioner of Lakota medicine, who owns the allotment that is the focus of the novel's action.

Hazel eventually uncovers an embezzlement scheme being run by George Wanbli, a tribal member and rival of Hazel's in the practice of medicine, who works for the BIA as the bureaucrat in charge of the accounts of tribal members who are leasing their allotments to mostly white farmers because, like Hazel, they "hadn't the money or the credit to buy the equipment that farming would take."[21] But even before Hazel uncovers the scheme, she is primed to be suspicious because of the colonial situation of tribal nations and Wanbli's manipulation of this situation, blurring the line between medicine man and bureaucrat. Hazel says categorically: "I do not trust the government, federal, state, local, or tribal. Of course I do not trust George, either, as the head and administrator of the lease program"—and, the novel makes clear, as a practitioner of medicine.[22] So when Wanbli decides to distribute the allottees' checks by mail instead of in person, Hazel remarks:

> I was not even particularly upset about all this. Such things as this happen all the time when you are dealing with tribal officials or the Bureau of Indian Affairs, and nothing surprising about that when you think that most tribal government systems are modeled after the United States federal system and look at the breaking of the

Christian's ten commandments that goes on up there, even though until recently, a lot of those offices had an oversized display of those ten commandments displayed in a prominent place. You can hear the sound of words and ethics being smashed all the way to the moon and back. Our tribe does the same thing; we just do it bilingual, throwing in a little breakage of traditional spiritual practice as well as Christian commandments, which makes iniquitous, illegal, immoral practices doubly double dealing.[23]

As this sketch of *The Sacred White Turkey* suggests, if readers want to understand the historical context of the novel, which is to say *if they want to understand the novel,* they need to know the *Cobell* case and its context, which represents the colonial condition of tribal nations.

As it functions, the trust relationship, in addition to being continually violated by the United States, contradicts what since 1975, with the passage of the Indian Self-Determination and Education Assistance Act, has been the stated federal policy of increased "self-determination" for Indian tribes.[24] Yet the tribes rightly resist any congressional attempts to dissolve the trust relationship (indeed, only Congress has the authority to do so) because all such attempts—the Dawes Act of 1887, and the termination and relocation policy enacted by Congress in the 1950s and 1960s—have only offered the dismemberment of the tribes and the dispersal of tribal lands as an alternative.

As noted, the Dawes Act gave the president the power to translate Indian communal land into property and to turn Indians into individual property holders. The act was meant to compel Indians to become individuals—that is, competitive and acquisitive persons pitted against one another in a market economy—through the socialization process of property ownership. To borrow words from Laguna author Leslie Marmon Silko's novel *Ceremony,* which is set in Indian Country in the post–World War II period but nevertheless echoes the federal ethos of the allotment era, allotment, reproduced in the era of termination, tried to compel Indians to displace words like "we" and "us" with "I."[25] Quoting Merrill E. Gates's comments made to the "Friends of the Indian" at the Lake Mohonk Conference in 1900, President Theodore Roosevelt described allotment in his message to Congress of December 3, 1901, as "'a mighty pulverizing engine for breaking up the tribal mass' whereby 'some sixty thousand Indians have already become citizens of the United States.'"[26] As if to emphasize the social force of allotment in its effort to displace Indian communalism with Western individualism, along with the act came an official renaming program that replaced traditional Indian names with Western names that would redefine the kinship-based family in terms of the Western nuclear family for the purposes of land ownership and inheritance.[27]

In order to understand the violence allotment visited on Indian land and people, a violence precisely reproduced in the termination era, I want to analyze further the radical difference between Native land and what the West terms "property."

U.S. federal Indian law is grounded in the history of Western imperialism in the Americas and thereby in what were and remain the central issues in the resistance of Native nations to European powers: land and sovereignty. It is not only that the Euramericas are built on stolen Native land but also that the traditional Native relation to that land has always constituted a set of practices based in values radically opposed to what was emerging in sixteenth-century Western Europe as a capitalist relation to land, particularly in England, where, by certain accounts, that capitalist relation had been developing since the thirteenth century.[28] Hawaiian scholar and activist Haunani-Kay Trask summarizes the conflict: "The constant fighting over land and water that we see throughout Indian Country, in Hawai'i, New Zealand, Australia, and other parts of the world is played out in the language of property law. The inevitable conflict between land that is collectively held and land that is individually owned will never cease because it is a conflict between cultures whose values are directly opposed."[29] This conflict is at the core of Native American literatures and among its many compelling representations is powerfully focused in the work of Linda Hogan. In her novel of Native women's resistance to Western environmental destruction, *Solar Storms*, the narrator, Angela, a young Native woman returning to her community after a life alienated in white foster homes, speaks of the conjuncture of that life with the traumatized life of her mother, Hannah Wing, broken by the same capitalist system, which led to the abandonment of her daughter: "My beginning was Hannah's beginning, one of broken lives, gone animals, trees felled and kindled. Our beginnings were intricately bound up in the history of the land. I already knew that in the nooks of America, the crannies of marble buildings, my story unfolded. [. . .] It was the systems we ended up fighting. But it went even farther back than that, to houses of law with their unkept treaties."[30]

In her book of environmental essays, *Dwellings: A Spiritual History of the Living World,* Hogan writes what could be a comment on that passage from *Solar Storms:* "Here is a lesson: what happens to people and what happens to the land is the same thing."[31] The "systems we [Native people] ended up fighting" are systems of property. Western law is grounded in property rights. The treaties that are the ground of the law are documents that translate Native land into property. A key Supreme Court case in this process of translation, a 1988 case that can be read as exemplary of the passages just cited, is *Lyng v. Norwest Indian Cemetery Protective Association.*[32] Justice Sandra Day O'Connor sums up the conflict in the case between property and Native land in declaring the opinion of the Court: "This case requires us to consider whether the First Amendment's Free Exercise Clause prohibits the Government from permitting timber harvesting in, or constructing a road through, a portion of a National Forest that has traditionally been used for religious purposes by members of three American Indian tribes [Yurok, Karok, and Tolowa] in northwestern California. We conclude that it does not."[33] In essence, what the decision in this case asserts is that the government's property rights supersede Native rights to use the land traditionally in spiritual practice.

In his dissent, Justice William Brennan focuses the violence of translation in the case: "As the Forest Service's commissioned study, the Theodoratus Report, explains, for Native Americans religion is not a discrete sphere of activity separate from all others, and any attempt to isolate the religious aspects of Indian life 'is in reality an exercise which forces Indian concepts into non-Indian categories.' Thus, for most Native Americans, '[t]he area of worship cannot be delineated from social, political, cultur[al], and other areas o[f] Indian lifestyle.'"[34] The report thus makes the point that there is no separate category of religion in Native life but that the sacred and the secular are synonymous. Brennan continues to elaborate the Native relation to land:

> A pervasive feature of this lifestyle is the individual's relationship with the natural world; this relationship, which can accurately though somewhat incompletely be characterized as one of stewardship, forms the core of what might be called, for want of a better nomenclature, the Indian religious experience. While traditional Western religions view creation as the work of a deity 'who institutes natural laws which then govern the operation of physical nature,'

tribal religions regard creation as an on-going process in which they are morally and religiously obligated to participate. Native Americans fulfill this duty through ceremonies and rituals designed to preserve and stabilize the earth and to protect humankind from disease and other catastrophes. Failure to conduct these ceremonies in the manner and place specified, adherents believe, will result in great harm to the earth and to the people whose welfare depends upon it.[35]

Hogan's dictum, quoted previously, parses this passage: "Here is a lesson: what happens to people and what happens to the land is the same thing." One notices as well that Brennan takes pains to note that his translation of Native concepts is imperfect, which emphasizes the cultural differences that the Court is ignoring in its decision—a reversal of the decisions of the lower federal courts that found for the Indians.

Brennan continues in his dissent to make a crucial distinction between property and Native land:

The site-specific nature of Indian religious practice derives from the Native American perception that land is itself a sacred, living being. Rituals are performed in prescribed locations not merely as a matter of traditional orthodoxy, but because land, like all other living things, is unique, and specific sites possess different spiritual properties and significance. Within this belief system, therefore, land is not fungible; indeed, at the time of the Spanish colonization of the American Southwest, "all [. . .] Indians held in some form a belief in a sacred and indissoluble bond between themselves and the land in which their settlements were located."[36]

Property is "fungible," able to be bought and sold, whereas Native land is not, precisely because it is "living," an integral part of Native kinship systems. Note that Brennan is careful to distinguish Native "stewardship" of the land from ownership, which is the prime relationship of the property complex.

Above, I use the key but by no means transparent word "traditional" in describing the Native relation to land. This word inevitably comes into play in relation to Indigenous peoples in the contexts of the cultural ruptures that occurred because of the European invasion that began in 1492 and that continue under the name of globalization. Marshall Sahlins has defined "tradition" "as a *culturally specific mode of change.*"³⁷ Following Sahlins, Arnold Krupat has defined it as "the means by which changes are integrated into what has been known before."³⁸ Following Sahlins and Krupat, I use "traditional" in the present context not to denote unchanging cultural practices, the notion of which is in any case a fiction because all societies are dynamic and typically interactive, that is to say, historical; but rather to signify an ongoing resistance marshaled in the postinvasion period against the European translation of Native land—the inalienable ground of Indigenous economic, social, and cultural life constructed through kinship relations—into property: land commodified and thus made alienable through its fungibility.³⁹

Such Native resistance is exemplified in the present by the continued refusal of the Sioux Nation to accept from the federal government a monetary settlement for what was judged by the Supreme Court in 1980 to be an illegal taking of the Black Hills in 1877.⁴⁰ Lumbee legal scholar David E. Wilkins notes:

> Despite an apparently impressive monetary award in the amount of 105 million dollars, plus the earlier approved [by the U.S. Court of Claims] 17.5 million, today's 60,000 constituted Lakota people [...] have thus far refused to accept any payment. [...] Meanwhile, the award for the taking of the Black Hills rests in the Federal Treasury where interest continues to accrue. It is now [as of 1997] estimated at 350 million dollars.⁴¹

Wikipedia notes that as of 2011, the award was "valued at over $1 billion."⁴² In spite of pressing poverty in the Sioux communities, the Black Hills, central to their identity as a people, are not fungible. That is, the land is not a commodity that can be traded in a market but rather is the very matrix of an historic community. It is this Native view of the relationship between land and community that I term traditional. For Tlingit poet Nora Marks Dauenhauer, the traditional is an "enduring relationship between the Tlingit people, the fish [centrally salmon] and animals, and the land, and the connection of all these to our social structure, [which] took many generations to evolve."⁴³ Originally, then, Tlingit social structure existed in a space beyond the commodification that establishes the capitalist market. Thus, Tlingit resistance, as Dauenhauer understands it, is composed in the continual struggle with capitalism to maintain that social structure: "With the arrival of Euro-Americans, many Tlingit and other Alaska Native people were separated from their land and resource base. For example, many canneries were built at the mouth of salmon streams traditionally claimed by Tlingit clans and used for subsistence fishing. Tlingit people historically practiced subsistence hunting, fishing, and logging without dominating or destroying the natural resources."[44] The conflict is clear between capitalist domination and Native subsistence. The former lives *against* "the natural resources" and ultimately, as we are witnessing in the Anthropocene, destroying them. The latter traditionally lives in cooperation *with* them and struggles to make the West understand both in activist movements, some of which I will reference in what follows, and in Indigenous literatures that the only way to continue living is to adopt an ethics of subsistence.

Central to the traditional Native relationship with the world is the part that land plays in forming Native identity. Anishinaabe novelist Louise Erdrich makes this relationship and the threat to it posed by federal Indian law the focus of her 2020 Pulitzer Prize–winning novel, *The Night Watchman*. The action of the novel, which is grounded in the experience of Erdrich's grandfather, Patrick Gourneau, takes place in 1953 on the Turtle Mountain Chippewa reservation in North Dakota, where Erdrich is an enrolled member of the tribe, and concerns the attempts of members of the community to stop the termination of their reservation from being enacted under the policy created by House Concurrent Resolution 108, passed by Congress in July 1953, "thereby initiating a termination policy movement in the 1950s that lasted through the early 1960s. [. . .] Although the measure was not enforceable as law, it expressed congressional approval for the federal government to redefine imperative, fundamental changes in Indian policy."[45] In the novel's afterword, Erdrich gives us the results of termination, which officially came to an end in 1970 under the Nixon administration: "In all, 113 tribal nations suffered the disaster of termination; 1.4 million acres of tribal land was lost. Wealth flowed to private corporations, while many people in terminated tribes died early, in poverty. Not one tribe profited. By the end, 78 tribal nations, including the Menominee [. . .] regained federal recognition; 10 gained state but not federal recognition; 31 tribes are landless; 24 are considered extinct."[46]

As a result of termination and the relocation of American Indians that followed, 72 percent of Native Americans, both enrolled and non-enrolled members of Native nations, now live in urban areas.[47] The policy, implemented incrementally through distinct congressional acts, resulted in the further erosion of tribal sovereignty not only through the termination of "approximately 109 tribes and bands" and the loss of "about 3.2 per cent" of trust land[48] but also through the transfer of areas of tribal and federal jurisdiction, such as criminal law, to particular states in the form of Public Law 280, passed in 1953.[49] "Although the great majority of Indian spokesmen were opposed to the legislation," the law went forward until—in the face of pantribal resistance, particularly that of the National Congress of American Indians (NCAI), founded in 1944, and governmental policy shifts beginning in the Kennedy administration—termination was officially abandoned during, and with the support of, the Nixon administration.[50] Still, "termination stands as a chilling reminder to Indian peoples that Congress can unilaterally decide to extinguish the special status and rights of tribes without Indian consent and without even hearing Indian views."[51]

Thomas Wazhashk, the figure of Erdrich's grandfather in the novel, sees this "chilling reminder": "the passage of [the termination] bill indicated Congress was fed up with Indians. Again."[52] This "again" has numerous referents, which Thomas has no need to elaborate, from preemptive war to statute law. Within this context, the force of termination fragmented targeted Native communal land, dissolved the trust relationship with the dissolution of targeted reservations, and forced the targeted Indians to become property-holding individuals or displaced them entirely. Termination is the clear successor and companion to allotment, which in the process of fragmentation, as noted, left 90 million acres of Native land to be sold as surplus by the federal government. Just as allotment had been, termination was an attack on Native identity, which is intrinsic to the land. Thinking to himself about the pending termination bill, which he is determined to resist, Thomas concisely articulates the attack and its "unbelievable intent. Unbelievable because the unthinkable was couched in such innocuous dry language. Unbelievable because the intent was, finally, to unmake, to unrecognize. To erase as Indians him, Biboon [his father], Rose [his wife], his children, his people, *all of us invisible and as if we never were here, from the beginning, here.*"[53] As with allotment, the government couches this process of "erasure" in the euphemism of "emancipation."[54] But it is clear that emancipation means extermination.

Published at the end of the termination–relocation period, Kiowa author N. Scott Momaday's landmark novel *House Made of Dawn*

(1968) charts in its second half the impoverished urban Indian landscape of relocation in post–World War II Los Angeles. In his novel *There There*, published in 2018, Tommy Orange, an enrolled member of the Cheyenne and Arapaho tribes of Oklahoma, represents the result of termination-relocation in the present day among the Native residents of Oakland, California, Orange's hometown, who are struggling in various ways with ruptures of identity embedded in their separation from homelands. In the final section of the novel's prologue, "Urbanity," Orange writes about this separation as if it is not a separation at all:

> Urban Indians were the generation born in the city. We've been moving for a long time, but the land moves with you like memory. An Urban Indian belongs to the city, and cities belong to the earth. Everything here is formed in relation to every other living and nonliving things from the earth. All our relations. The process that brings anything to its current form—chemical, synthetic, technological, or otherwise—doesn't make the product not a product of the living earth. [. . .] Cities form in the same way as galaxies. Urban Indians feel at home walking in the shadow of a downtown building. We came to know the downtown Oakland skyline better than we did any sacred mountain range. [. . .] We know the sound of the freeway better than we do rivers. [. . .] We know the smell of gas and freshly wet concrete and burned rubber better than we do the smell of cedar or sage or even fry bread—which isn't traditional, like reservations aren't traditional, but nothing is original, everything comes from something that came before, which was once nothing. Everything is new and doomed. [. . .] Being Indian has never been about returning to the land. The land is everywhere or nowhere.[55]

Is this rationalization for the dispossession of termination, or is it resistance—the virtual possession of the cities sprung from the land, which is always the ground from which everything grows, both rural and urban? The passage deconstructs the "traditional" in a familiar Derridean move of infinite regress. The word "doomed" adds a fatalistic note to the passage, which begins with the birth of Native urbanity as a grounded response to termination: we are still on the land. The novel, however, ends in doom: mass Indian-on-Indian violence at the Oakland powwow, with the last sentence striking an ironic note of virtual hope. This sentence focuses on Tony Loneman, also the first character we meet in the novel. He is a Cheyenne Native, facially deformed from fetal alcohol syndrome, acutely aware of his people's dispossession. At the end of *There There,* Tony is dying from gunshots, the result of his participation in an attempted robbery of the powwow, from which, at the last moment, when uncontrollable violence has erupted, he tries to pull away: "Tony isn't going anywhere. And somewhere in there, inside him, where he is, where he'll always be, even now it is morning, and the birds, the birds are singing."[56] *There There* ends, then, ambivalently, both in termination, Tony's, and a beginning where "the birds are singing."

In reading American Indian literature and its central engagement with land, readers should be clear that under federal Indian law, any tribe occupying reservation land is considered a "dependent Indian community" in relation to the federal government, most of whose land the federal government holds in trust. Further, as readers can understand through enactments like allotment and termination, through novels like *The Sacred White Turkey* and *The Night Watchman,* and through cases like *Lyng,* the federal government treats land as property—that is to say, as fungible. There are also tribes, like the Oklahoma Cherokees, numerically the largest in the United States, that, while not occupying a reservation per se, still come under federal superintendence and are thus considered a "dependent Indian community." In carrying out U.S. Indian policy today, the BIA counts on the collaboration of elected tribal councils, which were first put into place under the auspices of the IRA. The decision whether or not to adopt IRA-sponsored constitutions was left up to the tribes. At the time, 181 tribes voted to adopt them and 77 tribes voted to reject them.[57] However, each federally recognized tribe needed a governmental mechanism (tribal council) in order to deal with the BIA for the resources the BIA controlled under congressional mandate, which included principally (as it does today) tribal lands, so that whether or not a tribe constructed a constitution as the BIA requested, it had to comply in one way or another with BIA pressure to form a representative government. For example, the Navajo Nation, the tribe with the largest reservation land mass in the United States, does not have a constitution to this day. But it has developed a highly organized Western-style government, with a tribal council composed of elected representatives from districts called chapters, a president elected by the whole tribe, and a judiciary.

Tribal councils have faced various forms of resistance from the grass roots of their communities. Because of the resistance of traditional village leaders (Kikmongwis), a Hopi tribal council was unable to form successfully between 1934 and the early 1950s. And, to take another example, on the Pine Ridge Reservation, home of the Oglala Lakota, resistance has at various times over the last thirty years taken the form of advocacy for traditional modes of Native governance (direct democracy by informal consensus) rather than Western-style representative governments, where power and wealth can too easily become concentrated in the hands of the representatives at the expense of the community.[58] Thus, in Indian Country, one finds democratically elected tribal governments that are at the same time opposed by or alienated from the grassroots population precisely because they are perceived as arms of U.S. colonial power. As I have noted, Washburn's novel *The Sacred White Turkey* represents this state of affairs. However, it is important to emphasize that a tribal council may also oppose U.S. colonial power and so claim the support of its constituency on certain issues, particularly those dealing with land and sovereignty. This was the case with the Dakota Access Pipeline protests in February 2016–17 until then-tribal president David Archambault II and the Standing Rock Council worked to stop the protests, fearing, according to Archambault, for the safety of the protestors. Lakota scholar and activist Nick Estes comments on the situation as it played out in the DAPL protests on the Standing Rock Sioux reservation in February 2017: "In February, the Cannon Ball District and the Standing Rock Council passed resolutions calling for the evacuation of remaining campers at Sacred Stone and defunct Oceti Sakowin Camp. It was a controversial move that pitted factions against each other at a critical juncture when unity was needed most."[59]

These kinds of within-tribe divisions have a long history, which is a direct result of European colonial "divide and conquer" policies in the Americas. Moreover, this complex colonial situation is further complicated by the Indian Citizenship Act of 1924, wherein Congress imposed citizenship on all Indians living in the United States. In conjunction with allotment, which linked citizenship and holding land as property, a majority of Indians had already been made citizens by congressional mandates.[60] The 1924 act granted no particular rights to the Indians. The right to vote came subsequently on a state-by-state basis, and Fourteenth Amendment rights did not apply to tribal Indians on the reservation. In 1968, Congress passed the Indian Civil Rights Act, which granted certain constitutional rights to Indians on reservations.

But in 1978, in a landmark case, *Santa Clara Pueblo v. Martinez*,[61] a female member of the Pueblo, Julia Martinez, sued the Pueblo, contesting a rule that denied membership to the children of all Santa Clara women, but not men, marrying outside of the tribe. The suit asserted that this rule discriminated against Santa Clara women on the bases of both sex and ancestry in violation of Title I of the Indian Civil Rights Act of 1968 (ICRA), 25 U.S.C. §§ 1301–1303. The Act provides in relevant part that "no Indian tribe in exercising powers of self-government shall . . . deny to any person within its jurisdiction the equal protection of its laws."[62] However, granting certiorari, the Supreme Court effectively decided for

> tribal sovereignty's precedence over [the] civil rights [of an individual tribal member], except in the case of habeas corpus appeals to federal courts sanctioned under 25 U.S.C. § 1303 (ICRA). However, in this case *Martinez* makes it clear that the respondent is not the tribe but the individual tribal official holding the prisoner. Thus, today, the ten constitutional rights of Indians in their tribes, as enumerated in 25 U.S.C. § 1302, come under the sole authority of tribal courts; and the tribes are protected from federal lawsuits in this area through the principle of "sovereign immunity."[63]

The Indian Citizenship Act was and remains at best a double-edged sword, at once an assimilationist attack on tribal existence and leverage for empowerment in the larger nation. But—and this is crucial—the act only empowers one as an individual, operating beyond the reservation, the home community. As *Santa Clara* demonstrates, if an Indian remains on the reservation, which, despite all its economic hardships due to colonial underdevelopment, is still the place of identity—the nurturing nexus of kin and land—then that person is constrained to live under the colonial regime of federal Indian law without the constitutional guarantees of U.S. citizenship, excepting the right to vote in U.S. state and national elections. The relationship, or lack thereof, between the citizenship of individual Indians and the colonial status of the tribes is succinctly stated in 1921 in *Winton v. Amos,* where one cannot help but notice that in the case of Indians the fundamental ground of citizenship is a *"mere* grant": "It is thoroughly established that Congress has plenary authority over the Indians and all their tribal relations, and full power to legislate concerning their tribal property. The guardianship arises from their condition of tutelage or dependency; and it rests with

Congress to determine when the relationship shall cease; the *mere* grant of rights of citizenship not being sufficient to terminate it."⁶⁴

The Indian Citizenship Act of 1924, then, in no way affects the colonial status of federally recognized Indian tribes but rather presents the legal paradox of sovereign U.S. citizens who are at the same time colonial subjects of the United States if they are tribally enrolled. While because of reforms instituted by the IRA, the BIA is today administered from top to bottom largely by Indians, and while all Indians are now citizens of the United States, the colonial politics and policies of Indian Country continue, resulting in the general impoverishment of Indian people. In classic colonial fashion, Indian Country continues to be by far the most underdeveloped part of the United States, even though it encompasses some of its richest mineral resources. The relatively optimistic (glass half full) Taylor and Kalt report for the Harvard Project on American Indian Economic Development, published in 2005 and covering Indian economic development in the 1990s, points to the effects of underdevelopment in Indian Country, even after a decade of gaming revenues and what the report understands as increasing "self-determination" for the tribes:

> Notwithstanding evident socioeconomic improvement in Indian Country between 1990 and 2000, the glass is also half-empty. The Census data make it clear that, on average, Indians on both gaming and non-gaming reservations have a long way to go to [sic] with respect to addressing the accumulation of long-enduring socioeconomic deficits in Indian Country. Across many indicators—even those displaying remarkable improvement—the gap remained large in the 2000 Census: real per capita income of Indians living in Indian Country was less than half the U.S. level; real median household income of Indian families was little more than half the U.S. level; Indian unemployment was more than twice the U.S. rate; Indian family poverty was three times the U.S. rate; the share of Indian homes lacking complete plumbing was substantially higher than the U.S. overall level; and the proportion of Indian adults who were college graduates was half the proportion for the U.S. as a whole.
>
> In sum, the gains made by the tribes in the 1990s did not eliminate the socioeconomic disparities between Indian Americans and other Americans. Much remains to be done to close the gap: If U.S.

and on-reservation Indian per capita incomes were to continue to grow at their 1990s' rates, it would take half a century for tribes to catch up. More critically, the reality of falling real incomes and worsening socioeconomic conditions on reservations during the 1980s are testament to the vulnerability of the gains made in the 1990s. Solidification and extension of the gains of the 1990s will require steady hands on the policies of self-determination in the decades to come. Without that—or worse, under policies that actually erode tribal powers essential to self-government—the gains in Indian Country could easily be reversed. Such a reversal would dash prospects for socioeconomic progress in Indian Country and would increase demands that federal and state governments address the problems of reservation poverty. That would be a losing proposition for all.[65]

The National Community Reinvestment Coalition (NCRC) report (2022) shows that the economic situation of Indian Country recorded by the Harvard report has not fundamentally improved over the last twenty years: "Based on the data from the 2018 U.S. Census cited by Poverty USA, Native Americans have the highest poverty rate among all minority groups. The national poverty rate for Native Americans was 25.4%, while Black or African American poverty rate was 20.8%. Among Hispanics, the national poverty rate was 17.6%. The White population had an 8.1% national poverty rate during the same period."[66] Sociologist Beth Red Bird in February 2020 reported an even higher poverty rate: "Across the United States, 1 in 3 Native Americans are living in poverty, with a median income of $23,000 a year. These numbers from the American Community Survey highlight the stark income inequality the nation's first peoples face,"[67] even as income inequality in the United States continues to grow.

While Gover acknowledges the complicity of, indeed the central part played by, the BIA in the "ethnic cleansing" of Native Americans and understands this cleansing as having continuing devastating social effects in the present, he also makes a distinction between the BIA "in the past" and now, "in this era of self-determination, when the Bureau of Indian Affairs is at long last serving as an advocate for Indian people in an atmosphere of mutual respect." But this all-too-clean separation of institutional past from institutional present requires overlooking or denying certain salient facts, such as the mismanagement of trust funds. In his statement Gover also conflates "self-determination" with "self-governance." Federal Indian law in effect prohibits the former and allows the latter in certain circumscribed civil and criminal matters. Another fact that complicates Gover's sense of history is the ongoing Navajo–Hopi land dispute, which, begun in 1882 by the BIA's machinations, since 1974 has resulted, under the BIA's direction, in the displacement of twelve to fourteen thousand Navajos from their traditional lands, with catastrophic social results.[68] Despite Gover's claims of "an atmosphere of mutual respect," the colonial structure of federal Indian law, which the BIA administers, dooms the BIA to be a certain kind of classic colonial bureaucracy. Since the ratification of the Constitution, this colonial structure has been articulated in laws of Congress, decisions of the federal courts, and administrative regulations emanating from the Department of the Interior and put into action by the BIA within the context of federal Indian law.

The colonial structure of Indian Country has its roots in European imperialism in the Americas, which begins with Columbus's invasion of the Caribbean in 1492. For the Indigenous peoples of what Europeans would name the Americas, Columbus's appearance heralded an apocalypse. Between 1492 and 1504, Columbus made four voyages into the Caribbean, believing all the while that he was traveling the margins of Asia and would therefore come upon the limitless supplies of gold that Europe wove into its Orientalist narratives of the Great Khan ("El gran Can," as he is referred to in Columbus's journal). Columbus's gross error in geography—that is, his confusion of the Caribbean with the Indies—caused him to homogenize under the name of "Indians" the Indigenous peoples he encountered.

While there were apparently trace amounts of gold in the Caribbean islands that Columbus invaded, his commitment to finding the precious metal in abundance caused him to hallucinate the mines of his imagined Asia until the day he died. His journal obsessively notes every fleck of gold he sees, or thinks he sees, in Indigenous artifacts. He translates rumors of gold into testimony of fact, when really these rumors are translations of Native languages that the invaders could not have known before arriving in the Caribbean, and would have taken a long time to learn even if they had been interested. In other words, when it came to his fantasies of gold in this place he imagined to be Asia, Columbus understood what he wanted to believe, regardless of the linguistic barriers—an epistemology that was typical of the European invasion of the Americas.[69]

Columbus's hallucination of gold proved deadly for the Indigenes. On his second voyage to the Caribbean, which lasted from 1493 to 1496, Columbus, along with his two brothers, Diego and Bartolomé, organized the colonization of Hispaniola (present-day Dominican Republic and Haiti) for the principal purpose of extracting the fabled gold through the forced labor of the Arawak communities on the island.[70] Native resistance developed, and by fall 1494, it had turned into a revolt against the Spanish settlers. According to Columbus's son, Hernando, who was not present at the time but who composed an account from his father's papers, the revolt was caused by the occupiers indiscriminate brutality against the Arawaks, a result of the failed leadership of Pedro Margarit, whom Columbus had left in charge of "pacifying" the Indian population of Hispaniola and instituting the gold extraction while "the Admiral" continued his incursions throughout other parts of the Caribbean between the end of April and the end of September 1494.[71] Columbus had left his brother, Diego, in charge of the settlement on Hispaniola, but apparently he could not control Margarit, and internal factions developed among the settlers. During this time, Columbus's other brother, Bartolomé, arrived, and Margarit used one of his ships to return to Spain and begin fomenting resistance to Columbus.[72]

On his return to Hispaniola, Columbus, along with his brothers, took control of the situation. Aided by internal conflicts among the Arawaks, they suppressed the revolt and pacified the population. According to Hernando's account, "the region became so peaceful that a Christian could go anywhere he pleased alone and in complete safety. Indeed, the Indians would carry him on their shoulders in the way they carry letters, wherever it pleased him to go."[73] The language of "peace" here only serves to accentuate the actual violence that converted Arawaks into beasts of burden for the Spanish. In effect, under the restored regime of the brothers Columbus, the Margarit's violence was systematized; the pogrom became the concentration camp. Here is Hernando's account:

> Hispaniola was reduced to such peace and obedience that all promised to pay tribute to the Catholic sovereigns every three months. That is to say: in the province of Cibao, where the goldfields lay, every person over the age of fourteen would pay a large bell-full of

gold dust, and everywhere else twenty-five pounds of cotton. And in order that the Spaniards should know what person owed tribute, orders were given for the manufacture of discs of brass or copper, to be given to each every time he made payment, and to be worn around the neck. Consequently if any man was found without a disc, it would be known that he had not paid and he would be punished.[74]

Because there was virtually no gold, punishment, which was death by having one's hands cut off, was inevitable. Armed Arawak resistance having been suppressed by the occupiers, the Indians resorted to mass suicide using cassava poison: "During those two years of the administration of the brothers Columbus, an estimated one half of the entire population of Hispaniola was killed or killed themselves. The estimates run from one hundred and twenty-five thousand to one-half million."[75]

In his novel *Heirs of Columbus* (1991), Anishinaabe novelist, poet, and essayist Gerald Vizenor imagines a different Columbus:

> Christopher Columbus saw a blue light in the west, but "it was such an uncertain thing," he wrote in his journal to the crown, "that I did not feel it was adequate proof of land." That light was a torch raised by the silent hand talkers, a summons to the New World. Since then the explorer has become a trickster healer in the stories told by his tribal heirs at the headwaters of the great river [the Mississippi].[76]

Vizenor's Columbus does not commit genocide but leaves the life of the West for Native life. With a Native woman, a hand talker, he gives birth to a "crossblood" progeny who populate the novel: "Five centuries later the crossblood descendants of the explorer and the hand talker declared a new tribal nation" whose history began in "Samana [. . .] an island in the ocean sea that would be imagined but never possessed in the culture of death," the culture of the West.[77] Like Indigenous literature more broadly, *Heirs of Columbus* represents an alternative history to that of the West, which has brought the living world to the brink of the abyss.

Columbus inaugurated what demographer Russell Thornton aptly terms the American Indian Holocaust: the ongoing destruction of Indian communities throughout the Americas by a variety of means "stemm[ing] from European contact and colonization: introduced disease, including alcoholism; warfare and genocide; geographical removal and relocation; and destruction of ways of life."[78] It is important to emphasize Thornton's contextualization of "introduced disease," for it has been the strategy of official Western histories to depoliticize disease in order to make Indian extermination appear to be the result of uncontrollable natural processes rather than of political will. In fact, even when diseases such as smallpox were not strategically introduced into Native communities (by providing them with infected blankets, for example), cures or medical help were not made widely available until the end of the nineteenth century.[79] As Thornton's list of deadly agents makes clear, disease fit perfectly into an arsenal aimed at Native destruction so that we should properly speak of it in terms not of natural causes but of biological warfare.

Thornton "estimate[s] [. . .] a total population of 72+ million Indigenous people in the Western Hemisphere in 1492. This 72+ million declined in a few centuries to perhaps only about 4 to 4.5 million."[80] Of this Native population at invasion, Thornton estimates a population of more than 5 million in "the conterminous United States area,"[81] which by the end of the nineteenth century had been reduced by the forces of European colonization to around 250,000,[82] a figure that today is up to from 2 to almost 10 million, depending on what institution is doing the counting and what population they are counting for a database that is at best inaccurate. This increase should be taken as a sign not that the colonial war of attrition against American Indians is over but rather that its strategies have shifted in certain ways and that Native resistance, which has been persistent since the Columbian invasion and has accounted for Native survival, has itself taken on new forms.

Since the massacre of approximately three hundred Lakota men, women, and children by the Seventh Cavalry (Custer's regiment) at Wounded Knee, South Dakota, on December 29, 1890,[83] the continuing genocide of Native peoples in the United States has taken on a predominantly legal/economic form, which among its other effects, as noted, keeps Indians the poorest of the poor. Although the Canadian situation must be viewed in detail within the particular circumstances under which Canadian federalism developed,[84] it is in broad outlines similar to the contemporary U.S. trajectory of legal/economic conflict, likewise deriving its fundamental colonial relations to the Indians from the British imperial system. This system is articulated in the Royal Proclamation of 1763, which, among its other provisions, assumed control of Indian lands for the crown, with the language of protection used as justification. Contemporary North American Indigenous–government conflict is centered in the legal/economic arena, primarily focused on Indigenous land rights, which are typically being violated by government-backed corporations. Throughout the Americas, conflicts that occur between Indigenous peoples defending civil and land rights—including armed conflict as well as peaceful modes of protest like civil disobedience—and the government–corporate sector's violation of rights, typically with armed force, are an ongoing part of the history of Indigenous resistance to European genocide.

In 1973, in the second Wounded Knee, Indian activists from around the United States, most of whom were associated with the American Indian Movement (AIM), joined with traditional Lakotas on the Pine Ridge Reservation against the BIA-supported tribal government, which was using violence to suppress dissent, and a heavily armed federal military force called in to support that government.[85]

In 1990, at Kanehsatake, Québec, a small group of Mohawks protecting traditional lands from urban development in the form of a golf course faced the Canadian military.[86] Historically, Latin American governments have pursued terrorist wars against Indigenous peoples. In the post–World War II era, these wars have had the strategic support of the United States. The thirty-four-year genocidal civil war in Guatemala, which ended in 1996, clearly demonstrates such support. The official report of this war, which was "established through the Accord of Oslo on 23 June 1994, in order to clarify with objectivity, equity and impartiality, the human rights violations and acts of violence connected with the armed confrontation that caused suffering among the Guatemalan people," unequivocally articulates the overwhelming state violence (physical, social, cultural, and economic) perpetrated against Mayan communities, who historically were and are seeking social justice, as well as the part played by the United States in supporting this violence.[87] In this respect, the U.S. genocide against Native Americans at home and their ongoing resistance to this genocide cannot be separated from U.S. support for genocidal movements against Native Americans in Latin America and the Indigenous resistance to these movements, of which Bolivia is a key example.

After an Indigenous- and worker-led revolutionary movement against the neoliberal privatization of key resources (water and natural gas) in Bolivia from 2000 to 2003, Evo Morales, an Aymara Indian, was elected in 2005 as president of the country, 62 percent of whose people identify as Indigenous. After subsequently being elected twice more (2009–14 and 2014–19), he was deposed by a right-wing coup supported by the United States in November 2019. Then, in October 2020, his political party, MAS (Movement to Socialism), was returned to power in the national election, and in November 2020, Morales returned to Bolivia from exile in Argentina. Under the Morales government, the constitution of the Plurinational State of Bolivia[88] was enacted by national referendum in 2009, although its drafting in the preceding three years by a popularly elected constituent assembly was complicated in terms of representation. However, to quote Miguel Centellas, "there can be no denying that the 2009 Constitution [recognizing 35 Indigenous languages (article 5, paragraph 1)] is a significant advancement for multiculturalism in Bolivia—and for the rights of indigenous peoples in particular."[89] The constitution is an attempt to represent the plurinational sovereignty of diverse Indigenous communities within a nation-state formation, a model that potentially presents an anticolonial alternative to the "domestic dependent nation" status of U.S. Indian tribes, though it is not without its problems, which I turn to in the following paragraphs.

The constitution, a document of 130 pages encountering the present while projecting a yet-to-be realized future, repudiates in its introduction "the colonial, republican, and neo-liberal State" of the past in order to "found Bolivia anew" on the values of Indigenous kinship. The complication, indeed the contradiction, in this promise is the problem of founding a state (a vertical system of rights) on kinship (a horizontal system of responsibilities). This is the problem of founding a sovereign unitary structure on a structure of heterogeneous autonomous communities (plurinationalism) without the state becoming a neocolonial force privileging its own rights over those of the nations within the nation—that is, without those nations becoming a version of U.S. "domestic dependent nations."

Under Morales, Bolivia has faced from its beginning, as a revolutionary state, conflicts with Indigenous communities arising from the incompatibility of the responsibilities within rights model. This has centrally come into play in the Amazon basin over the conflict between the state's right to development versus the community's responsibility to sustain the biodiversity of the environment, with the former taking precedence even though the constitution reads: "Rural native indigenous autonomy consists in self-government as an exercise of free determination of the nations and rural native indigenous peoples, the population of which shares territory, culture, history, languages, and their own juridical, political, social and economic organization or institutions."[90]

In theory, the Bolivian constitution, in contrast to U.S. federal Indian law and the U.N. Declaration of the Rights of Indigenous Peoples, which in its final article subordinates Indigenous rights to the nation-state,[91] offers a faithful translation of kinship responsibilities into nation-state rights. In practice, the two forms remain in conflict. Centellas puts it this way:

> Looking explicitly at the relationship between Bolivia's indigenous peoples and the state, there is little evidence of a multicultural consociational model. Indigenous peoples are now constitutionally granted autonomy, but in a rather limited way: it is restricted by preexisting territorial boundaries; it is limited to small rural communities; it places significant restrictions on the use of *usos y costumbres* [traditional values]; and it does not grant communities veto rights on decisions involving their resources. Like people in many other countries, Bolivians have been forced to wrestle with potential conflicts between practices that fall under *usos y costumbres* and their commitments to human rights. Thus, for example, one can understand restrictions on the use of capital or corporal punishments—a practice sometimes defended as falling under the category of *usos y costumbres*. However, it is less understandable why far less controversial elements of *usos y costumbres*—such as traditional ways of selecting community leaders—should be brushed aside.[92]

Centellas understands Indigenous autonomy within the Bolivian nation-state as follows: "Overall, the evidence suggests that despite indigenous autonomy originating as a grassroots demand, the application of indigenous autonomy is still primarily understood as structured and applied 'from above' in ways that privilege the central state. Despite legal and constitutional assurances, indigenous autonomy is still very fragile in Bolivia."[93]

From the models I have analyzed, it would appear that a regime of responsibilities, an egalitarian kinship regime, is in the end incompatible with regimes of rights that are grounded, as such regimes necessarily are, in nation-state sovereignty. The moment we move from a kinship to a nation-state regime, from responsibilities to rights, is the moment we move from democracy to something that the nation-state calls democracy but is more accurately a majoritarian form of representative politics in which power is not circulated horizontally and thus equally but is distributed vertically and unequally from the top down. That is, we move from regimes of sustainability to regimes of growth, of production and consumption, based on extractive industries, which today are engineering climate collapse. The West calls this progress, but thinking from a different place—a place of responsibility—one might understand it as regression. We need a regime of not only human rights but also environmental rights, strictly enforced, because we have abandoned a regime of responsibility to the living world.

By insisting on this responsibility to the living world, Indigenous communities across the globe have been leading movements of sustainability. In Canada, for example, the Idle No More grassroots movement, founded in 2012 by four Indigenous women, continues to oppose extractive industries on First Nations land as concomitant with asserting First Nation rights. Analyzing the movement at its inception, Yellowknives Dene scholar and activist Glenn Sean Coulthard notes:

> As long as the land remains in jeopardy, supporters of movements like Idle No More will continue the struggle. "We're in this for the long haul," explains Pamela Palmater. "It was never meant to be a flashy one month, then go away. This is something that's years in the making. [. . .] You'll see it take different forms at different times, but it's not going away anytime soon." Indeed, the recent escalation and increased public visibility of Indigenous anti-fracking protests [. . .] along with the ongoing anti-oil sands activism [. . .] and the unrelenting antipipeline campaigns [. . .] are a clear demonstration of Indigenous peoples' continued resolve to defend their land and sovereignty from further encroachments by state and capital.[94]

In the United States, following on Idle No More, we have witnessed antipipeline protests against the Dakota Access Pipeline (DAPL), which threatens the land and water of the Standing Rock Sioux reservation, and were met by the brute force of the government–corporate industrial complex before the federal government allowed the pipeline to go through. As Colville scholar and activist Dina Gilio-Whitaker notes: "The resistance movement, organized around the hashtag #NoDAPL, #Miniwiconi, #Waterislife, and #Standingwithstanding rock, officially began in April 2016 when a small group of women from the Standing

Rock Sioux Tribe (SRST) set up camp and named it Camp of the Sacred Stones, or Sacred Stone Camp."[95] Nick Estes characterizes the protest this way: "The protestors called themselves Water Protectors because they weren't simply against a pipeline; they also stood for something greater: the continuation of life on a planet ravaged by capitalism. This reflected the Lakota and Dakota philosophy of Mitakuye Oyasin, meaning all my relations or 'we are all related.' Water Protectors led the movement in a disciplined way, by what Lakotas call Wocekiye, meaning 'honoring relations.'"[96] Kinship was the principle on which the protest camp was organized: "The ultimate goal for Dakotas, and therefore the Oceti Sakowin [Sioux Nation], 'was quite simple. One must obey kinship rules, one must be a good relative,' wrote the Dakota scholar Ella Deloria."[97]

Beginning in November 2020, Minnesota Anishinaabe began protests against the Enbridge Line 3 "replacement pipeline," the installation of which was supported by the Biden administration. Enbridge, a Canadian company, is also part of the corporate conglomerate that owns and operates the DAPL, which conveys particularly toxic tar-sand oil from Canada to the United States. As Anishinaabe activist and writer Winona LaDuke points out, this so-called replacement is actually a new pipeline to replace the old defective one—without any U.S. or Minnesota government plans for dismantling the old one and cleaning up its environmental damage.[98] Line 3 was completed in September 2021. LaDuke responded: "They've created their jobs. They put in their pipe. They won. They've committed a crime. And someone needs to stop them from making a profit off of that crime. Do something for the people. Stop Line 3 and give us a 'just transition.'" Theia Chatelle, who reported this response, sums up the situation:

> But, the story of Line 3 is not that of "safety standards" and "operating capabilities" [Enbridge's justification for the new pipeline]. Instead, it is the story of Honor the Earth and the Anishinaabe's resistance against Line 3. It is the story of "manoomin" [wild rice] and Turtle Island [the earth] again being attacked by the "Black Snake" [crude oil]. And it is the story of the MPUC's [Minnesota Public Utilities Commission] failure to honor treaty rights and protect the Earth. Line 3 was not a failure of the State of Minnesota but rather the logical consequence of a settler-colonial political system determined to destroy the Earth and any potential for Native

sovereignty. Enbridge knew it would face a fight, as with the Dakota Access Pipeline and Keystone XL. But, this time, it came prepared. It assembled the Northern Lights Taskforce, "brought jobs to Minnesota," and pursued every legal and illegal option available to nullify resistance to Line 3. Enbridge wielded its power to its advantage, and it won. But, that doesn't mean that the resistance failed.[99]

As the resistance to these pipelines indicates, the Columbian invasion of the Americas was only the first wave of forces put into play by the emerging Western European nation-states of Spain, England, France, Holland, and Portugal as part of an expansionist movement whose most recent manifestation has come to be known as globalization (in which the energy sector plays a crucial role) but whose early modern manifestation is known retrospectively as imperialism: the creation of European empires through the mechanism of colonization. Although the word "imperialism," along with its companion, "colonialism," only emerged in the middle of the nineteenth century (both, according to the *Oxford English Dictionary*, with connotations of exploitation that have since become denotations), the emerging Western European nation-states of the sixteenth century clearly thought of themselves as empires and their transatlantic adventures as planting colonies on the classical model of imperial Rome, which was for them to be emulated. The United States followed suit.

Two monumental works of American Indian literature that deal with resistance to the predations of corporate capitalism and its rationalization in U.S. federal Indian law are *Fight Back: For the Sake of the People; For the Sake of the Land* by Simon Ortiz (1980) and *Almanac of the Dead* (1991) by Leslie Marmon Silko.[100] Both of these works look forward to the Indigenous values embedded in the Bolivian constitution that resist the invasion of corporate capitalism.

Ortiz's *Fight Back* was originally published in 1980 "in commemoration of the Pueblo Revolt of 1680 and our warrior Grandmothers and Grandfathers," as the front matter comments. In her preface to Ortiz's book, Roxanne Dunbar-Ortiz notes that the book's dedication to the revolt "reminds us that the Revolt left a legacy of [Indigenous] resistance. Resistance continues in the mines, in the fields, in the factories."[101] The book is a memoir composed in poetry and prose that chronicles microcosmically and macrocosmically the resistance of the Native peoples of the Southwest to Spanish and then U.S. colonialism.

The first part of the book consists of twenty poems that focus on workers, both Native and non-Native, in the Grants Uranium Belt, which ran from west of Albuquerque to Gallup, New Mexico, between the early 1950s and the publication of the book.

The second section of *Fight Back,* "No More Sacrifices," is a political and personal history—or, more precisely, a history in which culture and politics are inseparably intertwined. It details the usurpation of Native land and water rights beginning with the Spanish invasion of the Southwest in 1540 and continuing through the U.S. invasion (the Mexican War), which culminated with the Treaty of Guadalupe Hidalgo (1848), to the contemporary moment, when U.S. corporations, signing sweetheart leases with tribal councils under the auspices of the Department of the Interior, exploit Native land for the deadly uranium as well as Native labor to mine the poisonous metal, which fueled the atom bomb. Of the sacrificial labor, Ortiz writes in 1980: "Mining is dangerous work, whether underground or surface, but people continue to work there because there is no other employment available. It is total and intensive work, and the New Mexican and national economy requires it. It is not the safety or health or lives of the miners that there is concern for; it is in the national interest that the mine operators, oil corporations, utility companies, international energy cartels, and investors sacrifice these men and women."[102]

Mary F. Calvert and Andrew Romano report in 2022 on the continuing legacy of uranium mining for Native people, principally Navajos, in the West:

> After the invention of atomic weapons in 1945 and the subsequent development of nuclear power plants, mining companies dug more than 4,000 uranium mines across the Western U.S. Though other tribes were affected—including the Hopi, the Arapaho, the Southern Cheyenne, the Spokane and [. . .] Laguna Pueblo—roughly 1,000 of these claims were located on Navajo Nation, which encompasses 27,000 square miles where Arizona, Utah and New Mexico meet. Over the next four decades, miners contracted by the U.S. government blasted 30 millions of tons of ore out of Navajo land with little environmental, health or safety oversight. Eventually, demand declined, deposits played out and the pits were abandoned. Much of the damage, however, had already been done.
>
> When the mines were active, companies recruited Navajo men to

work them. They hired women and children as support staff; to save money and avoid leaving a paper trail, they "paid" them with sacks of sugar, flour, potatoes and coffee. Exposure to radioactive ore and toxic by-products such as arsenic, cadmium and lead was commonplace—a fact of everyday life. Navajo families crushed the poisonous rock to make concrete. Homes were built from abandoned mine tailings. Kids played in waste piles. Herders watered sheep in open, unreclaimed pits. Husbands came home covered in uranium dust; wives washed their clothes. Everyone drank the contaminated groundwater; everyone inhaled mine dust borne on the hot desert winds. They still do today.[103]

Ortiz makes clear that this history of U.S. imperialism ("of a ruthless, monopolistic U.S. empire" from east to west) is a history of Western law: "To cast away Indians was easy enough [. . .] and there was even something called Manifest Destiny which ordained the U.S. with a religious mission. There was no need for conspiracy to steal and defraud; rather there was a national goal to fulfill and godly purpose to be done. Laws, in fact, could be made and changed and new ones made which would legally serve economic and social interests with more proficiency."[104] As a citizen of Acoma Pueblo, which along with Laguna sits in the Grants Uranium Belt, Ortiz must have in mind among the laws he references federal Indian law, which under the plenary power of Congress could be made and unmade to serve the interests of the country. Of special provenance here are the Supreme Court decision in *U.S. v. Sandoval*[105] and the Pueblo Lands Act of 1924, both of which, though for different reasons, converted lands titled to the Pueblos by the Spanish crown in the eighteenth century into Indian trust lands in order to protect them from depredations by white settlers, which began in force after the Treaty of Guadalupe Hidalgo (1848). While both *Sandoval* and the Pueblo Lands Act protected Pueblo territory from white claimants, they did so within a colonial system where the best position was still limited. Before *Sandoval*, the Pueblos as communal freeholders were left open to settler land claims within a legal system where they were being defrauded; after *Sandoval*, as government wards, they were left open to government control of their lands.[106] In *Fight Back*, Ortiz not only references a complex legal history but also intertwines it with an equally complex history of resistance to European imperialism, by Indians and by working peoples of all kinds. Ortiz conceives of this resistance as specifically anticapitalist: "If the survival and quality of the life of Indian peoples is not assured, then no one else's life is, because those same economic, social, and political forces which destroy them will surely destroy others. [. . .] But it will take real decisions and actions and concrete understanding by the poor and workers of this nation. [. . .] They will have to be willing to identify capitalism for what it is, that it is destructive and uncompassionate and deceptive."[107]

Ortiz identifies this resistance historically with a specifically pan-Indian, panethnic movement that began in 1680 with the Pueblo Revolt, which has been referred to as "the first American Revolution":

> In August of 1680 when the Pueblo people rose against the ruling Spanish oppressor, they were joined in the revolt by the mestizo and genizaro ancestors of the Chicano people, and the Athapascan-speaking peoples whose descendants are the peoples of the Navajo and Apache nations, and descendants of Africans who had been brought to the New World as slaves. They were all commonly impoverished. These people rebelled against the oppressive rule of the civil, church, and armed guard of the Spanish colonialist. They were forced to submit to the control of the wealthy and so-called royalty and religious fanatics who forbade native spiritual practice and beliefs because of the social integrity and strength upon which they were based.[108]

The oral tradition plays a central role in Ortiz's narrative of resistance: "In the oral tradition, war, crisis, and famine are spoken about. The people had to cope with epochs when catastrophe came suddenly, inevitably, and perhaps necessarily when the people had not paid careful heed to their responsibilities. [. . .] The oral tradition does not ignore bad times and mistakes the people made throughout their history. And they are told in mythic proportions in order to impress upon those hearing that there are important lessons, values, and principles to be learned."[109] *Fight Back* itself is an example of the oral tradition translated into written form, where the redistributive agenda of Marxism and Indigenous values of kinship intersect.

Silko's *Almanac of the Dead* begins and ends at Laguna Pueblo, Acoma's sister pueblo, in the Grants Uranium Belt. As in *Fight Back*, the atomic bomb is a focus of the narrative. At the end of the novel, Sterling, a native of Laguna, returns home, walking at the end of his journey through the tailings of the abandoned Anaconda Jackpile-Paguate mine:

> Sterling still had two miles to walk, but already the mountains of grayish-white tailings loomed ahead. He had not understood before why the old people had cried when the U.S. government had opened the mine. Sterling was reminded of the stub left after amputation when he looked at the shattered, scarred sandstone that remained; the mine had devoured entire mesas. "Leave our Mother Earth alone," the old folks had tried to warn, "otherwise terrible things will happen to us all." Before the end of the war, the old folks had seen the first atomic explosion—the flash brighter than any sun—followed weeks later by the bombs that had burned up a half a million Japanese. "What goes around comes around."[110]

Almanac of the Dead, which coincides in time with *Fight Back,* imagines pan-Indian/panethnic revolution in the Americas in an intellectual context where traditional Indian communal views of land, kinship, and storytelling coincide with a kind of pure Marxism. Angelita La Escapía, Marxist revolutionary and explicator of Marxism in the novel, ruminates on this coincidence:

> Marx had been inspired by reading about certain Native American communal societies, though naturally as a European he had misunderstood a great deal. Marx had learned about societies in which everyone ate or everyone starved together, and no one being stood above another—all stood side by side—rocks, insect, human being, river, or flower. Each depended upon the other; the destruction of one harmed all others. [. . .] Marx of the Jews, tribal people of the desert, Marx the tribal man understood that nothing personal or individual mattered because no individual survived without others. [. . .] Marx, tribal man and storyteller. Marx with his primitive devotion to the workers' stories. No wonder the Europeans hated him! Marx had gathered official government reports of the suffering of English factory workers the way a tribal shaman might have, feverishly working to bring together a powerful, even magical assembly of stories.[111]

The plot of *Almanac of the Dead* centers on issues stemming from federal Indian law, as Silko makes clear in the figure of "Wilson

Weasel Tail, Poet Lawyer," who appears near the novel's end at "the International Holistic Healers Convention in Tucson": "Weasel Tail was Lakota, raised on a small, poor ranch forty miles from the Wounded Knee massacre site. Weasel Tail had dropped out of his third year at UCLA Law School to devote himself to poetry. The people didn't need more lawyers, the lawyers were the disease not the cure. The law served the rich. The people needed poetry; poetry would set the people free; poetry would speak to the dreams and to the spirits, and the people would understand what they must do."[112] Weasel Tail is at the convention "not as a lawyer-poet" but "as 'a Lakota healer and visionary.'"[113] Yet we are told by Lecha (one of the central characters in the novel), who listens raptly to Weasel Tail's revolutionary lecture-poem on the Ghost Dance,[114] "Still, Weasel Tail was a lawyer at heart; Lecha noted that he had made the invaders an offer that couldn't be refused. Weasel Tail had said to the U.S. government, 'Give back what you have stolen or else as a people you will continue your self-destruction.'"[115]

"Lecha had met Wilson Weasel Tail on a cable-television talk show originating in Atlanta years before."[116] Before Weasel Tail was forcibly removed, he had seized control of the show long enough to recite a revolutionary poem about the U.S. government's theft of Indian land, couched entirely in the language of Anglo-American law in general and of federal Indian law in particular. I quote the poem in its entirety because of the way it figures the central argument of my book, the imbrication of U.S. Indian literatures and federal Indian law:

> Only a bastard government
> Occupies stolen land!
>
> Hey, you barbarian invaders!
> How much longer?
> You think colonialism lasts forever?
> *Res ipsa loquitur!*
> Cloud on title
> Unmerchantable title
> Doubtful title
> Defective title
> Unquiet title
> Unclear title
> Adverse title

Adverse possession
Wrongful possession
Unlawful possession!
[...]
We say, "Adios, white man," to
Five hundred years of
Criminals and pretenders
Illicit and unlawful governments,
Res accedent lumina rebus,
One thing throws light on another.

Worchester v. Georgia!
Ex parte Crow Dog!
Winters v. United States!
Williams v. Lee!
Lone Wolf v. Hitchcock!
Pyramid Lake Paiute Tribe v. Morton!
Village of Kake, Alaska v. Egan!
Gila River Apache Tribe v. Arizona!

breach of close
breach of conscience
breach of contract
breach of covenant
breach of decency
breach of duty
breach of faith
breach of fiduciary responsibility
breach of promise
breach of peace
breach of trust
breach of trust with fraudulent intent!

Breach of the Treaty of the Sacred Black Hills!
Breach of the Treaty of the Sacred Blue Lake!
Breach of the Treaty of Guadalupe Hidalgo!

Res judicata!
We are at war.[117]

This poem, composed using legal terms and citing federal Indian law cases and treaties, is in the form of a verdict, pronounced by a transtribal voice, which judges the U.S. government guilty of colonialism and thereby declares an anticolonial war against it—a war that by implication is both legal and just. Although Wilson Weasel Tail's ultimate cry is transnational, a cry for all the dispossessed (Indians, African Americans, and the poor across races and ethnicities—that is, beyond identity politics) "to take back the Americas!,"[118] he necessarily grounds that cry, in both his Ghost Dance poem and this one, in nationalist terms, in both the Native (tribal or Indigenous) and the nation-state sense. Both are imbricated within the context of U.S. colonialism structured by federal Indian law. This transnational cry must be grounded in the national because revolutions can only take place in specific locales by overturning specific institutions. Federal Indian law is the one on which Weasel Tail focuses. The Marshall Trilogy (see below) is text and context evoked by Weasel Tail's anticolonial poem. Of the three treaties mentioned in the poem, we should note that there is no "Treaty of the Sacred Blue Lake" specifically. But in 1906 the federal government took Blue Lake from Taos Pueblo and made it part of Carson National Forest, thereby violating one of the provisos of the Treaty of Guadalupe Hidalgo, which "guarantee[d] protection of all property rights recognized by Spanish and Mexican law."[119] Congress restored the lake to the pueblo as trust title land in 1970—a rare concession in the history of federal Indian law, where financial compensation is typically offered for land the Indians traditionally consider nonfungible. In this context, Weasel Tail's reference to "the Treaty of the Sacred Black Hills" invokes the refusal of the Sioux to accept money for the government theft of their most sacred ground.

Weasel Tail's poem, then, invokes the colonial history of the U.S. translation of inalienable Indian communal lands into property as well as the ongoing Indian resistance to this imperial process. It is this ongoing resistance, not some timeless cultural essence, that is represented by the word "traditional" in an Indigenous context. The chant of "title" (of various synonyms for "Doubtful" and "Defective title") in the second stanza and the chant of "breach" in the fifth invoke the violent taking of Native land instituted in the cornerstone of federal Indian law, the Marshall Trilogy, named after the principal author of the decisions in three important Supreme Court cases, Chief Justice John Marshall. *Johnson v. M'Intosh*, the first of these cases, is from the U.S. nation-state perspective a lawful claim to title of all Indian lands based on the medieval legal "doctrine of discovery," formulated by European powers to legalize their invasion of the Americas.[120] *Johnson* is scandalously still the ground of U.S. federal Indian law. However, from the Indian nationalist, or tribal, perspective—and clearly the perspective of justice—the doctrine is a decided "breach of close," or "the unlawful or unwarrantable entry on another person's soil, land, or close."[121] The Cherokee Nation came to the Supreme Court in 1831 to remedy this breach in the second case in the Marshall Trilogy, *Cherokee Nation v. Georgia*.[122]

The third case, *Worcester v. Georgia*[123] (misspelled "Worchester" in Weasel Tail's poem), is invoked as the first line of the fourth stanza. This case triangulates the legal relationship between the U.S. nation-state, Indian "domestic dependent nations," and the several states. In his opinion's conclusion, Marshall asserts: "The Cherokee nation, then, is a distinct community occupying its own territory, with boundaries accurately described, *in which the laws of Georgia can have no force*, and which the citizens of Georgia have no right to enter, but with the assent of the Cherokees themselves, or in conformity with treaties, and with the acts of congress. *The whole intercourse between the United States and this nation is, by our constitution and laws, vested in the government of the United States.*"[124] In relation to the several states, Marshall makes it clear that Indian sovereignty is absolute, while he appears at points in his decision to accord considerably more sovereignty to tribes than he does in both *Johnson* and *Cherokee Nation,* terming the tribes in one instance "distinct political communities, having territorial boundaries, *within which their authority is exclusive, and having the right to all the lands within those boundaries,* which is not only acknowledged, but guaranteed by the United States."[125] In a concurring opinion, however, Justice McLean references the qualification of Indian sovereignty in the first two cases of the Marshall Trilogy: "At no time has the sovereignty of the country been recognized as existing in the Indians, but they have been always admitted to possess many of the attributes of sovereignty. All the rights which belong to self-government have been recognized as vested in them. Their right of occupancy has never been questioned, but the fee in the soil has been considered in the government."[126]

Following *Worcester* in the Weasel Tail poem, the rest of the cases cited, which, including *Worcester,* span from 1832 to 1972, have to do with legal conflicts resulting from the triangle of sovereignties established by the Marshall Trilogy and always played out at the local level, where Indian nations struggle for their sovereignty over land (*Lone Wolf v. Hitchcock* [1903]), their water (*Winters v. United States* [1908], *Pyramid Lake Paiute Tribe v. Morton* [1972], *Gila River Apache Tribe v. Arizona*[127]), the sovereignty of tribal law (*Ex parte Crow Dog* [1883], *Williams v. Lee* [1959]), and the right to use their natural resources in order to survive (*Organized Village of Kake v. Egan* [1962]). As the poem tells us, despite local or temporary victories,[128] the game is rigged in favor of the colonial power, which stages it. *Lone Wolf*, which appears conspicuously in the fourth stanza of the poem, by articulating the doctrine of plenary power, collapses *Worcester*'s triangle of sovereignties and shows the government's hand by asserting virtually absolute power of Congress to keep the game under its control. This results in the inevitability of the declaration of "war" that concludes the poem.

Almanac of the Dead thus displays a keen interest in the national issues of U.S. federal Indian law—as well it might, because, as Silko herself narrates in a book of essays, *Yellow Woman and a Beauty of the Spirit*, her development as a writer, like that of her character Weasel Tail, began during her brief stint in law school, where she recalled that when she "was only five or six years old [and her] father was elected tribal treasurer," Laguna Pueblo was pursuing a land claims case:

> I should have paid more attention to the lesson of the Laguna Pueblo land claims lawsuit from my childhood: The lawsuit was not settled until I was in law school. The U.S. Court of Indian Claims found in favor of the Pueblo of Laguna, but the Indian Claims Court never gives back land wrongfully taken; the court only pays tribes for the land. The amount paid is computed without interest according to the value of the land at the time it was taken.[129]

The Laguna people, in a response typical across Indian communities, did not want money; they wanted their land. Ultimately, Silko understood "that injustice is built into the Anglo-American legal system" and decided to leave law school and pursue a career in literature and the arts; she thought that "the only way to seek justice was through the power of the stories."[130] But her sojourn in law school was far from a waste of time: "It seems to me there is no better way to uncover the deepest values of a culture than to observe the operation of that culture's system of justice."[131] Silko joins Cook-Lynn at this point in emphasizing the intimate connection between Native American literatures and U.S. federal Indian law. As the citations I have been marshaling testify, the ground of that connection is Native land. The law's agenda is to transfer that land into "property," both of which I will define precisely in the following paragraphs, and the literature's exposé of that agenda and resistance to it.

Traditionally, land is the absolute resource of the Native community. Land mediates all relationships on a plane where the Western distinction between the sacred and the secular does not exist, as Justice Brennan asserted in his dissent in *Lyng*. In Western terms, all we can say is that Native land is sacred, the ground of a complex of spiritual beliefs and practices that have traditionally governed Native societies. In traditional Native kinship economies, land was not marketable or alienable by an individual or group acting as an individual within the community. Thus, any treaty signed by chiefs or other designated leaders in which, centrally, the Native nation alienated a portion of its land in exchange for payment of various kinds is a literal imposition of Western terms on Indigenous communities. Treaties were always written in Western languages, which used Western legal vocabularies grounded in the term "property." Native land is therefore not what the West understands as property—a decidedly secular institution—but is, as a traditional value, the antithesis of property.

Property, in both concept and fact, is the foundation of Western capitalist democracies, in the history of which land is the fundamental form of property. These democracies, in their ideal (or ideological) form as nations and in their instrumental form as states, are particular articulations of property. Property in this sense is not simply a material relation but is also, as implied in the very history of the word, a moral and social relation (that is, what is proper) as well as a metaphysical one: the particular properties that define what the West has come to understand as an individual.[132] When the United States was founded, for example, only property-holding white men by and large had the franchise—that is, only white men were considered individuals in the political realm. Even today, not to hold some substantial form of property in the West (typically a house and the land on which it stands) is to have one's individuality bracketed, to find one's recognition as a person seriously compromised in the social, economic, political, and cultural realms. It is worth remembering in this regard that the Virginia Declaration of Rights, written by George Mason, the model Thomas Jefferson used in drafting the Declaration of Independence, in its first section explicitly equates "the means of acquiring and possessing property" with the "unalienable Rights" of "Life, Liberty, and the pursuit of Happiness." In his "Plymouth Oration" of December 22, 1820, Daniel Webster succinctly sums up the centrality of property to the emerging Western nation-states in the age of democratic revolutions: "A republican form of government rests not more on political constitutions, than on those laws which regulate the descent and transmission of property."[133]

At the beginning of the republic, land was the fundamental form of property. Even today, it can be argued, land remains the fundamental form worldwide: the foundation of real estate, for example, and of mineral wealth, indeed of the nation-state itself, which, however transformed by new corporate and political forms of globalization, remains the territorial arena for the two fundamental political issues of the modern era: sovereignty, and the radically unequal distribution of wealth both within and between nations. These are certainly the twin issues facing Indigenous communities throughout the world, including Indians, Alaska Natives, and Native Hawaiians within the United States. It has been the overriding purpose of U.S. federal Indian law, from its inception in the Commerce Clause of the U.S. Constitution to the present, to translate Native land into property—not to entitle Natives to it (except in the special case of Alaska's Native villages) but to legally entitle the federal government to it, and thereby compromise the sovereignty of Native communities.[134]

Over and against the property relation to land, which comprehends land as a commodity, alienable by an individual or an entity acting as an individual, such as a corporation, I can best describe the traditional Native American conception of land as the inalienable ground of the communal, defined exclusively in terms of extended kinship relations. In his poem "We Have Been Told Many Things but We Know This to Be True," Simon Ortiz puts it this way:

> The land. The people.
> They are in relation to each other.
> We are in a family with each other.
> The land has worked with us.
> And the people have worked with it.[135]

Referencing the Hawaiian situation specifically, Trask also sums up the kinship between all Native lands and all Native peoples: "The people cannot exist without the land, and the land cannot exist without the people."[136] To return to Linda Hogan's succinct point: "Here is a lesson: what happens to people and what happens to the land is the same thing." Whether, to take some examples from the Native Americas, we are referring to such different social and cultural formations as those of Native Hawaiians, Alaska Natives, the pueblos in what would become the southwestern United States (or the Mayan pueblos in Mexico), the Iroquois Confederacy in the territory that is now the northeastern United States and Canada, the Creek or Cherokee towns in what became the southeastern United States, or the *tiospaye* of the Oceti Sakowin (Sioux) on the Great Plains of North America, the traditional Native community can be described as an extended family or system of interlocking extended families, often referred to as clans, working in concert for mutual sustenance. Larger formations such as tribes or nations, which typically are centralized political responses to the European invasion, remain based in decentralized extended family relationships. However, it is important not to conflate the Western nuclear family paradigm with the Native paradigm of family—or, as I prefer, kinship. The relational terms of English (father, mother, brother, sister, aunt, uncle, cousin) and their linguistic counterparts in other Western languages do not translate into the terms of Native kinship. In *Navajo Kinship and Marriage,* Gary Witherspoon explains this crucial problem of cross-cultural translation: "The point here is that there is no set of biological or sexual ties *unless they are said by the culture to exist*" (my emphasis):

> For those who follow American and European cultural beliefs, according to which "real" or "true" kinship is limited to those human beings who are blood relatives, it must be pointed out that Navajo define kinship in terms of action or behavior, not in terms of substance.
>
> Although the Navajo believe that through sexual intercourse and birth some kind of common substance is shared, their culture attaches no meaning to this alleged common substance. The Navajo never mention common substance in finding or invoking kinship ties and norms. Kinship is discussed in terms of the acts of giving birth and sharing sustenance.
>
> The primary bond in the Navajo kinship system is the mother–child bond, and it is in this bond that the nature and meaning of kinship become clear. In Navajo culture kinship means intense, diffuse, and enduring solidarity, and this solidarity is realized in actions and

behavior befitting the cultural definitions of kinship solidarity. Just as a mother is one who gives life to her children through birth, and sustains their life by providing them with loving care, assistance, protection, and sustenance, kinsmen are those who sustain each other's life by helping one another, protecting one another, and by the giving or sharing of food and other items of subsistence. Where this kind of solidarity exists, kinship exists; where it does not exist, there is no kinship.

Thus, "kinsmen are differentiated kinds of mothers who give and share according to need. [. . .] To put it simply and concisely, true kinsmen are good mothers."[137]

Within Navajo society, then, one is not defined as a mother by the biological fact of birth but by what it symbolizes: ideally, the act of giving and sharing according to the needs of your kin. Crucially, "there is an effort by the Navajo to think of, and to relate to, everyone in terms of kinship. Everyone is addressed as a kinsman; affinal terms and personal names are seldom used."[138] Whereas in the Navajo case the primary kinship term is *-ma,* traditional Native communities, whatever their particular vocabularies, are, like the Navajos, fundamentally bound together through the extension of kinship terms. In the language of the Diné (meaning "the people," the term the Navajo use to designate themselves), the term *-ma* is not equivalent to the Western term "mother." Compared to the class and sex/gender hierarchies of Western nation-states, which, as Mark Rifkin argues, are based in the structures of heteronormativity,[139] Native communities were marked by egalitarian social and political structures, where group action was based on consensus, precisely because (from an economic perspective) the labor of all—female, male, and "two-spirited" persons[140]—was equally valuable for the sustenance of the group. Refuting the Western stereotype of preinvasion Hawai'i as a feudal society, Trask notes: "And when they [Europeans] said that our chiefs were despotic, they were telling of their own society, where hierarchy always resulted in domination. Thus, any authority or elder was automatically suspected of tyranny."[141] In contrast to the stereotype, Trask defines traditional Hawaiian leadership by two terms: *mana,* which "requires specific identification by the leader with the people, just as the *ali'i,* or chiefs, in days of old were judged by how well they cared for their people"; and *pono,* "balance between people, land, and the cosmos."[142] *Pono* seems to find its translation in the Navajo word *hozho*, which I discuss below. The Navajo origin narratives take as their central theme the struggle or striving to maintain sex/gender balance. *Hozho*, the central term in Navajo philosophy, synonymous with notions of psychic and social balance, translates variously into English as "happiness," "harmony," and "beauty." Witherspoon remarks, "Through their distinctiveness, males and females are related to each other as complementary equals."[143] Ideally, that is, they are in *balance*, a term that translates across Native societies as the key goal of life. Native kinship terms extend as well into the part of the world that the West has increasingly alienated, subordinated, and exploited as "nature." Such extended kinship, made by folding nature into the Native community, sets conservative limits to the use of natural resources precisely because they are valued as kin. William Bevis puts it this way: "Native American nature is urban. The connotation to us of 'urban,' suggesting a dense complex of human variety, is closer to Native American 'nature' than is our word 'natural.' The woods, birds, animals, and humans are all 'downtown,' meaning at the center of action and power, in complex and unpredictable and various relationships. [. . .] Nature is part of tribe."[144]

Santa Clara Pueblo scholar Gregory Cajete notes: "Most Native languages do not have a specific word for 'animals.' Rather, when animals are referred to they are called by their specific names. The fact that there are no specific generic words for animals underlines the extent to which animals were considered to interpenetrate with human life. Animals were partners of humans even when humans were abusive."[145] In the Navajo language, "essential parts, as well as the earth itself, are called mother. Agricultural fields are called mother, corn is called mother, and sheep [central to Navajo lifeways at least since the eighteenth century] are called mother. These applications of the concept *-ma* certainly make it clear that motherhood is defined in terms of the source, sustenance, and reproduction of life."[146]

In this regard, Witherspoon speculates that "mother earth" is not a metaphor but the literal ground of the notion of motherhood itself: "Maybe it is the earth who is really mother, and human mothers merely resemble the earth in some ways and are not really mothers"—that is, I take it, not literal mothers.[147] However, such may be the power of Native kinship terminological systems that they break down the distinction between the literal and the metaphoric—a distinction fundamental to Western notions of identity. James Axtell's study of seventeenth- and eighteenth-century captivity narratives informs us that European captives, taken in frontier conflicts, were often adopted into Indian communities after going through rigorous ceremonies of cultural conversion to take the place of kin lost in battle.[148] Arguably the first U.S. Indian autobiography published, *A Narrative of the Life of Mrs. Mary Jemison* (1824), as told to and written down by James E. Seaver,[149] is the narrative of a Euramerican girl who was captured by the Seneca in 1758, when she was sixteen years old, adopted into the community, and lived with them her entire life. Her descendants are members of the contemporary Seneca community.

Literary critic Kenneth Lincoln understands Native kinship relations as the basis of the oral tradition, what he terms "tribal poetics," "an extended family that reciprocates among people, places, history, flora, and fauna, spirits and gods. [. . .] As with the land itself, the artists cannot presume to possess the living arts entrusted to them."[150] Tribal poetics, then, are the poetics of kinship, of communality; and these poetics expressed in the various Native oral traditions and literatures "interconnect through a poetics resisting Euro-American literary conceptions," which fundamentally pit the individual (artist) against nature.[151]

In theory and practice, the Indigenous conception of community does not exclude conflict either within or between communities, as Indigenous oral traditions clearly attest. That is, kinship is not an ideal but a real mechanism for managing conflict in societies that were without penal institutions until the twentieth century, and in which, because of the importance of every person to the sustenance of the group, exile was an extreme and last resort. As Patrice H. Kunesh writes:

> Indian tribes have historically used banishment as a means of social control and punishment. The custom has been recently revived to help tribes cope with a host of socially deviant and criminally dangerous activities within their respective communities. Hindered by their limited civil and criminal jurisdiction [under federal Indian law], frustrated with their inability to impose meaningful sanctions, and fearful of further disruption, harm, and violence to their communities, tribal governments recognize that the old customs of banishment and exclusion are powerful and effective means of reestablishing order and safety in their communities.
>
> The use of banishment in contemporary tribal society, however, has engendered serious strife and contention because, in effect, it

pits traditional values and customs against modern notions of fairness and due process. In traditional Indian societies, banishment or other sanctions were agreed upon through community consensus and thus were abided and respected by all of the people. Traditional communities rarely contested or disobeyed banishment decisions because they understood that such opposition could seriously jeopardize the social and political cohesiveness of the tribe as a whole. In tribal societies today, however, such decisions and actions are being directly challenged and their fairness questioned, particularly with respect to those decisions that banish or disenroll tribal members for political dissension.

Federal courts have become the arbiters of tribal banishment disputes under an array of unique legal theories. The central issue for the federal court is whether the banishment order imposes a sufficiently severe restraint on the individual's liberty interests as to constitute a detention for purposes of habeas corpus review under the Indian Civil Rights Act of 1968 (ICRA). Other challenges under the ICRA have contended that banishment orders violated the Act's due process and equal protection provisions, constituted cruel and unusual punishment, were unlawful bills of attainder, or were unauthorized or excessive uses of power.[152]

If banishment means being removed from tribal rolls ("disenrolled")—and if the tribes have autonomy in determining the rules of enrollment—then it is indeed a catastrophic measure because it in effect takes away a person's legal identity as an Indian and the federal benefits of health, welfare, and education that come with it, along with any tribal revenues to which the person may be entitled. Banishment may include disenrollment, but as David E. Wilkins and Shelley Hulse Wilkins note, "These two concepts are often conflated, but they are in fact distinctive terms." That is, one can be banished—"physical expulsion from tribal lands"—without being disenrolled, although in "some contemporary tribal cases [. . .] they become functionally similar."[153] The Wilkinses go on to note:

> *Disenrollment* is a legal term of art that arose most prominently during the Indian Reorganization Act period in the 1930s. Disenrollment can broadly be divided into two categories: nonpolitically motivated disenrollments and politically motivated disenrollments. The former are arguably justifiable when due process

is provided because of fraudulent enrollment, error in enrollment, dual membership, or failure to maintain contact with the home community. The latter, we argue, are never justified when driven by economic greed, political power, or personal vendettas, among other reasons. Banishment, in contrast, is an ancient concept that has been utilized by societies and states throughout the world dating back to at least 2285 BCE.[154]

The Wilkinses argue "that far too many tribal nations are engaging in banishment or politically or economically motivated disenrollment practices in clear violation of their own historic values and principles, which at one time utilized peacemaking, mediation, restitution, and compensation to resolve the inevitable disputes that occasionally arose within the community." In a January 2, 2022, article in the *New York Times*, Mike Baker comments on what I would term the disenrollment crisis, writing of the over three hundred disenrollments of the Nooksack tribe of Washington: "Tribes around the country have moved in recent years to trim their membership rolls, scrutinizing family trees and cutting out those deemed to have tenuous or insufficient ties to tribal heritage in an effort to strengthen tribal identity. The disenrollment fights have escalated as casinos and other businesses have brought in new revenue, development, growth and job opportunities."[155] Disenrollments are often part of intratribal resource wars—attempts by those in power in the tribes to purge tribal rolls for economic gain.

In Linda Hogan's novel *Power*, the narrator, a young Indian woman named Omishto, remarks "that in our language the word for 'banish' and the word for 'kill' is the same word; it's the same because in the traditional belief, banishment is equal to death. It is death to be split from your own people, your self, to go away from the place you so love."[156] Banishment is death because in kinship-based cultures, as the syntax of the preceding sentence illustrates, the self is not opposed but apposite to the community. Within the context of this social universe, Standing Rock Sioux lawyer and legal scholar Vine Deloria Jr. and his coauthor, Clifford Lytle, explain the philosophy underpinning traditional Native systems of justice, based as they are in kinship systems:

> The primary goal was simply to mediate the case to everyone's satisfaction. It was not to ascertain guilt and then bestow punishment upon the offender. Under Anglo-American notions of criminal ju-

risprudence, the objectives are to establish fault or guilt and then to punish. The sentencing goals of retribution, revenge, and deterrence and isolation of the offender are extremely important (though the system often pays much lip service to the concept of rehabilitation as well). Under the traditional Indian system the major objective was more to ensure restitution and compensation than retribution. [...] In most instances the system attempted to compensate the victim and his or her family and to solve the problem in such a manner that all could forgive and forget and continue to live within the tribal society in harmony with one another. [...] Banishment was extremely rare in most tribes and represented a very serious breach of the fundamental folkways that bound the tribe together. [...] Self-help was prevalent in many tribes and the specter of continuing blood feud between powerful families, with its subsequent disruption of community life, was sufficiently distasteful to prevent family revenge from getting out of hand.[157]

In Native communities, the killing of a member of one group (family or clan) by a member of another might be balanced by a single counterkilling or, alternatively, a payment of some kind, either of which, as agreed to by the aggrieved party, would close the circuit of violence. Anthropologist Circe Sturm references the Cherokee example:

One of the clan members' most important obligations to one another was to respect and maintain the law of blood revenge. This "law of blood" meant that if a member of the Paint Clan were killed by someone of the Wolf Clan, even if by accident, then all Paints were morally bound to avenge the death of their kinsman. The clan of the victim would usually exact vengeance by taking the life of the original killer, at which point "both clans involved would consider the matter settled because harmony had been restored."[158]

Interclan conflicts within the Hopi villages have been resolved historically by the formation of new villages, which nevertheless remain within the Hopi fold through clan ties that link village to village on the three Hopi mesas in northeastern Arizona.[159] As Deloria and Lytle note, the last resort for maintaining balance in Indigenous social systems was exile. Psychic, economic, and social survival outside the kinship community was precarious at best, and no person was superfluous to the community. These Native values of balance, the consequences of their rupture, and the communal mode of their restoration by exiling transgressors are the subject of the Inuit film *Atanarjuat* (The fast runner), released in 2000 and directed by Inuit filmmaker Zacharias Kunuk, based on traditional narratives of the Inuit people. As Arnold Krupat's detailed analysis of the film's narrative indicates, the murder of Atanarjuat's brother is revenged in blood by Atanarjuat, who, like his brother, goes by variations of his name in the narratives. Krupat reports that when Kunuk was asked at a lecture he gave in 2002, "Did you make any changes to the original legend?," he responded with, "We all changed the ending." Regarding the killings that are a consistent element of the story, Kunuk said, "Paul [Apak Angilirq, coproducer and cowriter] felt that doesn't make any sense. That is going to go on and on. We also knew they used to just send people away instead of killing them and that was a better ending so we chose that."[160] Apak's sense that murdering the murderer "doesn't make any sense" comes from a sense that it would not bring the community back into balance but lead to a trajectory of killings "on and on." So the filmmakers substituted what they understood is a traditional solution of banishment as a form of rebalancing the community. The film ends, then, with a "song, one in which all the remaining community members join, and the story concludes with an intact Inuit community."[161] In email correspondence with Dr. Louis-Jacques Dorais, I wondered if the words in Inuktitut for "banishment" and "kill" might be synonymous because I was thinking about Linda Hogan's remark in *Power,* cited previously, "that in our language the word for 'banish' and the word for 'kill' is the same word; it's the same because in the traditional belief, banishment is equal to death." Dr. Dorais responded:

> In the Eastern Arctic dialects, banishing and killing are definitely not the same. Banishing (*piiqtittiniq,* "making someone [put] themselves away") was a means to solve community problems without provoking death, because the banished individual(s) could always come back after a number of years if they repented and were not considered dangerous any more. Killing (*inuarniq,* "getting at a human being") was only resorted to when one individual who had become murderous was considered an immediate danger. In such a case, a relative of the murdered person would actually kill the murderer, or one man chosen by the community would kill him, then taking his wife and children in his household.[162]

The emphasis on community in both the case of banishment and the case of killing is important to note. Banishment need not be permanent because the community is forgiving if the banished person is "repentant" and no longer considered dangerous—that is, in effect is rehabilitated. It is also clear that the killing of the "murderous" person is a community decision and that the one who does the killing, whether a relative of the murdered person or someone chosen by the community, takes in the family of the executed person, which is an act of communalism—a way, it would seem, of bringing the community back into balance. So the way the killing was accomplished in traditional Inuit communities ensured that the killings would not, in Apak's sense, go "on and on." The common element in both the punishment of banishment and killing, then, is communal "balance."

A key case in U.S. federal Indian law that depended on the difference between Native concepts of restorative justice, resolving conflict through communal balance, and Western concepts of agonistic justice based in isolating and punishing the guilty *individual*, is *Ex parte Crow Dog* (1883).[163] Legal scholar Sidney Harring summarizes the case:

> Early in the afternoon of August 5, 1881, on a dusty road just outside the Rosebud Indian Agency on the Great Sioux Reservation in Dakota Territory, Kan-gi-shun-ca (Crow Dog) shot to death Sin-ta-ga-le-Scka (Spotted Tail), a Brule Sioux chief. Great confusion followed as Crow Dog was hunted down by Indian police on the orders of the reservation chief clerk and locked in a military cell at Fort Niobara, Nebraska. The families of both men met and, following tribal law, settled the matter for $600 in cash, eight horses, and one blanket. A year later, Crow Dog, still in jail, was tried in Dakota territorial court in Deadwood, convicted of murder, and sentenced to hang. In December 1883, the U.S. Supreme Court reversed the conviction, holding that the United States had no criminal jurisdiction over Indian tribes in "Indian country," because the tribes, inherently sovereign, retained the right to administer their own law [under the Trade and Intercourse Acts] as an element of that sovereignty. Crow Dog returned to his people a hero and a "troublemaker" in the eyes of his Indian agent, living out his life a traditional leader, resisting U.S. government authority until the end, even refusing to accept his allotment until the year before he died at the age of seventy-five in 1911.[164]

The dispute between Crow Dog and Spotted Tail that led to the shooting was political. As Harring notes, Crow Dog resisted U.S. imperialism and settler colonialism, while Spotted Tail, who had been a resister, reconciled himself to the colonial status quo after armed Sioux resistance was no longer possible. Two years after *Ex parte Crow Dog*, Congress enacted the Major Crimes Act of 1885, which nullified the tribal right to try Indian on Indian major crimes in Indian Country.[165] Then, in *U.S. v. Kagama* (1886), a challenge by a Native plaintiff to the Major Crimes Act, the Supreme Court in effect reversed its decision in *Crow Dog*, upholding the plenary power of Congress in Indian matters and concomitantly effectively nullifying the Court's constitutional powers of judicial review in these matters.[166] As David Wilkins has pointed out, "The judiciary has never voided a single congressional act that diminished or abrogated any inherent or aboriginal tribal rights."[167] More importantly, the Major Crimes Act imposed agonistic justice in major felonies on what had been systems of restorative justice for resolving conflicts in Indian Country.

As for intergroup conflict—what the West terms "war"—it is enough to say here that whatever its function (ritual, territorial, raiding) between Native communities, it cannot be understood in terms of modern Western warfare, which has been based in an imperial-colonial paradigm: the clash of nation-states over issues of occupying property. These property issues persist even in what might appear to be the postmodern paradigm of a war on terror, for here too violence centers on the nation-state, which still struggles to maintain its territorial integrity, defined in terms of entitlement, in the face of attacks by extranational and highly mobile organizations. Even Pekka Hämäläinen, who argues for a Commanche empire dating from the middle of the eighteenth to the middle of the nineteenth centuries, notes, "The Commanches [. . .] were an imperial power with a difference: their aim was not to conquer and colonize, but to coexist, control, and exploit. [. . .] The idea of land as a form of private, revenue-producing property was absent in Commanche culture."[168] Given this difference, can one accurately term the Commanches an empire? Or is this naming simply a classic Western move, going back to early days of the European invasion of the Americas, of translating Indigenous political systems into Western political terms in order to absorb these systems into a Western epistemology?[169]

Once capitalist economies disrupted Native economies, Native kinship relations to land were disrupted by property relations, and Natives were forced to come to terms with them. But Native communities have also managed to mount a continuing, if often divided, resistance to the institution of property. That is, the Western imperial invasions of Native America have brought collaborations. I use "collaboration" as noted in the introduction, in the range of its meanings from cooperation to coercion, emphasizing that in a colonial context, cooperation is always more or less inflected by coercion. In the post–Revolutionary War period in particular, treaties negotiated between the United States and Indian tribes were forms of coerced collaboration, a phrase that to this day characterizes the relationships established between Indians and the federal government by federal Indian law. The ascription of the interchangeable terms "tribe" and "nation" to Indian communities is itself a sign of this collaboration: the projection in the first instance of European conceptions of centralized governance and hierarchical social structure onto various kinds of extended kinship-based communities. Even the ceremonially centralized Iroquois Confederacy governed itself by a mode of consensus located in the matrilineal clan structure of the five (and ultimately six) confederated tribes; decisions were locally not centrally made. Thus, the confederacy could never act with the unanimity of a nation-state, a sign of organizational failure, perhaps, in Western terms but a sign of egalitarian flexibility from a Native perspective.[170]

In time, to resist and deal with invading European powers, the kinship-based communities that shared language and other cultural patterns were compelled to build tribal or national, and sometimes pantribal, structures to conduct foreign relations such as defensive warfare and treaty negotiations and later to deal with and resist U.S. federal bureaucracies. The history of these pan-Indian movements forms an important part of the colonial contexts of Native American literatures: most of them marshaled to resist the European subversion of Native sovereignty in one form or another, from the Pueblo Revolt of 1680 against the Spanish[171] through the resistance movements of Pontiac against the British in the mid-eighteenth century[172] and Tecumseh against the United States in the early nineteenth century,[173] to the formation of the Red Power movement in the late 1960s.[174] Today, the terms "tribe" and "nation" are common parlance in referring to Native communities, though Indians and whites often mean very different things when they use these terms because each is grounded in sovereignty.

Sovereignty, which has been at the heart of Native politics since the European invasion, is vexed, for in the first place, it is a Western term of international law. In the third of the three foundational Supreme Court cases in federal Indian law comprising the Marshall Trilogy, *Worcester v. Georgia* (1832), Chief Justice John Marshall makes clear the context in which the Court is applying "sovereignty" to the status of Indian communities, which it does throughout the case: "The words 'treaty' and 'nation' are words of our own language, selected in our diplomatic and legislative proceedings, by ourselves, having each a definite and well understood meaning. We have applied them to Indians, as we have applied them to the other nations of the earth. They are applied to all in the same sense."[175]

In international law, only "nations" have the right to sign "treaties" with other nations; this right signals their "sovereignty." However, under federal Indian law, "sovereignty," rather than being a mark of the autonomy of Native nations, is instead a mark of their subordination to the colonizing sovereign—the United States. Thus, in *Cherokee Nation v. Georgia* (1831), which the Court decided the year before *Worcester*, Indian nations were oxymoronically defined as "domestic dependent nations,"[176] which contradicts the definition of a "nation" in international law as being "foreign" and "independent." We recognize, then, the discourse of sovereignty in relation to Indigenous peoples as a foreign discourse into which Indigenous peoples have been translated as a constitutive part of colonialism.

In "Sovereignty," Kanien'kehá:ka (Mohawk) scholar Taiaiake Alfred locates the origin of the term in Western legal discourse:

> The discourse of sovereignty upon which the current *post facto* justification [for European sovereignty] rests is an exclusively European discourse. That is, European assertions in both a legal and political sense were made strictly vis-à-vis other European powers, and did not impinge upon or necessarily even affect in law or politics the rights and status of indigenous nations. It is only from our distant historical vantage point, and standing upon a counterfactual rock, that we are able to see European usurpations of indigenous sovereignty as justified.[177]

Here, while rejecting "the discourse of sovereignty" at this point in the essay, Alfred is using key terms from that discourse: "nations" and "sovereignty." However, he later suggests redefining the terms from an Indigenous point of view:

> The challenge for indigenous peoples in building appropriate postcolonial governing systems is to disconnect the notion of sovereignty from its Western legal roots and transform it. It is all too often taken for granted that what indigenous peoples are seeking in recognition of their nationhood is at its core the same as that which countries like Canada and the United States possess now. In fact, most of the current generation of indigenous politicians see politics as a zero-sum contest for power in the same way that non-indigenous politicians do. Rather than a value rooted in a traditional indigenous philosophy, indigenous politicians regard the nationhood discourse as a lever to gain bargaining position. [. . .] Until sovereignty as a concept shifts from the dominant "state sovereignty" construct and comes to reflect more of the sense embodied in Western notions such as personal sovereignty or popular sovereignty, it will remain problematic if integrated within indigenous political struggles.[178]

Alfred moves from rejecting the term "sovereignty" to considering reforming or revolutionizing it so that it signifies Indigenous forms of governance. Vine Deloria Jr., for example, notes that Native ideas of sovereignty "can be said to consist more of continued cultural integrity than of political powers."[179] In Vizenor's novel *Heirs of Columbus*, federal judge Beatrice Lord remarks, "The essence of sovereignty is imaginative, an original tribal trope, communal and spiritual, an idea that is more than metes and bounds in treaties."[180] Alfred himself asks, "Is there a Native philosophical alternative?"[181] His answer is worth reproducing at length, reflecting as it does fundamental values centered on the land that intersect the range of cultures represented in Native literatures:

> Many traditionalists hope to preserve a set of values that challenge the destructive, homogenizing force of Western liberalism and materialism: they wish to preserve a regime that honors the autonomy of individual conscience, noncoercive forms of authority, and deep respect and interconnection between human beings and the other elements of creation. The contrast between indigenous conceptions and dominant Western constructions in this regard could not be more severe. In most traditional indigenous conceptions, nature

and the natural order are the basic referents for thinking of power, justice, and social relations. Western conceptions, with their own particular philosophical distance from the natural world, have more often reflected different kinds of structures of coercion and social power.[182]

Alfred, echoing the Native novelists, poets, and essayists I have been referencing, as well as the Native Latin American discourse of the rights of Pachamama (mother earth), remarks, "Indigenous philosophies are premised on the belief that the human relationship to the earth is primarily one of partnership [. . .] reflecting a spiritual connection with the land established by the Creator [that] gives human beings special responsibilities with the areas they occupy, linking them in a natural and sacred way to their territories," whereas the Western relation to land is one of *property*, in which "the industry and enterprises center on natural resource extraction. Trees, rocks, and fish become resources and commodities with a value calculated solely in monetary terms."[183]

Alfred finally focuses on the idea of a sovereignty-free world, a world governed by the Indigenous values that he articulates and that Native writers espouse: "For people committed to transcending the imperialism of state sovereignty, the challenge is to de-think the concept of sovereignty and replace it with a notion of power that has at its root a more appropriate premise. [. . .] Before their near destruction by Europeans, many indigenous societies achieved sovereignty-free regimes of conscience and justice that allowed for the harmonious coexistence of humans and nature for hundreds of generations."[184]

In his book *Peace, Power, Righteousness: An Indigenous Manifesto*, Alfred specifies the model of sovereignty-free Indigenous governance, based in kinship, he has in mind:

> The Native concept of governance is based on what a great student of indigenous societies, Russell Barsh, has called "primacy of conscience." There is no central or coercive authority, and decision-making is collective. Leaders rely on their persuasive abilities to achieve a consensus that respects the autonomy of individuals, each of whom is free to dissent from and remain unaffected by the collective decision. The clan or family is the basic unit of social organization, and larger forms of organization from tribe through nation to confederacy, are all predicated on the political autonomy and eco-

nomic independence of clan units through family-based control of lands and resources. [...] The indigenous tradition sees government as the collective power of the individual members of the nation; there is no separation between society and state. [...] By contrast, in the European tradition power is surrendered to the representatives of the majority, whose decisions on what they think is the collective good are then imposed on all citizens.[185]

At the present moment, the Indigenous Zapatista movement in Chiapas, Mexico, represents an important experiment in sovereignty-free governance. Alvaro Reyes and Mara Kaufman, who continue to work closely with the Zapatistas, encapsulate the experiment, which enacts in the Zapatista autonomous villages the values Alfred articulates, as follows:

> We argue that the singularity of the Zapatista struggle arises in the practice of *mandar-obedeciendo* (rule by obeying). [...] *Mandar-obedeciendo* has allowed the Zapatistas to formulate their struggle not as one for the establishment of sovereignty or even some form of sovereignty (concepts that they show us are ultimately tied to the history of conquest as well as to the regime of social control proffered by contemporary global capitalism), but rather as the practical and tendential unmaking of sovereignty, be it in classical or contemporary forms. This possibility for the active unmaking of sovereignty presents itself in Zapatista territory through a new spatialization of an intricate system for the development of what the Zapatistas have termed "autonomy." This is an autonomy that the Zapatistas claim is central not only for the struggles of indigenous peoples but also as an antidote to the dispersed form of global "paracoloniality" that accompanies the appearance of what the Zapatistas have called "the Empire of money."[186]

Historically, Reyes and Kaufman continue, sovereignty is defined by "a relation of command obedience" (*mandato-obedecer*), whatever form that relation of subjection might take, autocratic or democratic.[187] In contrast, the "Zapatista method for implementing 'autonomy' took the form of what they called rule by obeying [*mandar-obedeciendo*]. In direct contrast to *mandato-obeceder*, which lies at the base of the sovereign tradition, rule by obeying draws on the community practices of self-organization through assembly that tendentially disperse power (through a series of mutual obligations, shared responsibilities, and the accountability and revocability of delegates), effectively preventing the accumulation of power that might ensue from delegation."[188] What we have here is in effect the traditional governance mode of consensus used by Indigenous societies. Importantly, these forms of sovereignty-free governance are not regimes of rights, which are a component of sovereignty to protect citizens from overreach by sovereigns, but of responsibilities based in kinship.

The method of Indigenous governance described here is historically integrated with the traditional social and economic values articulated by Alfred and practiced, as is governance, by the Zapatistas. This mode of economic life is articulated by the Quechua phrase *sumak kausay,* or *buen vivir,* a way of living antithetical to capitalism and its contemporary manifestation, neoliberalism. In his pamphlet *Buen Vivir,* Thomas Fatheuer, following the indigenous Andean traditions from which it emerges, defines the term:

> It is important to distinguish this concept from the Western idea of prosperity. *Buen Vivir* is not geared toward "having more" and does not see accumulation and growth, but rather a state of equilibrium as its goal. Its reference to the indigenous world view is also central: its starting point is not progress or growth as a linear model of thinking, but the attainment and reproduction of the equilibrium state of *Sumak Kausay.* [. . .] *Buen Vivir* is a culture of life based on the ancestral knowledge of indigenous peoples that aims to strike a balance, striving for harmony between humans and nature alike, and which foresees a return to a way of life that had been suppressed by colonization. "We must return to being, because colonization has made us into 'wanting to be.' Many of us want to be, but as of yet, we are not. We now want to return to our own path to our being."[189]

In contrast to this form of political, social, and economic life, as Alfred suggests, the Native nations in the United States and Canada govern themselves with variations of sovereignty, following the supersovereign that governs them, the nation-state, within the framework of federal Indian law. These forms of sovereignty, as Glenn Coulthard argues in *Red Skin, White Masks,* confer on these Indigenous governments the "recognition" of the supersovereign; this system of recognition ensures the continuation of the settler-colonial state. Writing in "the Canadian context" of federal Indian law, which parallels (with differences) that of the United States thanks to their common origin in British colonial politics, Coulthard notes that "colonial relations of power are no longer reproduced primarily through overtly coercive means, but rather through the asymmetrical exchange of mediated forms of state recognition and accommodation."[190] Next, following Frantz Fanon's book *Black Skin, White Masks,* he continues to elaborate the argument that animates Fanon:

> Fanon's analysis suggests that in contexts where colonial rule is not reproduced through force alone, the maintenance of settler-state hegemony requires the production of what he liked to call "colonized subjects": namely, the production of the specific modes of colonial thought, desire, and behavior that implicitly or explicitly commit the colonized to the types of practices and subject positions that are required for their continued domination. However, unlike the liberalized appropriation of Hegel that continues to inform many contemporary proponents of identity politics, in Fanon recognition is not posited as a source of freedom and dignity for the colonized, *but rather as the field of power through which colonial relations are produced and maintained.*[191]

Fanon's analysis, as Coulthard suggests with his use of the term "hegemony," recalls Antonio Gramsci's definition of the term in his prison writings, where he defines it as "the spontaneous consent given by the great masses of the population to the general direction imposed on social life by the dominant fundamental group."[192] This "consent" must be scrutinized within the context of ongoing forms of Native resistance to colonialism. That is, it is coerced consent—a contradiction in terms. Coulthard appears to recognize this when he terms Fanonian "recognition" as a "field of power."

THE COLONIZATION OF NATIVE IDENTITY THROUGH BIOLOGIC

Is it possible to find a way out of the bitter disputes about identity which characterize a great deal of the interaction among Indian people today? Can tribes take identity issues seriously without being destroyed by them? What role can American Indian academics play in contributing to questions about racial identity? Those are questions that will require some more work, but they have profound implications—not only for tribal communities but also for the academy.

Eva Marie Garroutte, Real Indians: Identity and the Survival of Native America

There's no way to talk about blood quantum in Blackfoot, because it's not a concept that belongs to us, that comes from our cultural history. In our language belonging has everything to do with who you are related to, and who claims you as a relative, and being related to someone doesn't necessarily have anything to do with "blood."

Sterling HolyWhiteMountain, "Sterling HolyWhiteMountain on Blood Quantum, Native Art, and Cultural Appropriation"

As noted in the previous chapter, allotment translated communal Native land worked by clan relationships into small property holdings titled to members grouped in patriarchal nuclear families. This marked a major attack on traditional Native identity formations, as I have been rehearsing these formations in the preceding pages, based on a relationship between kinship and land. Although not incorporated into the Dawes Act, a principal weapon in the arsenal was the federal invention of blood quantum regulations for determining a person's degree of Indianness, which developed as part of allotment policy in the wake of the Burke Act of 1906.[1] The idea of blood quantum, which was a particular culmination of the scientific racism that had been developing throughout the nineteenth century, supplanted (or at least significantly modified by a particular biologic of identity) Indian cultural logics of identity that were based on kinship relations.[2] The biologic of blood quantum brings into focus the vocabulary of racial mixing (termed amalgamation before 1860 and miscegenation after 1860), which in U.S.–Indian relations took a particular form, now quite familiar to us. This form embodies the identity of mixed-blood people in opposition to full-blood people. This is a central figure of conflict in both federal Indian law and Native American literatures.

Because of Cherokee importance in the development of both U.S. federal Indian law and Native literatures (among other texts, the Cherokees gave us the first Native syllabary, the first Native newspaper, and the first Native written constitution), the Cherokees provide an important and readily available history of the shift in emphasis from cultural logic to biologic in the colonial and antebellum United States. While in certain respects the trajectory of Cherokee history in terms of identity shifts is not universal in Indian Country, particularly in its involvement with the Western institution of chattel slavery, it is broadly instructive, if not always representative, as regards the biologic of blood quantum in Native identity.

Theda Purdue summarizes the processes of political change in Cherokee society that are imbricated with the shift in logics of identity:

> Beginning in 1730 [. . .] Cherokee political history is the chronicle of the centralization of power in response to white pressure for Cherokee land and to the need for regulating the behavior of their own people for the protection of increasing maldistributed property. The process culminated in 1827 when the Cherokees organized a republic under a constitution patterned after that of the United States government.[3]

From a decentralized town structure—each community was governed through a process of consensus involving all members, and towns were informally linked through a matrilineal clan system[4]—the Cherokees changed, first, under the British, into a tribal society with a centralized council representing all the towns, primarily in diplomatic relations, and then, under the United States, beginning in the early nineteenth century and culminating in the adoption of the Cherokee constitution in 1827, into a nation that administered both domestic and foreign affairs through a republican form of government divided into legislative, judicial, and executive branches, with "the office of the principal chief [. . .] remodeled in the Cherokee Constitution in imitation of that of the president of the United States."[5]

By 1828, this national formation, thoroughly permeated by market relations, had made significant inroads in transforming Cherokee society into a class-based, patriarchal structure, in which, in the words of Wilma Mankiller, former principal chief of the Cherokee Nation, "the strength of our people diminished. [. . .] The clan system and the time-honored practice of descent through maternal lines began to erode. The Cherokee Constitution further limited women's rights by excluding them from all government offices and prohibiting them from voting. Cherokee women were expected to become subservient and domesticated like white women, who were home oriented."[6] The constitution also prohibited anyone of African ancestry from political participation.[7]

According to Purdue, "an economic class system began to emerge" in Cherokee society in the eighteenth century around the trade of "Indian deerskins and war captives" for "European ammunition, hoes, knives, hatchets, kettles, blankets, and other goods":

> Contributing to the inequality in wealth were the children of white traders and Indian women; such children inherited the mother's tribal affiliation along with the father's property. The warriors and descendants of traders began to dominate politics as well as economics. Previously, every man (and some women) had a voice in government, and leaders only advised and never coerced. But because Europeans desired the alliance of warriors and communicated more easily with bilingual descendants of traders, political power came to be concentrated in the hands of an economic elite.[8]

This economic and ruling elite was mainly composed of a small but nevertheless powerful slaveholding class: "over half the signers of the Constitution of 1827 owned bondsmen."[9] "According to the Census of 1835, the slaveholders cultivated more acres, produced more corn, and owned most of the nascent industries in the Nation."[10] Purdue offers an explanation for the ascendancy of this class, which in 1835 comprised 207 of an estimated Cherokee population of 17,000.[11] A total of 168 of these slaveholders "owned fewer than 10 slaves," and Joseph Vann, the largest holder, owned 110.[12]

Slaveholders controlled the government of the Cherokee Nation partly because they had created it, but also because their wealth and situation gained the respect of fellow tribesmen and enabled them to deal more effectively with whites. The slaveholders' advantage over non-slaveholders in relationships with whites stemmed from inter-marriage as well. Only 17 percent of the people living in the Cherokee Nation in 1835 had any white ancestors, but 78 percent of the members of families owning slaves claimed some proportion of white blood. Contact with a white parent or grandparent gave these people a headstart toward "civilization." Moreover, the Cherokee slaveholders seem to have identified linguistically with white society. Among the people (including infants and small children) living in slaveholding families, 39 percent could read English, while only 13 percent were proficient in reading Cherokee [the Cherokee government had adopted the syllabary of Sequoyah in 1821; and both the Cherokee Constitution and the Cherokee newspaper the *Phoenix* were printed bilingually]. In the case of non-slaveholding Cherokees, less than 4 percent were capable of reading English, but 18 percent could read Cherokee. Literacy in English clearly gave the slaveholders a tremendous advantage at a time when troubles with the whites were mounting.[13]

The preceding citations register revolutionary changes in Cherokee communal and personal identity in the hundred-year period from 1730 to 1830, though not without resistance from traditional forces within the community.[14] These changes worked to replace a nonprofit economy of kin-based communal land in which resources were equally distributed with a market economy of property relations in which certain people began to emerge as individuals, set distinctly and hierarchically apart through the production and investment of surpluses for profit. In Silko's *Ceremony*, white psychiatrists tell Tayo "that he would never get well as long as he used words like 'we' and 'us.'" Rather, "he had to think only of himself, and not about the others."[15] Two models of sociopsychic health, European and Native, are embodied in opposed languages containing opposed subject positions: individual and communal, "I" and "we." At Cherokee, a century of European and Indian collaboration was producing a new and antagonistic subject position. Purdue represents the antagonisms in relation to the introduction of chattel slavery in the Cherokee community, though elsewhere she suggests that they began to emerge earlier as a result of diverse pressures of postinvasion politics:

> Slaves were property and a form of wealth, but traditional Cherokee economics shunned both the accumulation of property and the acquisition of wealth and ridiculed the production of anything in excess of basic needs. A plantation system using slave labor necessitated some sort of centralized control and police power, but traditional Cherokee government bordered on *anarchy,* and enforcement of behavioral rules was strictly an individual or family matter. Although Cherokees recognized only human beings and possessed no sense of racial identity before extensive contact with whites, the enslavement of one race by another inevitably produced a feeling of racial superiority among the masters.[16]

In resistance to or compromise with this radical change of communal identity from one based on kin to an individualistic one based on property, the Cherokees, through their national council, formulated a set of laws that attempted to contain property relations in land within the nation while interdicting them in foreign relations. Persico summarizes:

> Another set of articles [to the Cherokee constitution] was adopted in 1825. Its primary objective was to confirm and to formalize the control of the General Council over the lands and other public property of the Cherokee Nation. Articles I and II stated that all lands and annuities were public property. Improvements on the land belonged to those who had made, or bought, them. Article III reserved to the General Council the exclusive right to dispose of public property. Articles IV and VIII denied the principal chiefs any power to dispose of public property, to make treaties, or to overrule the Council's decisions.[17]

Theda Purdue notes of the council's ultimate ruling to protect Cherokee land, "In 1829 the Council passed a law that made cession of tribal land a capital offense."[18] This is a compromise formation—communal property—that, from a traditional Native standpoint, is an oxymoron.

We can read in this history of Native identity the emergence of biologic and its intensifying inflection of cultural logic in forming a new vocabulary of race. Purdue attributes the introduction of "a feeling of racial superiority" in Cherokee society to the institution of slavery;

the identity of the masters in this case—an emerging entrepreneurial class of Cherokees—was already being reformulated beginning in the first quarter of the nineteenth century in terms of the new vocabulary of scientific racism that grounded the hierarchical opposition of civilized/savage in a theory of blood quantum. This theory held that the whiter one was, the more civilized, with a concomitant erasure/naturalization of the political agenda that defined both whiteness and civilization.

As noted, Purdue records the social circumstances of this shift in the emergence of a property-holding class composed of "the children of white traders and Indian women." In addition to inheriting the property of white fathers, these children also inherited the valuable cultural capital of access to English, which gave them a considerable edge, not to mention an inclination, in collaborating with the European community. The collaboration included fulfilling the strategic function of translating between the two communities. This process of acculturation, which preceded the institution of slavery among the Cherokees, brought with it the biologic of blood quantum in the vocabulary of racial hierarchy, which ultimately rationalized the enslavement of black people. Thus, a class of Indians nominated "mixed bloods" or "half bloods" or "half breeds" in discourses from the legal to the vernacular emerged in the antebellum United States. Such a class is referenced by these terms of blood quantum in the *Opinions of the Attorney General of the United States* in 1856: "Indians are not citizens of the United States, but domestic subjects. Half-breed Indians are to be treated as Indians in all respects so long as they retain their tribal relations."[19] Over time, the class of mixed bloods became identified with, if not wholly identical to, a class within tribal society that was linked to white society with terms such as "friendly" or "progressive" and that was (stereo)typically opposed to a class of full bloods, who in contradistinction were labeled "hostile" or "conservative."

The complicating factors in understanding such oppositions are well illustrated by John Ross, the first principal chief of the Cherokees under their constitution and a member of the emergent propertied class. Ross—a "half breed," according to the attorney general's report just cited, and one-eighth Cherokee in terms of contemporary blood quantum—was both a proponent of Cherokee adaptation of Western forms and an adamant opponent of removal.[20] He was thus both "progressive" and "conservative," "friendly" and "hostile" to U.S. designs, though we should also note that there were many traditionalists, most designated full-blood, who were opposed to both adaptation and removal. In the Cherokee Nation, these traditionalists were represented by the Keetoowah Society:

> Though the Keetoowah Society was open to Christian Cherokees, it did not admit members of mixed racial ancestry, and even educated full-bloods were suspect. Keetoowah meetings were conducted in Cherokee and the proceedings recorded in the syllabary, which provided a modicum of protection from curious outsiders. However, this "anti–mixed blood sentiment among Keetoowahs was strange, because several important leaders had mixed racial ancestry The categories of full and mixed were much more complex than mixed biological parentage." Again, we see how full-blood and mixed-blood were social, cultural, and political constructs. "Politically speaking, the terms served as shorthand. Mixed stood for accommodation with whites, a willingness to negotiate. Full bloods were uncompromising and religiously insistent."[21]

It is important to emphasize, then, at every turn, that while the terms of blood quantum represent an emergent biologic, this itself is an effect of a particular cultural logic. Thus, terms like "mixed- blood" and "full-blood" seek to ground cultural practices and political decisions in the imagined stability of categories attributed to nature.

These complicated alignments are the result of European colonialism, which instigated tribal factions that would continue to take shape in Indian Country over the next century and comprise today a powerfully divisive force in intratribal politics, where in various reservation communities, grassroots groups comprising people who identify with traditional cultural practices oppose tribal governments elected within the terms of Western democracies. Mankiller summarizes these new biocultural or biopolitical identity configurations as they unfolded in the Cherokee community: "By the 1820s, the mixed-bloods, some of them with blue eyes and light hair, had acquired most of the tribal wealth. Even though they still had to share their power with the full-bloods, they held at least 40 percent of the Cherokee government posts. Although the majority of the white blood in members of the tribe came from the male side, an 1824 Cherokee Nation census noted seventy-three white women as the spouses of Cherokee men, and 147 white men as husbands of Cherokee women."[22]

Mankiller maintains "that the influence of the United States government in the area of identifying Indians by degrees of native blood had not yet had its effect on our tribe. To the Cherokee mind at that time, one's identity as Cherokee depended solely on clan affiliation. Ross's mixed-blood mother was a Cherokee by definition because she and her sisters were members of the Bird Clan. Cherokee children belong to their mother's clan and retain membership for life, so Ross, too, was a Cherokee of the Bird Clan."[23] This biologic was a new discourse of identity in the West as well, in the process of forming and not fully distinguished yet from cultural logic, of which, as noted, it is merely a particular development. But in the antebellum period, biologic, however ambiguously, entered the discourse of federal Indian law in the landmark case of *U.S. v. Rogers* in 1846.

Wilkins gives this summary of the facts of the case:

[William S.] Rogers, a yeoman, got into a deadly scuffle in September 1844 with Jacob Nicholson, who, like Rogers, was Euro-American by race, had married into the Cherokee Nation, and was, by Cherokee law, a citizen of their nation. Rogers killed Nicholson by stabbing him in the side with a five-dollar knife. Rogers was arrested, then indicted by the grand jury in the district court of Arkansas in April 1845. When he was brought into federal court to hear the indictment, Rogers, representing himself, argued that the district court lacked jurisdiction to try him because both he and the deceased were regarded legally as *Indians* by the Cherokee Nation and under the 1834 trade and intercourse act the United States lacked jurisdiction in such cases [of Indian-on-Indian crime].[24]

The case came to the Supreme Court in 1846 "on a certificate of division," the two circuit court judges not being able to decide the matter.[25] Somewhat contrary to Wilkins's summary, Rogers, in his plea, did not assert that "he and the deceased were regarded legally as *Indians* by the Cherokee Nation" but that he and Nicholson were *Cherokee Indians*.[26] This is important because Rogers's identification of himself as a "Cherokee Indian" suggests an important tension between the cultural-political identity "Cherokee" and what was at this moment emerging as the racial designation "Indian." That is, the identity of "Cherokee Indian" articulates a coupling of cultural logic with biologic. A longer quote from Rogers's plea can help us understand this coupling, which represents the historic shift in emphasis from *Cherokee* Indian to Cherokee *Indian*—that is, from cultural logic to biologic:

> And the defendant further says, that, from the time he removed, as aforesaid, he incorporated himself with the said tribe of Indians as one of them, and was and is so treated, recognized, and adopted by said tribe and the proper authorities thereof, and exercised and exercises all the rights and privileges of a Cherokee Indian in said tribe, and was and is domiciled in the country aforesaid; that, before _____ and at the time of the commission of the supposed crime, if any such was committed, to wit, in the Indian country aforesaid, he, the defendant, by the acts aforesaid, became, and was, and still is, a citizen of the Cherokee nation, and became, and was, and still is, a Cherokee Indian, within the true intent and meaning of the act of Congress in that behalf provided.[27]

The syntax of the plea suggests that to be a "citizen of the Cherokee nation," which is to "exercise [. . .] all the rights and privileges" thereof, is to be a Cherokee Indian. On the one hand, we can say that Cherokee thinking incorporates a biological term of race, "Indian" (coined by Columbus and acquiring its biological meaning in the nineteenth-century discourses of law and anthropology), into a cultural-political term, "Cherokee," representing a particular postinvasion national formation that took shape in the eighteenth and nineteenth centuries in response to Anglo-American imperialism. Anthropologist James Mooney notes: "Cherokee, the name by which they are commonly known, has no meaning in their own language, and seems to be of foreign origin." We might speculate that before any national names took hold, clan and town names were the principal names of self-ascription for the peoples known now as the Cherokee.[28]

On the other hand, in contradistinction to the incorporation of biologic by cultural logic, Cherokee *Indian* can represent the invasion and displacement of cultural by biologic, as Chief Justice Taney suggests in his decision:

> And we think it very clear, that a white man who at mature age is adopted in an Indian tribe does not thereby become an Indian, and was not intended to be embraced in the exception [to the 1834 trade and intercourse act, which exempted Indian-on-Indian crime from federal jurisdiction] above mentioned. He may by such adoption

become entitled to certain privileges in the tribe, and make himself amenable to their laws and usages. Yet he is not an Indian; and the exception is confined to those who by the usages and customs of the Indians are regarded as belonging to their race. It does not speak of members of a tribe, but of the race generally,—of the family of Indians; and it intended to leave them both [Rogers and Nicholson presumably], as regarded their own tribe, and other tribes also, to be governed by Indian usages and customs.[29]

This passage suggests that for Taney, the issue is not whether Rogers and Nicholson are Cherokee Indians, but whether they are Indians. The former designation would mean simply that they are "members of a [particular] tribe," which Taney seems willing to concede. The latter designation, however, means not inclusion in a tribe but "in the race generally,—of the family of Indians." Taney's decision, in other words, gives us the generic "Indian," invented by Columbus and here refurbished in the language of biologic. By 1850, four years after the court's decision in *Rogers*, "formal racial classification [. . .] [became] operative on the census [. . .] and it was then left to white census enumerators to decide whether or not to accept the classification offered by those who were counted."[30]

Yet the passage also implies that Taney's biological Indian is still operating under cultural logic, suggesting that we are witnessing here the historical moment when the biological Indian was still emerging from the cultural logic of local Native communities. Note, for example, that Taney's implicit biological formulation—a white man cannot be an Indian—is contained within a cultural parameter: "a white man who at a mature age is adopted in an Indian tribe does not thereby become an Indian" suggests that white youths and white female subjects can become Indians through the cultural logic of adoption.[31] Whatever its cause, its effect is to circumscribe a certain biologic by a certain cultural logic. That is, the definition of "Indian" that the opinion offers "is confined to those who by the usages and customs of the Indians are regarded as belonging to their race." Thus, it would appear, the emergent biological category of Indians as a "race" is determined by "the usages and customs of the Indians" themselves—that is, by a cultural logic. The logic in Taney's decision is circular: the biologic is determined by cultural logic, which the biologic seeks to transcend. Before *Rogers*, as discussed previously, Indian communities under certain circumstances adopted Europeans, regardless of whether these communities referred to themselves as "tribes" or "nations" or with clan or kinship terms. But adoption by the community did *not* make an "Indian," a Western racial-political category. Instead, it made a community member, a person belonging to a Native cultural category—a member of the Cherokee Nation, for example, or of the Bitter Water Clan, to take an example from the Navajos, who only became a "tribe" when their traditional band/clan/kinship structure was forcibly centralized by the federal government in 1868. The Navajos did not adopt the term "nation" to describe themselves as a political unit until a hundred years later.[32] The biologic beginning to emerge in *Rogers* would not reach its full force in federal Indian affairs until the early twentieth century, when it would become a distinct component, first of government determinations of degrees of "Indianness," then, after 1934, of tribal determinations of their own enrollments. In the former case, the biologic of blood had its first major impact through policy stemming from the amendment of the Dawes Act in the Burke Act of 1906.[33]

The ostensible rationale for the Dawes Act was "progressive": the assimilation of Indians into the American dream of property-holding individualism. At first, allottees "born within the territorial limits of the United States" were automatically granted citizenship by the act, which in its original form placed their land "in trust" with the U.S. government "for the period of twenty-five years [. . .] for the sole use and benefit of the Indian to whom such allotment shall have been made," at the end of which time the allotment was delivered in fee to the allottee.[34] The citizenship provision was amended by the Burke Act, by which "the Indian became a citizen after the patent in fee simple was granted instead of upon the completion of his allotment and the issuance of a trust patent."[35]

Among the policies implemented in the wake of the Burke Act were authorizations for "competency commissions" to determine whether the newly compelled *individual* Indians should receive the patent to their land in fee or in trust. "Government policy" often, though not uniformly, "called for the issuance of fee patents to allottees of one-half or less Indian blood."[36] Just how autonomous the biologic of blood had become since its emergence in federal Indian discourses in the first half of the nineteenth century can be read in federal Indian discourses of the first quarter of the twentieth century. For example, *United States v. Shock*[37] finds that "varying degrees of blood most naturally become the lines of demarcation between the different classes, because experience shows that generally speaking the greater percentage of Indian blood a given allottee has, the less capable he is by natural qualification and experience to manage his property."[38] Similarly, the *Annual Report of the Commissioner of Indian Affairs* for 1917 states, "While ethnologically a preponderance of white blood has not heretofore been a criterion of competency, nor even now is it always a safe standard, it is almost an axiom that an Indian who has a larger proportion of white blood than Indian partakes more of the characteristics of the former than of the latter. In thought and action, so far as the business world is concerned, he approximates more closely to the white blood ancestry."[39] Pronouncements like these reveal the cultural logic of identity formation through the social act of intermarriage being translated into the biologic of blood—that is, naturalization or biologization of the social construction of race.

From the time of *U.S. v. Rogers* to the present moment, the biologic of Indian identity politics has achieved increasing autonomy, which has generated a new configuration of racism. Between the institution of the IRA in 1934 and 1940, the BIA began to issue Certificates of Degree of Indian Blood (CDIB)—though without, until the present, any written regulations for such issuance. Written rules were first proposed in 1986 and a draft was composed in 1992. The proposed rules were finally published in the *Federal Register* in 2000:[40]

> A Certificate of Degree of Indian or Alaska Native Blood (CDIB) certifies that an individual possesses a specific degree of Indian blood of a federally recognized Indian tribe(s). A deciding Bureau [BIA] official issues the CDIB. We issue CDIBs so that individuals may establish their eligibility for those programs and services based upon their status as American Indians and/or Alaska Natives. A CDIB does not establish membership in a federally recognized Indian tribe, and does not prevent an Indian tribe from making a separate and independent determination of blood degree for tribal purposes. The rolls of federally recognized Indian tribes may be used as the basis for issuing CDIBs. The base rolls of some tribes are deemed to be correct by statute, even if errors exist. All portions of the Request for Certificate of Degree of Indian or Alaska Native Blood (CDIB) must be completed. You must show your relationship to an enrolled member(s) of a federally recognized Indian tribe, whether it is through your birth mother or birth father, or both.[41]

The rules for applying for a CDIB are now published on the BIA website:

> BUREAU OF INDIAN AFFAIRS CERTIFICATE OF DEGREE OF INDIAN OR ALASKA NATIVE BLOOD INSTRUCTIONS   All portions of the Request for Certificate of Degree of Indian or Alaska Native Blood (CDIB) must be completed. You must show your relationship to an enrolled member(s) of a federally recognized Indian tribe, whether it is through your birth mother or birth father, or both. A federally recognized Indian tribe means an Indian or Alaska Native tribe, band, nation, pueblo, village, or community which appears on the list of recognized tribes published in the Federal Register by the Secretary of the Interior (25 U.S.C. 5131).
>
> - Your degree of Indian blood is computed from lineal ancestors of Indian blood who were enrolled with a federally recognized Indian tribe or whose names appear on the designated base rolls of a federally recognized Indian tribe.
> - You must give the maiden names of all women listed on the Request for CDIB, unless they were enrolled by their married names.
> - A Certified Copy of a Birth Certificate is required to establish your relationship to a parent(s) enrolled with a federally recognized Indian tribe(s).
> - If your parent is not enrolled with a federally recognized Indian tribe, a Certified Copy of your parent's Birth or Death Certificate is required to establish your parent's relationship to an enrolled member of a federally recognized Indian tribe(s). If your grandparent(s) were not enrolled members of a federally recognized Indian tribe(s), a Certified Copy of the Birth or Death Certificate for each grandparent who was the child of an enrolled member of a federally recognized Indian tribe is required.
> - Certified copies of Birth Certificates, Delayed Birth Certificates, and Death Certificates may be obtained from the State Department of Health or Bureau of Vital Statistics in the State where the person was born or died.
> - In cases of adoption, the degree of Indian blood of the natural (birth) parent must be proven.

- Please return your request and supporting documents to the Agency from whom you receive services. Incomplete requests will be returned with a request for further information. No action will be taken until the request is complete.

The bureaucratic language of Indian identity in the twenty-first century is markedly different from that of the explicit language of naturalized racial hierarchies, which rationalized competency commissions in the Dawes era. We immediately recognize the latter, with its claims of innate white superiority, as racist, while the language of identity in the federal regulations for the issuance of a CDIB appears in the bureaucratic rhetoric of neutrality. But in both cases, the same colonial bureaucracy, albeit at different historical moments, dictates the legitimate forms of Indian identity for the purpose of resource distribution. Whereas the language of the Dawes era unselfconsciously expresses the racial ideology that rationalizes the maldistribution of resources inherent in the colonial system of Indian Country, the language of identity in the era of Indian self-determination (the typical term used for the post-1970 phase of U.S. colonialism in Indian Country) represses or disavows this ideology both in the very form of its expression (the supposedly value-free language of bureaucracy) and in the source of its promulgation: the contemporary BIA, staffed by "about 87 percent" Indians, including the commissioner of Indian Affairs and "most of the high level Indian policy positions within the Interior Department."[42] An Indian-run BIA is the result of a provision in the IRA, which dictates Indian preference in hiring within the agency. This policy was challenged in 1972 by a group of white workers in the BIA, who claimed it violated the Equal Employment Opportunity Act of 1972, which prohibited racial discrimination in hiring. But the practice was upheld by the Supreme Court in the 1974 decision *Morton v. Mancari*: "The preference, as applied, is granted to Indians not as a discrete racial group, but, rather, as members of quasi-sovereign tribal entities whose lives and activities are governed by the BIA in a unique fashion."[43] In this case, it appears, the Court used cultural logic to trump biologic. Yet the regulation in the BIA manual, dictating the hiring preference and cited in the opinion, was itself contingent on the biologic of blood: "To be eligible for preference in appointment, promotion, and training, an individual must be one-fourth or more degree Indian blood and be a member of a Federally-recognized tribe."[44]

Contemporary regulations of blood, couched in a vocabulary that promises scientific objectivity and generated by an Indian-run bureaucracy, give the biologic of blood quantum legitimacy at a moment in which, in spite of the fact that race is a social construction, we still believe in the biologization of a whole range of cultural logics organized around a naturalization and universalization of the body both as a material object of knowledge and as a metaphor for human nature. Historian Patricia Nelson Limerick has articulated the subversive effects of blood quantum policy: "Set the blood quantum at one-quarter, hold to it as a rigid definition of Indians, let intermarriage proceed as it had for centuries, and eventually Indians will be defined out of existence. When that happens, the federal government will be freed of its persistent 'Indian problem.'"[45] Because of the way colonialism constructs Native bureaucracies, blood quantum also became a means in the twentieth century by which, along with disenrollment, Indians are doing away with Indians. In the post-IRA era, the tribes themselves adopted blood quantum standards as part of their rules for determining tribal membership. Though they generally keep to the federal benchmarks of one-quarter to one-half Indian blood, some tribes have considerably lower minimums:

> For the Cherokee in Oklahoma descent from a person on the 1906 roll (no matter how small the percentage of Indian blood may be) is all that is required. Therefore, in order to limit the fiscal impact on the federal government, the BIA has an informal agreement with the state of Oklahoma that the U.S. government will be responsible for the welfare payments of Indians with one-fourth or more Indian blood and the state will be responsible for those with less than one-fourth Indian blood. Various tribes specify one-half, one-fourth, or another degree of Indian blood for membership eligibility. The U.S. census counts anyone who declares himself or herself to be an Indian.[46]

Even given the official respectability (both federal and tribal) of blood quantum regulations at the present moment, the language of the BIA on CDIBs suggests that the biologic of blood quantum cannot escape its ground in the cultural logic of the political history from which it emerges. This language suggests the relative nonidentity of federally identified and tribally identified Indians: "A CDIB does not establish membership in a federally recognized Indian tribe, and *does not prevent an Indian tribe from making a separate and independent determination of blood degree for tribal purposes*" (my emphasis). *The Rights of Indians and Tribes* puts it succinctly: "Indian tribes have the authority to determine who is an Indian for tribal purposes but not for state or federal purposes."[47] That is, there is no stable answer to the scandalous question that frames the U.S. legal history of Native identity from *Rogers* forward: What or who is an Indian? In 1979, in its opinion in the case of *U.S. v. Broncheau*, the U.S. Court of Appeals for the Ninth Circuit pointed to the legal instability of Indian identity: "Unlike the term 'Indian Country,' which has been defined in 18 U.S.C. at 1151, the term 'Indian' has not been statutorily defined but instead has been judicially explicated over the years. The test, first suggested in *United States v. Rogers* and generally followed by the courts, considers (1) the degree of Indian blood; and (2) tribal or governmental recognition as an Indian."[48] *Broncheau* points to not only the legal instability of the term "Indian," which changes its shape from ruling to ruling and from federal to tribal regulations, but also to the way federal Indian law has rationalized the historical ambiguities of biologic and cultural logic found in *Rogers* into the apparent clarity of a two-pronged identity standard, of which, ironically, *Rogers* becomes the ground. However, the cultural prong of the standard is itself grounded in the biological prong: tribal membership is widely dependent on some degree of Indian blood.

The question of what an Indian is, formulated as such in the wake of *Rogers* and the Dawes Act, appears officially, perhaps for the first time as such, in the *Sixty-First Annual Report of the Commissioner of Indian Affairs* for 1892: "In close connection with the subject of Government control over the Indians and methods of administration, an interesting question has recently arisen, What is an Indian?"[49] Fifty years later, referring to historic shifts in the legal articulation of the term "Indian," Felix Cohen's classic text, *Felix Cohen's Handbook of Federal Indian Law*, begins by noting "the lack of unanimity which exists among those who would attempt a definition of Indians."[50] "Who is an Indian?" was the first question under the heading "Frequently Asked Questions" on the BIA website in the early twenty-first century, before Judge Lamberth ordered the site closed in December 2001 during the *Cobell* case, pending assurances that trust fund accounts were not vulnerable to hacking through the site. As of this writing in early 2023, under the "Frequently Asked Questions" section of the BIA website, we find the question posed this way: "Who is an American Indian or Alaska Native?" Here is the answer:

> As a general rule, an American Indian or Alaska Native person is someone who has blood degree from and is recognized as such by a federally recognized tribe or village (as an enrolled tribal member) and/or the United States. Of course, blood quantum (the degree of American Indian or Alaska Native blood from a federally recognized tribe or village that a person possesses) is not the only means by which a person is considered to be an American Indian or Alaska Native. Other factors, such as a person's knowledge of his or her tribe's culture, history, language, religion, familial kinships, and how strongly a person identifies himself or herself as American Indian or Alaska Native, are also important. In fact, there is no single federal or tribal criterion or standard that establishes a person's identity as American Indian or Alaska Native.
>
> There are major differences, however, when the term "American Indian" is used in an ethnological sense versus its use in a political/legal sense. The rights, protections, and services provided by the United States to individual American Indians and Alaska Natives flow not from a person's identity as such in an ethnological sense, but because he or she is a member of a federally recognized tribe. That is, a tribe that has a **government-to-government relationship** and a **special trust relationship** with the United States. These special trust and government-to-government relationships entail certain legally enforceable obligations and responsibilities on the part of the United States to persons who are enrolled members of such tribes. Eligibility requirements for federal services will differ from program to program. Likewise, the eligibility criteria for enrollment (or membership) in a tribe will differ from tribe to tribe.[51]

This criterion forms a loop with the requirement for a CDIB, mixing the fiction of blood with the political mandate of federally recognized tribal membership.

Under "Frequently Asked Questions," we also find population numbers for American Indians and Alaska Natives:

> According to the U.S. Bureau of the Census, the estimated population of American Indians and Alaska Natives, including those of

more than one race, as of July 1, 2007, was 4.5 million, or 1.5 per cent of the total U.S. population. In the BIA's 2005 American Indian Population and Labor Force Report, the latest available, the total number of enrolled members of the (then) 561 federally recognized tribes was shown to be less than half the Census number, or 1,978,099.

According to an August 19, 2021, CNN report, "in 2020, the number of people who identified as Native American and Alaska Native (AIAN) alone and in combination with another race was 9.7 million, up from 5.2 million in 2010. They now account for 2.9% of all the people living in the United States, according to the Census Bureau."[52] A report in the same year from the National Community Reinvestment Coalition (NCRC) conflicts significantly with the CNN report, although both claim the census as their source: "the Native American population has grown exponentially throughout the years. According to U.S. Census data in 2020, there were roughly 6.79 million Native Americans throughout the country. Therefore, this community only accounts for a mere 2.09% of the total population across all races and ethnicities." However, the NCRC report, acknowledging that the United States was built on stolen Native land, begins with a caveat about data collection in Native America: "The United States has too often hindered Native American advancement, not advanced it. Through years of intentional governmental policies that removed lands and resources, American Indians have been separated from the wealth and assets that were rightfully theirs. Today, we still see a lack of information on Native Americans and their socioeconomic issues. Data is sparse and inconsistent."[53]

In terms of these counting differences, the BIA website gives the following explanation:

- American Indians are the most under counted group in the U.S. Census. More than 80% of reservation lands are in hard-to-count (HTC) census tracts. Nation Wide, approximately one-third of all Indian people live in HTC census tracts In states with large Indian reservations, like South Dakota, that number is even higher: 52.4% of Indians in South Dakota live in HTC census tracts. The Census Bureau has identified twelve factors that are associated with census undercounts, including unemployment, poverty, linguistic isolation, lack of a high school diploma, and lack of a telephone. A recent study of these factors found that on-reservation Indians are, and Will [sic] continue to be, "very difficult to enumerate accurately" for the Census Bureau.

- In addition to problems with undercounting, Census Bureau data capture self-reports of racial identities and tribal affiliations. They do not accurately count enrolled Tribal members.
- By comparison, Tribal enrollment lists are comprehensive lists of all Tribal citizens enrolled in each Indian Tribe. Tribal enrollment data can be obtained from each Indian Tribe and verified by the twelve (12) Regional Offices in the Bureau of Indian Affairs.[54]

I cite these population figures because they complicate the question of Native identity—who or what is an Indian?—in the difference between the census figures, where self-ascription is counted, and the enrollment figures, which have strict parameters of blood and descent, as devised initially by the colonial government during the Dawes era and then in varying degrees of blood quantum adopted by the tribes. The enrollment disputes and academic controversies, which have resulted in scholars who have published under a Native identity being outed by other Native academics, have stemmed from the bureaucratic question of who or what is an Indian, and the indeterminacy of the answer. The fact that Indian Country is the poorest part of the United States has exacerbated these disputes because they always involve conflicts over limited resources, both of materiality and status.[55] These conflicts represent the internalization of a colonial system by the colonized.

Beyond the colonial bureaucracy that formulated it, we might wonder who exactly asks this most frequently asked question: who or what is an Indian? Is it the general public of non-Indians interested in the situation of Indigenous peoples in the United States? This seems doubtful. In a country where numbers (quantity) are a critical factor in gaining public visibility, Indians, as the statistics generated by the BIA show, form at most 2.9 percent of the population; and because the Native political agenda is historically one of sovereignty, not integration, it has only a marginal place in public discourse, where the Black–white binary remains the dominant paradigm for understanding race in the United States. Senator James Abourezk of South Dakota, who was a member of the Senate subcommittee on Indian Affairs during his years in the Senate from 1973 to 1979 and who is a strong advocate of Indian sovereignty, is quoted as saying (one assumes with full irony): "Basically, Congress has no interest in Indians."[56] If the people's representatives are fundamentally indifferent to a portion of the people for whom they nevertheless bear full responsibility (plenary power), then why should the people themselves be interested?

Or is it scholars like myself, non-Natives in the fields of Indigenous, postcolonial, and American studies, who ask, who or what is an Indian? There are very few of us as well. Postcolonial studies, which over the years has taken a growing interest in the situations of Indigenous peoples internationally, excluded these situations from its foundational discourses, which focused on the post–World War II nation-states in South Asia and Africa that were formed in the revolt against the European imperial powers that had colonized these regions.[57] This is emphatically true in relation to the situation of Native Americans in the United States. As for American literature and American studies, which ought to be centrally interested in these matters, there was relatively little attention in proportion to the importance of the issues and the richness of the literature, both oral and written, until relatively recently. Finally, that leaves Indians themselves, both inside and outside of academia. The federal government forces them to keep asking the BIA this question—one that should be phrased not as "Who is an Indian?" but as "Am I an Indian?" or "Are we Indians?"

Erdrich's *Night Watchman* contains a short chapter entitled "Who?," as if in response to the BIA's question. In the chapter, Thomas, described as a member of "the after-the-buffalo-who-are-we-now generation," thinks: "His generation would have to define themselves" and asks: "Who was an Indian? What? Who, who, who? And how?" Thomas has no direct answer to the question but instead asks a further question: "How should being an Indian relate to this country that had conquered and was trying in every way possible to absorb them?"[58] Later, returning home from Washington, D.C., Thomas thinks about the question of blood quantum as he recalls his appearance before a Senate committee on termination:

The senator [Arthur V. Watkins of Utah, a strong supporter of termination] had also asked every single Indian person who testified about their degree of Indian blood. The funny thing was, nobody knew exactly. No one had answered with a numeral. It wasn't something that they kept close track of and in fact Thomas hadn't parsed out his own ancestors—determined who was a quarter or half or three-quarters or full blood. Nor has anyone he knew. As the miles rolled on, this began to bother him. Everyone knew they were Indian or not Indian regardless of what the rolls said or what the government said, it was a given or not a given. Long ago, a guy in a bar had made a family tree for him. When Thomas looked at the tree, he pointed out the Indians and came out a full-blood, though he knew there was French somewhere. Then the person made the tree again and made him more white. It turned into a game. And it was still a game, but a game that interested Senator Watkins, which meant it was a game that could erase them.[59]

These two passages, taken together, deconstruct the fiction of Indian identity as nothing more than a construct of the federal government that is then utilized by tribal governments. This deconstruction distinguishes between how the federal government thinks of Indians and how Indians, who have not subscribed to the federal or tribal definitions, think of themselves. The two passages understand that the bureaucratic identity game is about the absorption/erasure of Indians.

From its beginnings in the 1970s, criticism of Native American literatures has made the question "what is an Indian?" central to its project. The problem is that for the most part, this criticism, particularly in its formative stages, does not recognize the political history of the question, which Rogers and its progeny represent. In the first book-length study of the American Indian novel, published in 1978, Charles R. Larson begins by noting: "The concept of Indian identity [. . .] is a difficult one."[60] After musing on the blood quantum and phenotype of several Native authors, including N. Scott Momaday and John Joseph Mathews (both now securely in the Native American literary canon), Larson asks: "In short, how can we determine that the writers discussed in this study are American Indians? How can we be certain, even, that they wrote the works attributed to them? I ask these questions because the two primary qualifications for inclusion of an author in this study are, first, the establishment that he or she is genuinely a Native American, and, second, that he wrote the novel himself without the aid of a collaborator or an amanuensis."[61] Larson is preoccupied with who is "genuinely a Native American," yet simultaneously, and unsurprisingly, he is unable to supply a precise definition of "genuine." Larson's rejection of fiction written in collaboration with non-Indians appears to be based on a desire not to dilute or compromise the Indianness of the works he includes: "It has been my intention to include in this study only those *novels* written by Native Americans without the aid of a collaborator. I have therefore eliminated the large corpus of American Indian writing that is autobiographical, and an equally large number of works either 'as told to' or written with someone's assistance."[62] Yet this issue of collaboration does not seem to bother him when he cites, without qualification, the as-told-to autobiography *Black Elk Speaks*, which I discuss later, for the "Plains Indians' concept of circularity."[63] Larson's obsession with purity or authenticity in Native fiction is representative of the bureaucracies—federal, tribal, literary, and academic—that colonialism has created, as the passages I have been and will be citing make clear. Thus, he marginalizes what is now considered to be a major Indian novel—indeed, the first major Indian novel published in the twentieth century, *Cogewea, the Half-Blood* (1927), by Mourning Dove, because she collaborated with a non-Native, Lucullus Virgil McWhorter, although he notes, "Since I believe that *The Half-Blood* is an important work, I include an analysis of it in an appendix."[64] I include my analysis of this "important" novel, as well as the issue of its collaboration, which Larson regrets,[65] below.

As for his working definition of Indianness in the first place, Larson turns to the tribal rolls:

> The inclusion of a writer's name on the rolls of his specific tribe (compiled by tribal leaders and kept in the tribal headquarters as well as in the Bureau of Indian Affairs) implies a kind of kinship with his fellow tribesman. [. . .] Although their importance should not be overemphasized, the rolls are valuable documents for establishing certain factual matters about these writers. [. . .] What is of especial interest for my study here is the "degree" of Indian blood suggested by the tribal rolls. This is not simply a matter of the earliest writers having increased educational opportunities if they were mixed bloods. Nor am I trying to suggest that the closer the writer is to being full blood the more truly "Indian" his writing is. [. . .]

My concern with these [enrollment] figures has only been to suggest that although a significant test of a writer's Indian origins falls back on the rolls themselves, compiled by the tribal councils, the "Indianness" of the writing may have little to do with these figures. What is of equal importance is historical or documentary information about the writers that attests to their general acceptance by their own people. [...] Known acceptance by one's peers, then, is probably a more meaningful test of Indianness. Along these lines, it should be pointed out that many of the writers discussed in this volume have had their work included in anthologies of American Indian writing, edited by American Indians—a further test of this acceptance.[66]

Larson's definition hinges on acceptance by an Indian community, either formal (tribal rolls) or, more important for Larson, informal (acceptance by a Native literary community, as represented by "anthologies of American Indian writing, edited by American Indians"). Such community-centered criteria are certainly used today to determine the Indianness of Indian writing. But Larson's presentation of them is circular. How do those Indians who edit Indian anthologies come to be recognized as Indians themselves if not by the identical processes (tribal enrollment, appearance in Indian anthologies) that Larson uses to establish his notion of Indianness in the first place? Hence, the way he presents his criteria does not answer the question of who is an Indian but begs it in an endless regression. The problem here is that Larson fails to query the politics of the question itself; that is, he invokes the tribal rolls initially but does not historicize them by connecting them to the colonial history of federal Indian law from which they arose. As I have noted, in that history, the very notion of Indianness is the product first of a European term (Indian) and then of a legal decision (*U.S. v. Rogers*) aimed at wresting Native community control of identity from individual communities and investing it first in the European imaginary and then, in this case, in the U.S. federal government. Outside the legal fence that *Rogers* and its progeny, as practical applications of the European imaginary, have constructed around Native identities by homogenizing them as *Indian* identity, we might imagine that there are no *Indian* writers, only Cherokee or Navajo or Lakota writers—and, even more locally defined, only writers with particular clan/kinship names to identify them. Then there are those Native writers with decidedly

Native genealogies but, because of the historical ruptures of colonialism, no tribal affiliations. All of these identities (federal, tribal, nonfederal, nontribal), which certainly depend on community recognition, nevertheless conform not to a single biologic but to multiple cultural logics, the kind that obtained in Native communities, and that still persist today in important ways (however unofficially), before the onset of federal Indian law—what Vizenor terms "word wars of the whiteman."[67] Within these "word wars," which generate the history of the question "Who is an Indian?," the question itself is nothing but a scandal of European colonialism.

Nevertheless, to repeat the question without emphasizing its political history perpetuates the scandal by naturalizing it. Fifteen years after Larson raised it in the literary realm, Louis Owens begins his influential study of the American Indian novel *Other Destinies* (1992) with the same question: "To begin to write about something called 'the American Indian novel' is to enter a slippery and uncertain terrain. Take one step into this region and we are confronted with difficult questions of authority and ethnicity: What is an Indian?"[68] For Owens, the central theme of the contemporary American Indian novel is the "question of identity": "For the contemporary Indian novelist—in every case a mixedblood who must come to terms in one form or another with peripherality as well as both European and Indian ethnicity—identity is the central issue and theme."[69] Owens's Wikipedia biography notes: "Louis Owens was born in Lompoc, CA on July 18, 1948. He was one of nine children born to Hoey and Ida Owens. His self-identified heritage included Choctaw and Cherokee ancestors. Despite not being enrolled as a citizen in any Native nation, writing that 'I'm not enrolled and did not grow up on a reservation,' he still identifies as Native American" and is accepted as a Native writer in the field of Native American studies.[70]

Informed by both postmodern and postcolonial studies, Owens quotes Vizenor to the effect that all "Indians" are "invented," pointedly noting, "For American Indians, the problem of identity comprehends centuries of colonial and postcolonial displacement."[71] Owens remarks that in addition to "some basic knowledge of the tribal histories and mythologies of the Indian cultures at the heart of these novels, readers should be aware of crucial moments in Native American history of the last two centuries [because] such moments figure prominently in writing by Indian authors."[72] But Owens devotes only the last two pages of his thirty-one-page introduction to those moments in the history of federal Indian law; then he conflates two key cases, *Cherokee Nation v. Georgia* (1831) and *Worcester v. Georgia* (1832). Thus, while pointing toward the importance of colonial history in understanding American Indian literatures, Owens does not specify the historic legal forces that give crucial definition to the notion of invented Indians, charging the phrase with its particular colonial valence/violence; nor does he query the cultural and biologics that construct the term "mixed blood." The history of these logics makes Owens's assertion that "every" contemporary Indian novelist is a "mixedblood" problematic. As we have seen, depending on the context, someone who is mixed blood biologically might be a full blood culturally, and vice versa.

Owens's ahistorical, or undertheorized, use of "mixedblood" allows him to stabilize it by assuming the word's transparency and thus to make the claim that "the dominant theme in novels by Indian authors [is] the dilemma of the mixedblood, the liminal 'breed' seemingly trapped between Indian and white worlds."[73] In Cherokee novelist Thomas King's postmodern trickster narrative *Green Grass, Running Water*, one of the Indian characters catches the schematic banality of the mixed-blood theme: "It was a common enough theme in novels and movies. Indian leaves the traditional world of the reserve, goes to the city, and is destroyed. Indian leaves the traditional world of the reserve, is exposed to white culture, and becomes trapped between two worlds. Indian leaves the traditional world of the reserve, gets an education, and is shunned by his tribe."[74] As King's character points out, the mixed blood between two worlds has been a standard trope in the literary history of twentieth-century Native writing, although the passage cited locates the trope in the writing per se, whereas I want to locate it in standard interpretations of that writing. The project of *Other Destinies* is to revive this exhausted topic by ringing some changes. In this vein, Owens remarks of Leslie Silko's 1977 novel *Ceremony* that she "writes again of a mixedblood protagonist lost between cultures and identities. However, in the character of Tayo, Silko turns the conventionally painful predicament of the mixedblood around, making the mixedblood a metaphor for the dynamic, syncretic, adaptive qualities of Indian cultures that will ensure survival."[75] Of Vizenor, Owens comments that he "rejects entirely the conventional posture of mourning for the hapless mixedblood trapped between worlds, identifying the mixedblood with the shape-shifting visage of trickster, who requires that we reexamine, moment by moment, all definition and discourse."[76] These remarks usefully complicate the figure of the mixed blood within a literary tradition where that figure always teeters on (and often falls over the brink of) sentimentality. However, once we place the term "mixed blood" back within the colonial history of cultural and biologic, the two-worlds paradigm, with mixed blood as the mediating term, requires revision as an interpretive model precisely because mixed blood and full blood are not dialectical opposites but ambiguous, overlapping signs, overdetermined by their simultaneous positions in a range of contexts (legal, social, cultural, Native, non-Native). Perhaps this is what Owens has in mind. However, the colonial world, where these terms signify, is not two worlds but rather one in constant conflict.

For example, who says Tayo is mixed blood? The narrative informs us that his mother is Laguna and his father a nameless white man. But in a world of intermarriage, Tayo is hardly alone or anomalous as a representative figure, however solitary in certain ways he may be because of the alienation of his World War II experience. As his aunt remarks, "Girls around here have babies by white men all the time now, and nobody says anything. Men run around with Mexicans and even worse, and nothing is ever said."[77] The Laguna constitution, as ratified in 1958, which makes no distinction between full bloods and half bloods, makes tribal membership contingent on the following:

(a) All persons of any Indian blood whose names appear on the 1940 United Pueblos Agency census roll for the Pueblo of Laguna as enrolled members: provided that any person of one-half or, more Laguna blood whose name the Council finds to have been erroneously omitted from said roll be added to it upon application by such person within one year from the approval of this revised Constitution, in the manner to be prescribed by ordinance of the Concil [sic]. Any such addition shall have the effect of recognizing such person's membership from birth. Application for recognition of membership may also be filed on behalf of a deceased person, if done for the purpose of establishing membership rights under subsections (b), (c), or (d) of this Section.
(b) All persons born since the 1940 census whose mother and father are both members of the Pueblo of Laguna.
(c) All persons of one-half or more Indian blood born after the 1940 census but prior to the approval of this revised Consti-

tution whose mother or father is a member of the Pueblo of Laguna.

(d) All persons of one-half or more Laguna Indian blood born after approval of this revised Constitution:

(1) whose mother is a member of the Pueblo of Laguna; or
(2) whose father is a member of the Pueblo of Laguna, provided the child is born in wedlock.

(e) Provided that the persons referred to in subsections (b), (c), (d) (1), and (d) (2), above, shall not be entitled to membership in the Pueblo unless enrolled or unless application for enrollment has been made by their parent, parents, or other persons for them, or by themselves, prior to their 22nd birthday; provided further, that all such persons shall have at least one year from the date of approval of this revised Constitution in which to enroll themselves or make application for enrollment as members of the Pueblo, in the manner to be prescribed by ordinance of the Council.

(f) All persons naturalized as members of the Pueblo of Laguna, provided that a person who has no Indian blood shall never be naturalized

In making tribal membership flexible (in terms of blood quantum) for the children of two Laguna parents, the rule suggests the pueblo's desire to try to limit a reasonably widespread practice of intermarriage, even as it is prepared to admit the children of intermarriage to tribal membership, though the gateway narrows considerably.[78] Because Silko never makes it an issue in *Ceremony,* we can assume that Tayo is a tribally enrolled member of Laguna Pueblo and a member of a clan—the latter because Laguna is a matrilineal society, so clan membership is determined through the mother.[79] In these terms, readers can thus assume Tayo is not mixed blood because there is no such designation in the Laguna constitution, although blood quantum plays a part in enrollment for those who have only one enrolled parent. Tayo, then, is a Laguna Indian. He is not positioned between two worlds but ceremonially searching for his balance within Laguna society after being unbalanced by the trauma of World War II, coupled with the colonialist thrust of his secondary school education, which denigrated Laguna epistemologies.

Within the novel, the first reference to Tayo as mixed blood comes from his aunt, who thinks of him as a "half-breed child."[80] But Auntie, it is clear, is the character in the novel who is the most alienated from traditional Laguna practices. Silko stresses not only her Christianity, which "separated the people from themselves [. . .] tr[ying] to crush the single clan name,"[81] but also her upbringing of her son, Tayo's cousin, Rocky, who, full-blood in terms of biologic, is virtually a white man in terms of cultural logic. The only other character in the novel who uses the language of racism about Tayo, referring to him as "white trash,"[82] is the violent Laguna veteran Emo, who has nothing but contempt for anything Indian and a murderous envy of everything white. Besides Auntie, the Laguna elders who figure importantly in Tayo's life (his grandmother, his Uncle Josiah, his Uncle Robert, and the Laguna medicine man Ku'oosh) never refer to him in blood quantum terms but matter-of-factly accept him as a full-fledged member of the community who needs their help. Thus, Tayo is only mixed-blood from the most alienated of perspectives. As Owens (along with others) notices, in *Ceremony*, Silko certainly is fascinated with mixture as a positive force—Josiah's cattle are hybrid Hereford/Mexican, and Betonie, the Navajo singer who provides the ceremony for Tayo's cure, is Navajo/Mexican—but Silko never refers to these combinations in the language of blood quantum. So Betonie is not mixed-blood; the cattle are not mixed-bloods; and Tayo is not mixed-blood, except in a biological language that Silko marks as alienated. In her book of essays *Yellow Woman and a Beauty of the Spirit*, Silko historicizes this language:

> It was not so easy for me to learn where we Marmons belonged, but gradually I understood that we of mixed ancestry belonged on the outer edge of the circle between the world of the Pueblo and the outside world. The Laguna people were open and accepted children of mixed ancestry because appearance was secondary to behavior. For the generation of my great-grandmother and earlier generations, anyone who had not been born in the community was a stranger, regardless of skin color. Strangers were not judged by their appearances—which could deceive—but by their behavior. [. . .] But I could sense a difference from younger people, the generation that had gone to the First World War. On rare occasions, I could sense an anger that my appearance stirred in them, although I sensed that the anger was not aimed at me personally. My appearance reminded them of the outside world, where racism was thriving.[83]

This passage begins by using the language of mixed-bloods between two worlds, though Silko does not use the term "blood" from the biologic of nineteenth-century racism and the related vocabulary of federal Indian law. Rather, she chooses "ancestry," simultaneously referencing cultural and biological kinship. More importantly, the second sentence and what follows emphasize the primacy of "behavior" (culture) over physical "appearance" (the biologic of "skin color") in determining Laguna identity for an older generation. In *Ceremony*, then, from the perspective of Grandma's generation, Rocky's behavior, however full his blood quantum and his enrollment status, marks him as not Laguna (as a kind of "stranger"), whereas Tayo's behavior ultimately marks him as fully Laguna.

Owens's insight—that "Silko turns the conventionally painful predicament of the mixedblood around, making the mixedblood a metaphor for the dynamic, syncretic, adaptive qualities of Indian cultures that will ensure survival"—makes sense. However, within the colonial history of federal Indian law, it still leaves us asking in what sense or senses Owens uses "mixedblood." What the sentence says is that all Indians are mixed-bloods—or virtually so, insofar as mixed-bloods are merely metaphors for the dynamism inherent in all Indian cultures. Owens thus invokes the importance of history in interpreting American Indian writing, but in interpreting Silko's *Ceremony*, he also bypasses its importance by situating the term "mixedblood" outside the colonial history of cultural and biologic, of appearance and behavior, which gives Tayo's "quest for identity" its particular historical weight.[84]

Similarly, in his reading of Vizenor's *Bearheart*, a novel I discuss in chapter 6, Owens omits the fact that the narrative of Vizenor's first novel, published in 1978, a year after *Ceremony*, locates his mixedblood tricksters in a flight from the bureaucratic strictures of the BIA and its allied tribal councils created under the Indian Reorganization Act (IRA) of 1934:

> The women continued to govern the circus [in the sense of circular ground] in the traditions of tribal families, the values of shared consciousness until the patriarchal whitemen rewarded the tribal men as chiefs and rulers. Meanwhile reservation governments were gaining new powers and new generations of evil politicians were seeking control of the sacred cedar. The Indian Reorganization Act created constitutional governments on reservations. The constitutions were

designed by white anthropologists and the elections of tribal people were manipulated by colonial federal administrators. Men of evil and tribal fools were propped up in reservation offices to authorize the exploitation of native lands and natural resources. The cedar nation and all the sovereign circuses surrounding the cedar wood resisted all government controls, federal and tribal.[85]

When Vizenor introduces the notion of invented Indians into the narrative, it is a response that emerges from the history of federal Indian law: "What does Indian mean?" asks a member of a vicious community of "hunters and breeders," a "proud people" who, in the postapocalyptic world of *Bearheart*, live in a walled community, Orion, restricted to people of their "own breed"—full-bloods, we might say, though decidedly white full-bloods in this case.[86] Ironically, the mixed-blood answer is a paraphrase of the BIA regulations governing Indian identity: "An Indian is a member of a recognized tribe and a person who has Indian blood." Doubling the irony, the immediate full-blood response is: "But what is Indian blood?" The immediate mixed-blood rejoinder is: "Indian blood is *not* white blood."[87] This exchange deconstructs the very notion of blood by making it no more than the absence of its hypothetical opposite in a continually circular logic that will never yield a signified. Thus, the logic of this encounter insists that the terms of blood quantum have no meaning outside the colonial discourses that enforce them. This insistence results in the apparent irony produced by Vizenor's substitution of the term "mixedblood" for the term "Indian." Both are produced by the same legal discourse.

However, the speech given by the tribal pilgrim, Belladonna Darwin-Winter Catcher, is not simply contained within the blood discourse of federal Indian law, though it slips into it at the point under scrutiny and keeps recurring as if blood is the ground of identity. However, Belladonna begins her speech by stating, "Tribal values is the subject of my talk. [. . .] We are raised with values that shape our world in a different light. . . . We are tribal and that means we are children of dreams and visions. . . . Our bodies are connected to mother earth and our minds are part of the clouds. . . . Our voices are the living breath of the wilderness."[88] One of the hunters replies: "'My father and grandfather three generations back were hunters. [. . .] They said the same things about the hunt that you said is tribal. . . . Are you telling me that what you are saying is exclusive to your mixedblood race?' [. . .]

'Yes!' snapped Belladonna. 'I am different than a whiteman because of my values and my blood is different. . . . I would not be white.'"[89] The conversation continues in this vein, with Belladonna trying to define Indian identity and the hunters and breeders continuing to erase the boundary that Belladonna asserts until, backed into a rhetorical corner, she asserts the BIA's definition of Indian identity.

On the one hand, the hunters' and breeders' attack on the definition of Indian identity is a familiar and ongoing one in the history I am rehearsing. In this history, since the Dawes Act of 1887, when, for the most part, with the exception of Wounded Knee (1890), mass murder but not genocide ceased, the object of the federal government has been the forced assimilation of Native peoples by various means: the creation of tribal rolls with the proviso of blood quantum, the boarding schools grounded in anti-Indian education, the Indian Citizenship Act of 1924, the strictly limited federal recognition of Indian tribes in the lower forty-eight states and attempts to decertify certain tribes, and disenrollment by the tribes themselves—to take some significant examples that are part of an ongoing genocide by means other than outright murder. On the other hand, this scene at Orion represents the problematics of identity politics, which is decidedly a politics produced by the racial boundaries established and enforced by colonial institutions. When Belladonna says "I would not be white" rather than "I am not white," she registers the reality that race is a social construction, not a natural fact—a point made by one of the hunters in the exchange that ensues in response to Belladonna's definition of Indian blood: "Indians are an invention. [. . .] You tell me that the invention is different than the rest of the world when it was the rest of the world that invented Indians. . . . An Indian is an Indian because he speaks and thinks and believes he is an Indian, but an Indian is nothing more than an invention. . . . Are you speaking as an invention?"[90]

The hunter's intent is malign: to erase Indian reality. But he makes a point, for the word "Indian" is an invention—a Western invention first projected by Columbus and ultimately the legal fiction that grounds U.S. federal Indian law. In his book *Manifest Manners*, published sixteen years after *Bearheart*, Vizenor makes this point:

> The word *Indian* [. . .] is a colonial enactment, not a loan word, and the dominance is sustained by the simulation that has superseded the real tribal names. [. . .] The Indian was an occidental invention

that became a bankable simulation; the word has no referent in tribal languages or cultures. The postindian is the absence of the invention, and the end of representation in literature; the closure of that evasive melancholy of dominance. Manifest manners are the simulations of bourgeois decadence and melancholy.[91]

A passage from Taiaiake Alfred's essay "Sovereignty" can act as a gloss on this passage from *Manifest Manners:* "The maintenance of state dominance over indigenous peoples rests on the preservation of the myth of conquest and on the 'noble but doomed' defeated nation status ascribed to indigenous peoples in the state sovereignty discourse. Framing indigenous people in the past allows the state to maintain its own legitimacy by disallowing the fact of indigenous peoples' nationhood to intrude upon its own mythology."[92] Manifest manners is "the myth of conquest" of Indigenous peoples by the West that allows the West to simulate the conqueror while lamenting the "noble but doomed" conquered, an attitude that Vizenor terms "that evasive melancholy of dominance." "Simulations of the other are instances of the absence of the real," writes Vizenor.[93] While the West continues to indulge itself in the "bourgeois decadence" of domination, the post-Indian is elsewhere, projecting a post-sovereignty plan of action.

THREE

COLLABORATIVE IDENTITIES

Even as it invokes the importance of history, Owens's approach to the Indian novel as a site of identity conflict is fundamentally philosophical, or theoretical. The result of this theory without history is the translation of the political-historical valences of Indian identity into a metaphysical topos: "Ultimately, whereas postmodernism celebrates the fragmentation and chaos of experience, literature by Native American authors tends to seek transcendence of such ephemerality and the recovery of 'eternal and immutable' elements represented by a spiritual tradition that escapes historical fixation, that places humanity within a carefully, cyclically ordered cosmos and gives humankind irreducible responsibility for the maintenance of that delicate equilibrium."[1] Within this metaphysical paradigm of Indian identity, which understands history as a "fixation" opposed by Native spirituality rather than as a complex of dynamics inseparable from Native spiritualities, Owens reads *Cogewea*, which he terms "the first novel by an Indian writer to attempt to define the complex dilemma of the mixedblood,"[2] without alluding to its explicit historical context, the period of allotment (1887–1934), during which, as I have emphasized, the biologic of blood quantum, stemming from *U.S. v. Rogers*, achieved its modern legal definition. This critical omission of colonial history is typical, until recently,[3] of interpretations of the novel, which, occluding the identity politics of allotment, focus instead on the kind of identity politics bent on distinguishing the Native American Mourning Dove from her Euro-American collaborator, Lucullus Virgil McWhorter. This is the literary identity politics of disenrollment: is this really a Native novel? The controversy over the part McWhorter played in the actual writing of the text is a typical accompaniment of as-told-to autobiographies, translations of Indian orality into Euro-American writing, which form a substantial part of U.S. Native literatures. Thus, before I begin a reading of *Cogewea*, I want to analyze the way the literary issue of collaboration, which bears on the legal issue of identity I have been elaborating, functions in three of the most visible as-told-to autobiographies in Native American literary history: *Black Elk Speaks: Being the Life Story of a Holy Man of the Oglala Sioux, as Told to John G. Neihardt (Flaming Rainbow)* (1932), the most popular book in the as-told-to autobiography genre; *Life of Ma-Ka-Tai-Me-She-Kia-Kiak, or Black Hawk . . . Dictated by Himself* (1833); and *A Narrative of the Life of Mrs. Mary Jemison,* by James E. Seaver (1824).

First published in 1932, *Black Elk Speaks* was reissued in 1961 and again in 1972 with different prefaces by Neihardt. In 2014, an edition was published compiled by anthropologist Raymond J. DeMallie, including prefaces, a foreword by Vine Deloria Jr., an introduction by Philip J. Delora (Vine's son), and an extensive editorial apparatus.[4] Beginning with the 1961 University of Nebraska Press edition of the book, the "to" in the title, "at the author's request" was changed to the vatic "through,"[5] as if Neihardt thought of himself as a kind of medium through which Black Elk channeled his voice. However, the translation history of the work points to worldly problems. In attempting to explain the collaborative process that produced the autobiography, Neihardt stated: "*Black Elk Speaks* is a work of art with two collaborators, the chief one being Black Elk. My function was both creative and editorial. [. . .] The beginning and ending [of the book] are mine; they are what he would have said if he had been able. [. . .] And the translation—or rather the *transformation*—of what was given me was expressed so that it could be understood by the white world."[6] Legally, obviously, Black Elk is an Indian and Neihardt is white, but the collaborative process raises the question of what they are when merged. What is the identity of this book? It cannot be defined in the terms of federal Indian law, but it raises questions about the law's limits in defining Native identity.

These limits are indelible in the Indian Arts and Crafts Act of 1990, which the Department of the Interior website describes as follows:

> The Indian Arts and Crafts Act (Act) of 1990 (P.L. 101-644) is a truth-in-advertising law that prohibits misrepresentation in the marketing of Indian art and craft products within the United States. It is illegal to offer or display for sale, or sell, any art or craft product in a manner that falsely suggests it is Indian produced, an Indian product, or the product of a particular Indian or Indian tribe or Indian

arts and crafts organization, resident within the United States. For a first time violation of the Act, an individual can face civil or criminal penalties up to a $250,000 fine or a 5-year prison term, or both. If a business violates the Act, it can face civil penalties or can be prosecuted and fined up to $1,000,000.

Under the Act, an Indian is defined as a member of any federally or officially State recognized tribe of the United States, or an individual certified as an Indian artisan by an Indian tribe.

The law covers all Indian and Indian-style traditional and contemporary arts and crafts produced after 1934. The Act broadly applies to the marketing of arts and crafts by any person in the United States. Some traditional items frequently copied by non-Indians include Indian-style jewelry, pottery, baskets, carved stone fetishes, woven rugs, kachina dolls, and clothing.

All products must be marketed truthfully regarding the tribal enrollment of the producers so as not to mislead the consumer. It is illegal to market art or craftwork using the name of a tribe if a member, or certified Indian artisan, of that tribe did not actually create the art or craftwork.[7]

Clearly, literary works are works of art not included under the Indian Arts and Crafts Act, with its restrictive federal definition of the term "Indian," which I have reviewed. If such works were included under the act, it would result in the erasure of some significant Native writers from the body of Native American literature whose identity as Indians within the literary field implicitly shines a critical light on the colonial boundary of the federal definition, so proscriptively defined. Under the act, potential Native writers who did not come under the federal definition of "Indian" would be barred from entering the field as Native writers. Finally, in terms of the present discussion, the identity of collaborative work, which bears on the question of Native identity, would become a legal issue under the cultural and political policing function of federal Indian law.

DeMallie, whose work has been crucial in representing the collaborative processes of translation that resulted in *Black Elk Speaks*, tries to define the respective parts of translator and translated: "The book is Black Elk's story as he gave it to Neihardt, but the literary quality and the tone of the work are Neihardt's."[8] Neither of these statements, I emphasize, serves to clarify the distinct part that either man played in the collaboration. Rather, in equating translation with "transformation," and in trying to separate form and content, these statements only complicate the collaborative process. This suggests that from the textual standpoint, a final determination of the identity of the author or authors of the book is impossible. However, in the annotated edition, DeMallie notes where Neihardt has added commentary to the English-language transcripts, which is all that we have—a trace of what Black Elk narrated in Lakota. As in the case of *Cogewea*, as I will elaborate, the attempts to sort out the identities of the collaborators has generated a debate about the production and reception of *Black Elk Speaks* that itself raises questions about the authenticity of Native texts and their authors—questions that trouble Native American studies to this day.

David Brumble III, whose *American Indian Autobiography* (1988) has been an influential book in the field, comments on the debate over the Indian-editor relationship in *Black Elk Speaks* in response to an introduction to the 1979 edition of the book by the best-known Indian activist and scholar of his generation, the late Vine Deloria Jr.:

> As early as 1979 Vine Deloria expressed concern about the effects of such "debates . . . on the question of Neihardt's literary intrusions into Black Elk's system of beliefs." Deloria goes on to conclude that it does not matter "if we are talking with Black Elk or John Neihardt." It is easy to understand Deloria's concern; he is speaking as a *believer*, as one for whom Black Elk's words "now bid fair to become the canon or at least the theological core of a North American Indian theological canon." To speak with specificity of Neihardt's contribution to *Black Elk Speaks* might seem to diminish what is Indian in the book.[9]

Brumble's characterization of Deloria as a "believer" points to the fact that as a reader of *Black Elk Speaks*, Deloria is not concerned with identity politics but rather with the force of the collaboration in its context, with its reception, as I believe citing the passage in full from which Brumble quotes will show:

> Present debates center on the question of Neihardt's literary intrusions into Black Elk's system of beliefs and some scholars have said that the book reflects more of Neihardt than it does of Black Elk. It is, admittedly, difficult to discover if we are talking with Black Elk or John Neihardt, whether the vision is to be interpreted differently,

and whether or not the positive emphasis which the book projects is not the optimism of two poets lost in the modern world and transforming drabness into an idealized world. Can it matter? The very nature of great religious teachings is that they encompass everyone who understands them and personalities become indistinguishable from the transcendent truth that is expressed. So let it be with *Black Elk Speaks*. That it speaks to us with simple and compelling language about an aspect of human experience and encourages us to emphasize the best that dwells within us is sufficient. Black Elk and John Neihardt would probably nod affirmatively to that statement and continue their conversation. It is good. It is enough.[10]

In order to arrive at an understanding of Deloria's reception theory, which marginalizes the identity debates surrounding *Black Elk Speaks*, it is necessary to read those debates within the context of the production of the book. *Black Elk Speaks* is the result of a complex conversation that took place on the Pine Ridge Reservation, beginning and ending in May 1931, although it had a preamble in August 1930, when Neihardt first met Black Elk. The narrative of these meetings compiled by DeMallie is by no means coherent. In his 1960 preface to the 1961 edition of *Black Elk Speaks*, for example, Neihardt names the Lakota interpreter who accompanied him at the first meeting "Flying Hawk,"[11] whereas DeMallie names him "Emil Afraid of Hawk."[12] Perhaps the discrepancy is a result of translation problems in relation to Lakota naming or of the twenty-eight years between the 1932 edition of *Black Elk Speaks* and the 1960 preface, though DeMallie does not mention the difference. Whereas Neihardt states in his 1960 preface that when he first met Black Hawk, "I had known many of the Oglala Sioux for some years, and had good friends among the old 'longhairs,'"[13] a point he does not mention in the preface to the 1932 edition, DeMallie initially says that "Neihardt probably did not know that both Black Elk and Afraid of Hawk were Roman Catholic catechists, pillars of the Church at Pine Ridge."[14] If, as he claims in 1960, Neihardt had familiars among the Indians at Pine Ridge, how could he not have been aware of Black Elk's highly public Catholicism?

In addition to Neihardt and Black Elk, those participating in the conversation that finally took place in May 1931 were Black Elk's son, Ben, and Neihardt's daughter, Enid. Neihardt's other daughter, Hilda, was also present. In addition, other tribal members, as Hertha Dawn

Wong notes, "met with Black Elk and Neihardt to modify, add to, and affirm Black Elk's stories."[15] Black Elk's narrative was translated/interpreted into English by Ben. Enid, as DeMallie tells us, also played a crucial part: "Neihardt's 1931 interviews with Black Elk exist in two forms, Enid Neihardt's original shorthand record in four spiral notebooks and her typed manuscript, from which Neihardt wrote *Black Elk Speaks*."[16] DeMallie describes the translation process as both painstaking and circuitous:

> Black Elk would make a statement in Lakota, which his son Ben then translated into English. Ben spoke the idiomatic "Indian English" typical of the time—a dialect that had arisen out of the need for Indian students in off-reservation boarding schools, coming from many tribes and speaking many different languages, to communicate with one another in English. Neihardt would repeat Ben's translation, rephrasing it for clarity in more standard English. When necessary, the sentence was repeated to Black Elk in Lakota for further clarification. As each sentence came forth in revised form from Neihardt's repetition, Enid wrote it down in shorthand.[17]

We can infer from the preceding passage that Neihardt, who apparently spoke no Lakota, communicated with Black Elk through Ben, although it would appear that Black Elk, by his own admission, spoke at least some English, which he gained during his travels between 1886 and 1889 with Buffalo Bill's Wild West Show, an episode given a chapter in *Black Elk Speaks*.[18] However, Neihardt states in his 1960 preface that Black Elk "knew no English"[19] even though Black Elk, in a letter from Europe in Lakota printed in 1888 in the monthly newspaper *Iapi Oaye*, had written, "I am able to speak some of the white men's language."[20] It could be, perhaps, that Black Elk understood a good deal of English after years of contact with white English speakers, both in his travels with Buffalo Bill and in his extensive missionary work for the Jesuits of Pine Ridge. In this context, Neihardt's statement that he "knew no English" would suggest either that Neihardt is dissembling what he must have known about Black Elk's history, at least by 1960—perhaps in order to keep his image of the Indian pristine in terms of what he believed his white audience expected a "real" Indian to be (one untouched by Western civilization, an impossibility in 1932)—or that Black Elk and the other informants were dissembling before Neihardt, who "chose" to remain in the dark because of his investment in a traditional literary figure like Black Elk, who is of the kind we recognize in the vanishing Sioux of Kevin Costner's starring turn in and direction of the film *Dances with Wolves* (1990). In the course of his narrative, DeMallie suggests the first of these possibilities: "In line with his assertion that this was to be 'the first absolutely Indian book,' Neihardt minimized everything that reflected Black Elk's knowledge and experience in the white man's world previous to his travels with the wild west shows."[21]

In pointing out an apparent contradiction in DeMallie's narrative, anthropologist William Powers inadvertently suggests a kind of collaborative dissembling, one based on an unacknowledged, almost unconscious agreement to tell a certain kind of story: one that fit into the Western romance tradition of the vanishing Indian:

> *Black Elk Speaks* was published in 1932. There is no trace of Black Elk's Christian life in it. But Neihardt was clearly aware of the old man's participation in the Catholic church. Although DeMallie states that Neihardt probably did not know about Black Elk's participation in the Catholic church, later in the book he states:
> "Black Elk told Neihardt [very] little about his later life, his experiences in the Catholic Church, his travels to other Indian reservations as missionary, and his work as a catechist at Pine Ridge. Neihardt was curious about why Black Elk had *put aside his old religion*. According to Hilda (Petri), Black Elk merely replied, 'My children had to live in this world,' and Neihardt did not probe any further."[22]

While Powers is rightly concerned with the contradiction in DeMallie's text that calls into question just exactly what Neihardt did or did not know about Black Elk's Catholicism at the time of their conversations that resulted in *Black Elk Speaks,* I want to point to the apparent reticence that DeMallie's narrative suggests on both Neihardt's and Black Elk's part about giving and exploring this information. Whatever the conflicts in this collaboration—and DeMallie's narrative, while taking account of these conflicts, emphasizes a mystical harmony between the two that Neihardt focuses in his 1960 preface—the concerted drive in the passage Powers quotes, expressed by both parties, appears to be away from the figure of Black Elk as a complex figure of modernity and toward the figure of Black Elk as a Lakota healer before a time when the Sioux came under U.S. colonial rule in the late 1870s. (Black Elk was born, according to *Black Elk Speaks,* in 1863.) Powers's notion that "there is no trace of Black Elk's Christian life" in *Black Elk Speaks*, however, must be bracketed. Although it certainly obtains on the explicit level of biographical detail, the question remains of how this life is represented in the Lakota spiritual practices described in the book. DeMallie, for example, notes: "It seems likely that for Black Elk, minimization of warlike themes in the vision resulted from his Christian perspective."[23]

In assessing the production of *Black Elk Speaks*, DeMallie comments on the problems of mediation: "The reader must understand [. . .] that these are not verbatim records of Black Elk's words, but that they are the combined efforts of the interpreters and of Neihardt to express in English the meaning of the old man's Lakota words," of which we have no record, for they were never written down.[24] DeMallie asserts, then, that "the intention of [his] book is to allow readers direct access to Black Elk, the historical personage; to make his life more fully understandable; and to publish at last the entirety of the teachings that he gave to John G. Neihardt."[25] The notion of "direct access" is already complicated, not to say ironized, by the narrative of what I term "the textual production of Black Elk speaking." How does this textual production complicate the legal question "what is an Indian?" This question is not rhetorical. Rather, it asks us, as Gerald Vizenor does, to question the restrictive federal definition, intended at its origin to eliminate Indians.

DeMallie's gesture of outlining the complexities of written mediation with one hand while erasing them in the service of a certain identity politics with the other is a problem in the translation of oral expression into writing. Hertha Wong, commenting on the textual production of Black Elk speaking, says, "Such a multilayered dialogic transmission of information compounds Neihardt's mediation of Black Elk's words as well as the complexity of the final form," yet asserts, "Despite Neihardt's many contributions, though, versions of Lakota autobiographical forms are found in Black Elk's autobiography. Discussion here will be limited to tracing traditional Lakota autobiographical forms and Black Elk's and Neihardt's modifications of them in *Black Elk Speaks*."[26] Despite the ubiquity of writing and its collaborative entanglements, Wong takes on the project of clearly identifying Neihardt and Black Elk, the written and the oral—as if this were possible. We might also note a bias in assigning active and passive roles to the figures of Neihardt and Black Elk; in Wong's formulation, it is Neihardt who mediates Black Elk ("an individual from a dominant culture shaping the experience of a member of a 'minority' culture"[27]). The question of how the Indian is also mediating the white man, of Neihardt as a complex figure of modernity (Indian and white) as well, is never raised. Further, in assuming the genre of autobiography as a universal form rather than a culturally and historically specific form, Wong, before she even begins her discussion of *Black Elk Speaks,* has already translated the oral tradition into writing.

The Black Elk who participated in the conversation at Pine Ridge in 1931 was already a figure of modernity, an actor/collaborator in a variety of scripts. A year after he was born in 1863, the Bozeman Trail permanently changed the actual and political topography of his birthplace, bringing his people, the Oglala Lakotas, "into active conflict with the white men. These hostilities continually escalated into warfare until 1877, when the western Oglala bands returned east of the Black Hills and joined their relatives on the Great Sioux Reservation in present-day South Dakota."[28] By 1881, Black Elk had become a medicine man like his father and grandfather. He settled the following year with the Oglalas on the Pine Ridge Reservation, where the traditional Lakota economy based on buffalo and interlocked with a warrior culture had been radically altered by buffalo herd depletion and the end of intertribal warfare, both a result of U.S. imperialism on the Plains.[29] In 1886, a year before the Dawes Act continued and intensified the Euramerican assault on the communal cultures and economies of Native America in the continental United States, Black Elk joined Buffalo Bill's Wild West Show, where it appears, from his letter previously cited, that he started to be interested in Christianity. In fact, based on the exclusive presence of Episcopalian missionaries on the Great Sioux Reservation from 1879 until 1888, when the first Catholic mission was built, and the requirement that all Indians joining Buffalo Bill be Christian, Powers argues that sometime before he joined the show, Black Elk had already converted to the Episcopal religion.[30]

Whatever the case, by 1889, Black Elk was back at Pine Ridge, where, during his theatrical sojourn, the Jesuits had gained a foothold.[31] During this period, Black Elk, who was still practicing traditional medicine, came "into conflict with the missionaries"[32] and also became involved with the Ghost Dance religion, itself a combination of Christianity and Native beliefs, which developed first in the late 1860s among some California and Northwest tribes, then subsequently among the Plains tribes, amid despair about and resistance to the U.S.

genocidal colonization of the West.[33] After the massacre of Big Foot's band of Lakota by U.S. cavalry at Wounded Knee in 1890 brought the first stage of U.S. genocide against the Indians to its brutal, official close,[34] Black Elk in 1892 married Katie War Bonnet, who, "it seems likely [. . .] joined the Roman Catholic Church." They had three sons, all of them baptized in the Catholic Church, between 1893 and 1899.[35] Katie died in 1903.

"Shortly after the turn of the century," DeMallie writes, "Black Elk turned his back on the entire practice of shamanistic healing and joined the Roman Catholic Church."[36] "As Black Elk's daughter Lucy later told the story, the turning point had come in 1904" in a conflict with a Jesuit priest, Father Joseph Lindebner, over the healing of a sick Indian boy, in which the priest physically prevented the shaman from completing his ceremony. Instead, he finished it according to Catholic ritual, then "invited Black Elk to return with him to Holy Rosary mission"[37]—though as Powers tells the story, it was "after curing a young Indian through traditional methods, that he chanced upon [. . .] Lindebner" and was converted.[38] In any event, Black Elk became a Catholic, though in all accounts there is an obscure space between the moment of his traditional practice and the moment of his conversion. Here is DeMallie's account: "There [at Holy Rosary Mission], after two weeks of instruction, he [Lindebner] baptized Black Elk on December 6, giving him the Christian name Nicholas in honor of the saint whose feast day it was. Black Elk's conversion was unquestionably genuine. By accepting Catholicism he at last put himself beyond the onerous obligations of his vision, and he never practiced the Lakota religious ceremonies again."[39]

The question of genuine conversion must, it would seem, be put in the forcible context that DeMallie provides: "there was real coercion on the part of the government to force Indians to join churches."[40] "From the beginning of the reservation period, the government had systematically suppressed all traditional social institutions—especially the tribal bands, the traditional chiefs, and the men's sacred and dancing societies—and tried to force the Lakotas to deal with the government as individual Indians rather than as a tribe."[41] In this situation of colonial repression, "such men's and women's sodalities as the Roman Catholic St. Joseph and St. Mary Societies could function as replacements for traditional men's and women's societies that had been fundamental social building blocks in earlier times."[42] Within this context, questions of correspondence certainly arise: if Catholic institutions displace Lakota ones, are the former unaffected by the latter? Everything we know about cross-cultural exchanges tells us otherwise. Of the statement that Black Elk "never practiced the Lakota religious ceremonies again," I would only ask, how do we know that? In fact, DeMallie gives an extended account of a Lakota ceremony, held on May 15, 1931, in which Black Elk was a central figure: the ceremony in which Neihardt was adopted into Black Elk's kinship group—hence the name "Flaming Rainbow," which appears in parentheses after "John G. Neihardt" on the title pages of all the editions of Black Elk Speaks. The ceremony marked "the day Black Elk would take Neihardt as his son, making the relationship between them public, preparing him to receive the teachings of his holy vision. After the prayer, Black Elk smoked the pipe and presented it to Neihardt for the ritual four puffs; then it was passed around the circle of the old men, who witnessed and validated the proceedings."[43] For students of Indian identity, this adoption ceremony might complicate the legal question of who or what is an Indian. Can Neihardt write as a Oglala Lakota?

In and of itself, this adoption ceremony would contradict, in any literal sense, the notion that Black Elk "never practiced the Lakota religious ceremonies again," unless, perhaps, one wants to make a clear distinction between the social and the religious, which the Lakota present do not seem to make; for, as DeMallie tells us, the ceremony functioned simultaneously both to adopt Neihardt as an Oglala, the "son" or "nephew" of Black Elk, and to admit him as a participant in Black Elk's sacred vision.[44] Further, DeMallie, whose narrative at crucial moments appears to contradict its own assertions about the changing identity of Black Elk, also recounts his participation from 1935 on in the "Sioux Indian Pageant," held in the Black Hills and sponsored by Alex Duhamel, "a businessman from Rapid City," in which "Black Elk demonstrated traditional religious activities including the offering of the pipe, the burial enactment, and the sun dance."[45] Apparently DeMallie does not consider such demonstrations to constitute actual practice, by which he perhaps means a practice the context of which is solely the Lakota community. He does hypothesize that "Black Elk's motivation in publicly performing these sacred rituals appears to have been to teach white audiences that the old-time Lakota religion was a true religion, not devil worship as the missionaries claimed."[46] This is strange educational work for someone who was a devoted Catholic— someone who had apparently signed a statement on January 26, 1934, written in Lakota and translated into English, entitled "black elk speaks again—the final speech." In this speech, in the wake of the Pine Ridge Jesuits' reaction against what they had perceived as the resurgent paganism of *Black Elk Speaks,* Black Elk affirmed his total commitment to Catholicism and renounced the Lakota practices that he affirmed in the book and was now rehearsing in the Duhamel pageant.[47] Within the complex interplay between Lakota and Catholic practice that mediates Black Elk's life, a life that is only available to us in writing, the question of Black Elk's intent in giving these paid performances, in which, as in the Wild West show, he appears to be representing himself for a largely white audience, has no clear answers. But we can remark on the relationship between these performances and the performance that constitutes *Black Elk Speaks,* if only to note the tangle of cultural practices that is itself tangled in a web of colonial coercion and resistance.

Nicholas Black Elk was no doubt a devoted "catechist," "help[ing to] speed conversion and maintain the faith,"[48] but the question arises, if only to remain unanswered, what is the collaborative relationship between that catechist, Nicholas; the Ghost Dancer; and the Lakota medicine man? Because "priests were able to celebrate Mass in the isolated communities on the reservation only about once a month, [. . .] in their absence catechists held Sunday services, led the prayers and hymns, read the Epistle and Gospel, and instructed the people—all *in the Lakota language.*"[49] What were the form and force of those services translated from Latin into Lakota and administered by a man whose life was powerfully structured by Ghost Dancing and the practice of Oglala medicine? To assert within the context of this dynamic of correspondent identities that Black Elk "never practiced the Lakota religious ceremonies again" is to suggest an impossible (because absolute) mechanism of surveillance over a community's practices. Black Elk's complex cultural identity makes it difficult to assert the ontological purity, or identity, of cultural practices in general, while intersecting lives like those of Black Elk and Neihardt contradict the purity, or stasis, of personal identity and thereby call into question the rigidities of the federal definition of "Indian."

DeMallie, in passing, gives possible examples of Lakota/Catholic correspondences, both in the relation of Christian charity to traditional Native communal relations and in the juxtaposition of "priestly garb" and "native finery" in the performance of Catholic ritual.[50] Near the end of his narrative, he asserts a position of correspondence that appears to reverse the identity-bound, or developmental, schema of Black Elk's life that he has previously offered: "Black Elk, like other Lakotas, could express his firm belief in the truth of the Catholic religion without the necessity of rejecting Indian beliefs. The two systems were not compartmentalized; rather, they were stages in his life. Unlike the missionaries, however, Black Elk did not conceive of the two religions as forming a developmental sequence. Both were intimately bound up in his being, and both sets of beliefs molded his character and personality."[51]

More pointedly than DeMallie, both Powers and Julian Rice[52] focus on Lakota/Catholic correspondence within the context of Black Elk's life while at the same time practicing an identity politics that seeks to resolve the correspondence into its component parts. For Powers, this means uncovering the correspondence that he reads Neihardt as trying to suppress at the same time that he seeks to discredit *Black Elk Speaks* as simply a white man's book written for the white man. For Rice, it means returning to the original transcripts of the 1931 and 1944 conversations in order to "cleanly disentangle" Black Elk's Lakota "voice" from Neihardt's Christian one.[53]

My own approach to this crucial question of identity, which writers like DeMallie, Powers, and Rice have brought to our attention in important ways, is in the first place to read it as much more conflictive than does DeMallie, who tends to read an identity, a harmony, between Lakota and Catholic practices and between the intentions of Black Elk and Neihardt, even as he describes a complex interplay between identity and difference, conflict and harmony, that does not allow us to come to rest on any one of these terms. My approach emphasizes the colonial context of the collaboration, which, even when not in the foreground, is nevertheless present as an inflection that keeps the meaning of the term "collaboration" oscillating between notions of coercion and cooperation.

Even as Black Elk's kinship relation to Neihardt is asserted in the Lakota terms for "son" or "nephew," or in the fact that Black Elk's son, Ben, and his wife named a son born in 1934 "John Neihardt Black Elk,"[54] letters in Black Elk's name or imputed to him (and how do we determine what hand he had in them?) accuse Neihardt of deceiving him about the financial outcome of *Black Elk Speaks* (the book was a failure at its publication) and castigate Neihardt for suppressing Black Elk's Catholicism in the book.[55] Here the Black Elk–Neihardt collaboration is defined by the conflict between kinship and property (communality and individualism), which is the classic conflict structuring Native American–Euramerican interaction, a point central to my argument. Considering Native American literatures within this particular collaborative configuration might significantly and productively reorder the forms of the field insofar as it might reorder the structure of Native identity. Brumble, for example, insists on making the distinction between preliterate and literate Indians in order to distinguish between two forms of Native American autobiography, the "as-told-to" and the "self-written": "Geronimo, Black Elk, Plenty-coups, and Black Hawk speak to us without benefit of such education [in letters], but they do speak to us through their editors—after many hours of storytelling and questions, all slowed by interpreters."[56] So while "there is a sense [. . .] in which every autobiography is a fiction of the self. [. . .] self-written autobiography is at least the subject's *own* fiction, the subject's own conception of the self, and so it must always be authentic in this sense at least. With the as-told-to autobiographies of the non-literate Indians, on the other hand, it is the Anglo editor, who decides, finally, what is to be the shape of his subject's 'autobiography.'"[57]

Brumble's apparently clear sense of agency/identity defines two forms of Native American autobiography here. But what does it mean to assert that the "self-written" is one's "own," whereas the literally collaborative is not? To term Black Elk, as Brumble does, "non-literate" is problematic in even the most literal sense. Black Elk apparently could write in the Lakota syllabary and signed his names in English as well to letters written in his name and to the contracts with Buffalo Bill.[58] Thus, in both as-told-to and self-written autobiographies, we are dealing with issues of the self and ownership in writing. In the West, the conjunction of self and ownership is classic, for it produces property, in the Lockean, liberal, or capitalist senses of the word, to deploy some crucial synonyms. As I have stressed, this conjunction is alien to Native American kinship cultures. Defining forms within the genre of Native American autobiography involves a distinction not simply between the oral and the written or as-told-to and self-written texts but between various forms of writing as property relations and resistance to those relations in the form of kinship. Neihardt and Black Elk are simultaneously kin and individuals with a property interest in *Black Elk Speaks*. What we might think about, then, in defining the forms of Native American literatures are the forms of contract, of which the first in Indian–European literary and legal relations is the treaty, the basis of U.S. federal Indian law. What, for example, in both the literal and figurative senses of the term, are the forms of contract that structure the collaboration between Black Elk and Neihardt?

"The mystic in Neihardt and the mystic in Black Elk were kindred souls," asserts DeMallie, yet he also asserts that "there has been a misunderstanding of purpose" in the composition of *Black Elk Speaks*: "Neihardt conceived of the project as writing Black Elk's life story, whereas Black Elk conceived of it as making a record of the Lakota religion."[59] While acknowledging differences in intention in noting the difference between the social function of Native oral expression and the aesthetic function of Western written expression, I want to complicate DeMallie's sense of separate and readable intentions in Black Elk and Neihardt. This sense returns us to the identity politics I am questioning in cases of collaborative art. Assertions of harmony or kinship and assertions of conflict suggest a complex of contractual obligations. These cannot be resolved in any simple, unified notion of identity of the kind that appears so seductive in much of Native American literary studies and is the norm in U.S. federal Indian law, where it is nothing if not reductive.

The collaborative dynamics of *Black Elk Speaks*, along with the problems they raise, can figure the field of Native American literatures. Deloria's reading of *Black Elk Speaks* focuses discussion not on the identity of the authors but on the text as a political or social performance rather than as a referent or key to transcendent identities. Deloria is in effect treating the text as social act, not aesthetic object—that is, as Native oral performance, which is always simultaneously both social act and artistic performance, as opposed to the emphasis on artistry in Western literature. In this sense, as performance, Deloria reads *Black Elk Speaks* as an effect of its social or political reception in Native communities:

> The most important aspect of the book, however, is not its effect on the non-Indian populace who wished to learn something of the beliefs of the Plains Indians but upon the contemporary generation of young Indians who have been aggressively searching for roots of their own in the structure of universal reality. To them the book has become a North American bible of all tribes. They look to it for spiritual guidance, for sociological identity, for political insight, and for affirmation of the continuing substance of Indian tribal life, now

being badly eroded by the same electronic media which are dissolving other American communities.[60]

Deloria's take on electronic media aside (it has both unifying and disintegrative effects), *Black Elk Speaks* does not claim its Indian identity through essence—the sorting out of European from Native American, of written from oral, of Neihardt from Black Elk—because such essence, in any absolute sense, is impossible. Rather, it claims its identity through practice of a particular pantribal, Indian community's resistance to the erosion "of the continuing substance of Indian tribal life." In this sense, identity, like the Indian practice of adopting European captives, is situational, not essential; it is the function of a position in a political/cultural debate, which is always ongoing and therefore subject to change—that is, to interpretation. This is to say that we can imagine *Black Elk Speaks* in the hands of a different community claiming a European identity for the book. These differing and conflicting identities can exist simultaneously as well as sequentially. Powers, for example, understands the Indian community that has claimed *Black Elk Speaks* as a revitalizing source of tradition as doing so only because it is alienated from what Powers understands as tradition—the "direct source of inspiration on the reservations"—both physically, in that it has moved to the cities, and mentally, in that it mistakes "a form [of] literary imperialism ... written by a white man" for a form of resistance to that imperialism.[61] Remember here the previously cited passage from Tommy Orange's novel *There There* erasing the boundary between reservation and urban Indian life, between tradition and modernity.

Clearly Deloria disagrees with this reading of *Black Elk Speaks* by a Western anthropologist. Questions of legitimacy arise—for example, who defines tradition?—because these questions drive historic issues of representation. As the work of Native American literary studies proceeds, the first and last question should be, who represents the Indians, in both the legal and literary senses of the term "representation"? The issues of representation that *Black Elk Speaks* manifests are integral to the genre of collaborative Indian autobiography at its inception. Vis-à-vis my earlier discussion of the conflict between Indian kinship and Western property relations to land, the very term "autobiography" is itself problematic when applied to traditional Indian narratives because of its emphasis on individual achievement within a framework that privileges the paradigm of property, as exemplified by Benjamin

Franklin's *Autobiography*, which remains the archetype of the genre in U.S. Euramerican literatures.

The two earliest examples of collaborative Indian autobiographies are *Narrative of the Life of Mrs. Mary Jemison* (1824), told to and written by James Everett Seaver, and *Life of Ma-Ka-Tai-Me-She-Kia-Kiak Black Hawk... Dictated by Himself* [to Antoine LeClair, "U.S. Interpreter for the Sacs and Foxes"] (1833).[62] Though Euro-American by birth, Mary Jemison was adopted by the Seneca after being captured in 1758 at the age of fifteen and lived with them until she was ninety. The name Jemison appears on tribal roles today. In line with Axtell's argument, rehearsed earlier, this pattern of adoption, in which whites became fully acculturated and accepted by Native communities, was not unique. Vizenor makes the same argument:

> The application of mixedblood geometric scores was not a form of tribal cultural validation. Skin color and blood quantums were not the means the tribe used to determine identities. The Anishinaabeg "classified a person Indian if he lived with them and adopted their habits and mode of life," according to David Beaulieu. [...] "Some tribal people... focus on style of dress as the main feature in distinguishing Indian and mixedblood. [...] Percentage of Indian and white blood was not a determining factor in distinguishing a mixedblood.... For the most part the distinction was cultural." These tribal distinctions, which were not racial but experiential, were not adopted by the federal government. Beaulieu pointed out that through treaties the government "attempted to render fixed and static definitions of mixedbloods and Indians not only for the people alive at the moment but to their descendants."[63]

Thus, as Susan Walsh suggests, citing Thomas S. Abler: "Read as the story of a Seneca woman, the Seaver/Jemison *Narrative* may well be 'the first Indian autobiography to reach publication.'"[64] Although Jemison, who apparently did not read or write English, told her story to Seaver in English, it was he who wrote the narrative.[65] In reading the Jemison autobiography, we face the same kinds of issues that *Black Elk Speaks* raises.

In the case of Black Hawk's autobiography, his collaborators were government translator Antoine LeClair, who was mixed-blood, being Potawatomi and French Canadian, and Illinois newspaper editor John B. Patterson. Before Black Hawk's story begins, there is a statement by LeClair testifying to the authenticity and accuracy of the narrative, which he assures the reader was dictated to him by Black Hawk (in Sauk) at Black Hawk's request, and checked by LeClair for accuracy after it had been put into literary English by Patterson.[66] Following this is a dedication by Black Hawk to General Atkinson, who in 1832 had directed the troops that defeated him and his band of Sauks, Mesquakies (Fox), and other Indians resisting removal from traditional lands in Illinois. This dedication appears both in English translation and in English transliteration from the Sauk.[67] The transliteration, we can assume, is meant to give further authenticity to the text, although in a strange way it serves to undermine the appearance of authenticity, both by the distance it figures between Sauk and English and by the very need to have it in writing to assure genuineness. After this dedication is a statement by Patterson, which in its last part also testifies to the authenticity of the narrative—its origin in the voice of Black Hawk through the writing of the translator and himself.[68]

Donald Jackson, the contemporary editor of *Black Hawk: An Autobiography,* tells us, "Since there are no known documents by which the authenticity of the work can be established, except the signed statements of LeClair and Patterson, much depends upon the evaluation of those men."[69] The most skeptical reader, then, might wonder if Black Hawk played any part in this text—more so than in the case of *Black Elk Speaks,* where a much more detailed record of the translation process exists and the subject appears to have been a more willing collaborator. (Black Hawk was a war captive.) The least skeptical reader, however, must wonder about the blurring of boundaries between Black Hawk, LeClair, and Patterson—although perhaps, following Deloria's thoughts on Neihardt and Black Elk, that is only a Western worry stemming from an obsession with individualism, which produces autobiography in the first place. As with *Black Elk Speaks,* my purpose is not to bypass or try to resolve this question of Black Hawk as either a literal or figurative presence in the text named after him but to deal with its politics.

The text itself, dictated and written only three years after the passage of the Indian Removal Act (1830),[70] is eloquently critical of federal Indian policy, with its aim of dispossession through removal, as well as sensitive to ethnographic details of American Indian social life. At the same time, the text at its end takes a conciliatory tone toward the United States that could be read as blunting or undermining that critique and as participating in the elegiac tone characteristic of one major movement in the genre of the nineteenth- and twentieth-century western, which projects American Indians through a haze of nostalgia as a noble but vanishing race—a nostalgia that characterizes the ending of *Black Elk Speaks* (which Neihardt admitted to crafting), which obscures both the violence being done to the Indians by the United States and the historical fact of continuing Indian resistance, as well as the ethnohistorical facts of the persistence of Indian cultures that drives this resistance.

As in the case of *Black Elk Speaks,* skepticism about the text, and the many others that follow it, can both serve and undermine Indian interests. As Jackson points out, for example, "the government attorneys participating in hearings before the Indian Claims Commission in Washington, August, 1953 [. . .] argued that the Sauk and Fox, seeking payment for lands taken from them in 1804, were basing some of their testimony upon statements in the Black Hawk autobiography—*a book which history had already discredited.*"[71] The quality of that skepticism is crucial—Western readers' awareness of their own motives. This means an awareness not only of the contexts within which texts are produced but also of the fact that context is also text. Context is open to interpretation because of the inevitably political form of what we often ingenuously call reality, as if it were a universal essence rather than an effect of cultures. What, for example, do government lawyers mean by the terms "history" and "discredited"? They speak as if there were only one uncontested history that had the transcendent power to determine the truth of discourses. But in fact the legal processes they are involved in suggest that history itself is no more than contests of discursive processes.

The context in which we must read Black Hawk's autobiography is crucially informed by *Johnson v. M'Intosh,* which I have reviewed in part. This was the second Supreme Court decision in the history of federal Indian law, and the most important because it denied the Indians ultimate title to their lands by placing this title in the hands of the U.S. government. Here, in a passage from the case, are some of the grounds for such a denial: "But the tribes of Indians inhabiting this country were fierce savages, whose occupation was war, and whose subsistence was drawn chiefly from the forest. To leave them in possession of their country, was to leave the country a wilderness: to govern them as a distinct people, was impossible, because they were as brave and as high spirited as they were fierce, and were ready to repel by arms every attempt on their independence."[72] Writing the foundational chapter in the literature of federal Indian law, Marshall first conjures ethnographic hallucinations about Indians: they are all warriors and hunters who do nothing productive with the land they live on, for it is a "wilderness" (and notice that there is no room in these hallucinations for Indian women). Next he stereotypes the Indians as noble ("brave and high-spirited") but vanishing (because this kind of bravery is savage and thus has no place in modern life), and combines the stereotype with partial truths about Indian resistance, which in most cases was a last resort after attempts at political accommodation did not end white violence. In fact, Indians did and do resist accommodation in significant, though clearly not in all, ways—and why shouldn't they? Their communal cultural forms are so antithetical to the property-centered forms of the West that to lose them is to lose their identities as Indigenous peoples. But historically they have been willing (with all the irony that the word entails under the circumstances of ever increasing Euramerican power) to be governed as distinct peoples, so long as they had sufficient share in that government to allow them political and cultural integrity. However, ever since the Marshall Court, in *Cherokee Nation v. Georgia*, defined, contradictorily enough, the relation of Indian peoples to the U.S. government as that of "domestic dependent nations," the federal government, as Deloria has pointed out, has increasingly emphasized dependency at the expense of nationhood.[73]

Black Hawk's autobiography, published ten years after *Johnson v. M'Intosh* and two years after *Cherokee Nation v. Georgia*, which elaborates and extends the usurpation of Native sovereignty decided in the *Johnson* case, takes on a particular strategic importance when read as one of the Indian voices of the time that, along with those of Elias Boudinot, William Apess, Mary Jemison, the Tuscarora David Cusick and the Ojibway George Copway, among others, emerged in writing to contradict in various ways the developing literature of federal Indian law, which is based on the ideology of "savagery" that Montaigne had contradicted, without any widespread cultural effect, 250 years previously. Maureen Konkle remarks of "Native intellectuals" in the antebellum period: "Their texts taken together dramatize a continuous process [. . .] of essentially thinking one's freedom into existence in a political and epistemological system that not only oppresses Native peoples but also renders them literally dead."[74] However, Konkle does not include the Jemison and Black Hawk texts, noting: "Whatever traces of Native agency remain in these accounts, both are versions of conventional forms—captivity narrative and frontier war story—and both close off their subjects by reiterating the narrative of Indians' providential doom."[75] The view of "Native agency" I am taking clearly extends, vis-à-vis Deloria's take on *Black Elk Speaks*, to Jemison and Black Hawk. Konkle's notion of conventional forms as, apparently, restricting agency could easily be applied to the work of Apess and others like him—those who used conventional Western forms like sermon, autobiography, and history to project their discourses. Of course, anyone using alphabetic writing has no choice but to use certain conventional forms; indeed, writing itself is a conventional form, one that, in its very structure and history, imposes certain restrictions. In this context, the question is thus not if one uses conventional forms but how. Walsh comments of the Jemison–Seaver collaboration: "Sought out at the advanced age of eighty by certain New York 'gentlemen of respectability' anxious to 'perpetuate the remembrance of' Indian atrocities committed during the French and Revolutionary wars, Jemison (undoubtedly to their surprise) told a tale extolling Indian virtue and denouncing the genocidal introduction of alcohol into the Iroquois nations."[76] The point here is that Jemison subverted or transformed conventions of the captivity narrative to include a critical Native voice. In determining the boundary between those Indian writers who have agency and those who do not, Konkle applies a metaphysics of presence and absence that I liken to the kind Brumble uses when distinguishing between self-written and as-told-to Native autobiographies. Certainly, there is a distinction to be made, but just exactly what it is or if it can be made remains to be specified. Meanwhile, specifying such difference, as Konkle and Brumble do, risks importing into Native American studies the very identity politics (of who is and is not a "real" Indian) instituted by federal Indian law, with rigid ideas of agency/identity in the intellectual realm taking the place of blood quantum regulations in the legal realm.

Following Deloria's reading of *Black Elk Speaks*, my notion of Indian voices is strategic. That is, this reading does not take the voice of Black Hawk as Indian because of a belief in an original presence, or verifiable contact, that generates the writing representing that voice. Rather, this reading takes the voice as Indian because of its position in a political/cultural debate. The identity of the voice is cultural, then, not biological. As the case of Mary Jemison articulates, a European voice, under certain rigorous circumstances that must finally be determined by the Native community involved, can speak as a member of that community. In this case, the dictum, as stated in *Black Elk Speaks*, is, "This they tell, and whether it happened so or not I do not know; but if you think about it, you can see that it is true."[77] Ward Churchill, who claims a Cherokee identity, though this claim is rejected by some within the Native community, is a contemporary case in point. Tried by the University of Colorado at Boulder, where he was a faculty member of the ethnic studies department, for "research misconduct," Churchill had the support of the Native students at Boulder, the faculty of ethnic studies, and several nationally known Native academics— precisely because his writings and public utterances represented for these Native people an authentic Native voice expressing resistance to the colonial rule of Indian Country. What matters here is not blood but behavior.[78]

Contra Marshall's characterization of Indians as fierce hunters and warriors in *Johnson*, in Black Hawk's autobiography, the reader learns that the Sauk led a way of life that combined agriculture and hunting along with fixed settlement with patterned movement in a seasonal economy.[79] The reader also learns that Indian bravery, as whites perceived it, was not based in some simple or savage warrior reflex but in a mental resistance to the kind of Western ideology that projected Indians as savage. As Black Hawk recounts, the Sauk resistance of 1832, which lasted for fifteen weeks and ended with a massacre of fleeing Sauk women and children by U.S. troops, was in response to what Black Hawk and his band understood to be a fraudulent 1804 treaty.[80] This treaty, which ceded a vast tract of land east of the Mississippi River between Wisconsin and Missouri, including the site of Black Hawk's village, had been negotiated under the most dubious of circumstances and without the mechanisms of tribal consent.[81] Even so, Article 7 of the treaty stated: "As long as the lands which are now ceded to the United States remain their property, the Indians belonging to the said tribes [Sauk and Fox], shall enjoy the privilege of living and hunting upon them."[82] This article clearly promises the extension of continuing usufruct rights to the Indians on what became federal land. However, under the pressure of expanding white settlement, the U.S. government sold the land to individuals (so it was no longer federal property) and ordered the Sauk and Fox tribes to remove west of the Mississippi in the early 1830s, forcing the Indians to abandon their traditional places, which were intimately involved with their traditional lifeways[83]—the heart of the *Lyng* case.

Black Hawk and his compatriots resisted this removal not only because of the treaty's fraudulence but also because, in threatening their traditional way of life, the removal threatened their economic survival. In fact, Black Hawk tells his readers that before resorting to armed resistance, he was willing to remove with the people of his village in exchange for the equivalent amount of corn that had been lost in the sale of the village to whites. But after signing an agreement with the Sauks for the corn, the government failed to deliver the necessary amount: "The corn that had been given us, was soon found to be inadequate to our wants; when loud lamentations were heard in the camp, by our women and children, for their *roasting-ears, beans,* and *squashes.* To satisfy them, a small party of braves went over, in the night, to steal corn from their own fields. They were discovered by the whites, and fired upon. Complaints were again made of the depredations committed by some of my people, *on their own corn-fields!*"[84] Black Hawk's acute sense of irony explodes Marshall's projection of a savage Indian as mere reflexive physical force; it simultaneously exposes federal Indian law for the parody of social justice that founds it.

From the Indian perspective, the treaty was always a form of force because within Native American societies, as Black Hawk tells his readers, and as this book stresses, *"land cannot be sold"* or ceded—that is, alienated in any form.[85] Also, contrary to European characterizations of Indian forms of government for their own political designs, Native governance consisted not in representative forms of government but in consensual forms in which no one could act for anyone else. Europeans brought to the Americas a whole battery of Western terminology, of which the notion of property was the central weapon, that helped translate the Indians into a Western legal system determined to thrust property on Native Americans so that they could then be "legally" dispossessed of it. Finally, as Black Hawk repeatedly states, treaties were always being broken by the Americans, whose written words could not be trusted.[86]

As Trask notes of European projections of their social ills onto Hawaiian society, Marshall's projection of the Indians as savage rationalizes or legitimizes their dispossession while serving to repress through projection ("We have met the enemy and he is us"[87]) a complex of Euramerican social problems that are still with us, but more virulently than ever because of continuous repression. For example, the projection of the Indian as savage warrior represses as it figures the Euramerican obsession with violence, the fetishization of guns and masculinity, which Euramericans have yet to confront and so continue to project on those they perceive as other both at home and abroad. The Marshall text also represses the movement of an unregulated capitalism—land speculation in this case—that put continual pressure on the government to violate treaties. The savagery of the Indians ironically allegorizes the actual savagery of untamed Western individualism, with its fierce acquisitive drives. The figure of the Indians as inhabiting a wilderness expresses even as it denies a Euramerican relationship to nature founded on dominance and submission, masking a terror of the natural world that even in the nineteenth century was beginning the environmental imbalances that today threaten to turn nature into an actual wilderness.

Keeping in mind the processes of translation by which American Indian oral traditions become Native American literatures, these oral literatures in translation are, if read with attention to the issues I have raised here, nevertheless part of the repertoire of texts we have available to understand Native American literatures insofar as, working across a wide range of cultural differences, they allow us not only to gain some insight into specific cultures but also to make comparisons and so construct a set of transcultural, or specifically Indigenous, values, particularly in relation to the central values of land and community, or kinship.[88] In this hazardous venture of cross-cultural understanding, some translations are more useful than others, as I have been suggesting—although as the example of *Black Elk Speaks* suggests, the criteria for judgment are controversial.

While translations into English make oral performance available in written contexts, however transformed, the oral tradition is an ongoing and dynamic process in Indian communities across the United States. In addition to traditional forms—ceremonial songs and chants, origin narratives, and stories of communal conflict exemplified by the culturally ubiquitous trickster, about which more in what follows—there are the everyday stories that people tell each other as part of the fabric of social relations: personal and tribal histories, anecdotes, and jokes, more or less formal. Anthropologist Keith Basso, for example, has recorded the way that Cibecue Apache jokes about white people play a formative role in social relations, providing a critical commentary on white behavior directed at Indians in colonial contexts, thereby ironically affirming Indian social relations while testing them. In this way, the jokes function akin to trickster narratives, but their origin is clearly colonial.[89] The jokes appear to develop spontaneously, and, at least in Basso's experience, usually take place between two men who have a close relationship, typically kin. One man, who initiates the action, will play a type of white functionary encountered on or near the reservation (anthropologist, doctor, teacher, bartender), and the other Apache will play (along) as the Apache butt of the aggressive, condescending language of the "whiteman." The joke, which is carried on in the infantilizing pidgin that colonizers typically adopt when talking to the colonized, and about which Frantz Fanon has written so probingly in *Black Skin, White Masks*,[90] ends when the Apache playing the Apache says, in Apache, what translates as "Whitemen are stupid." The punch line is clearly a commentary on the egocentric, racist behavior of the white man, thereby implicitly affirming Apache (and by extension Indigenous) values of communal respect for every person. The joke says, in effect: this is not how Apaches treat each other. Yet the joke is risky business: in commenting on the colonial situation, it recreates or summons it (because the colonial context is always present, in either foreground or background) and so threatens the violence inherent in the situation. That is why, Basso surmises, the two men involved in the joke must have a close bond to begin with—so that the Apache who is the ostensible butt of the joke does not read it as an attempt to belittle him but as a joint critique of white social behavior toward Apaches.

The transtribal Native values that emerge from these translations of the oral tradition help us understand the basis of Indigenous resistance to the European invasion from 1492 to the present. This resistance, implicitly and explicitly, has been the primary subject of U.S. Native American literatures since the works of the Pequot William Apess and others established a polemical, anticolonialist tradition of Indian writing in the late 1820s and the first half of the 1830s, when federal Indian law was in its formative stage. Casting the resistance in terms of collaboration may also be useful if we understand the term in the full spectrum of its meanings as I have elaborated them—from coercion to mutual cooperation, with all the nuances that occur in between. Apess himself is a case in point. A mixed-blood Pequot, he grew up in a world where his own tribal heritage had been brutally fractured through decimation by European diseases in the early 1630s, the Puritan massacre of Pequots in 1637, and the subsequent reduction in population in the eighteenth and nineteenth centuries, "in part because of the scattering of tribal members as a result of the loss of land and livelihoods," so that by 1860, there were only one hundred surviving tribal members.[91] Forced by these colonial circumstances to grow up as an indentured servant in a white, racist world, Apess nevertheless seemed to find in his conversion to Methodism, a religion that welcomed the marginalized, and in his vocation as a preacher a substitute for the Indian communalism that he lacked as a child but regained as an adult through his championing of Indian rights.[92] In his narrative *A Son of the Forest* (1829), the first published autobiography written by an Indian, Apess writes of his collaborative journey—of Native and Christian communalism, of Native oral tradition and an oral spontaneity that he discovered in particular in Methodist services. In his *Indian Nullification of the Unconstitutional Laws of Massachusetts* (1835), he presents an eloquent defense of human rights and Native sovereignty. In his *Eulogy on King Phillip* (1836), the seventeenth-century Wampanoag Indian leader who died resisting Puritan tyranny, he gives a powerful model of anticolonialist history written from a Native perspective. Native American literatures, then, are fully nuanced forms of collaboration. With origins in the colonial coercion of writing, they often become at crucial moments a countercolonial force.

As a collaboration between a European and an Indian, *Cogewea* is unique in the tradition of the U.S. Native novel.[93] William Penn, a novelist/critic of Nez Perce ancestry, remarks of the collaboration between McWhorter and Mourning Dove: "Even though Dexter Fisher [who has written a critical introduction to the modern edition of *Cogewea*] and Louis Owens seem willing to assume it is hers—and, indeed, she does bear the final responsibility as all writers do—I doubt much more than half of it is. Much of what we have in the published version of *Cogewea* is Lucullus V. McWhorter."[94] Penn tries to sort out where Mourning Dove begins and ends and where McWhorter takes over, but the analysis assumes that Mourning Dove's own writing somehow remained uninfluenced by a "Latinate" style that Penn identifies with McWhorter. In this sorting, Penn essentially identifies Mourning Dove with a pristine oral tradition and McWhorter, the white man, with a corrupted written tradition: "The language in this passage is not the language of storytelling. It is the Latinate language of someone who has read too many bad novels trying to stuff historical event into a chapter which, told simply and elegantly in Mourning Dove's way would express more ceremony and history than could ever be told by these addenda of the sympathetic white."[95] The test case for Penn, as it is for Fisher before him, is Mourning Dove's *Coyote Stories*, her versions of Interior Salish oral traditions, also edited by McWhorter, with Yakima city newspaperman Heister Dean Guie: "Thus, where the speech in *Cogewea* resembles this oral, simple (in the sense of poetic), repetitious and expanding style, we can find Mourning Dove."[96] However, Penn also has a critique of the way she "took out a good portion of what could be called Indian" in *Coyote Stories* under the influence of Guie and McWhorter.[97] Thus, *Coyote Stories*, rather than solving the problem of identity as style posed by *Cogewea*, seems to repeat the editorial intrusion. In the same manner, "McWhorter [in *Cogewea*] helped her make her voice the same as every other overwritten romantic novel. Where he failed was where her voice was the strongest, where her storytelling material was what she most believed in—the Stemteemä [Cogewea's grandmother] sections."[98] For Penn, Indian identity in the text is represented by what he terms "the digressive supplementation of the oral tradition": "Oral storytelling allows for digression. It allows for representation of dialect. And it allows for entertaining intrusions by the implied author-teller."[99]

In contrast, Choctaw scholar Michael Wilson sees the boundary between McWhorter and Mourning Dove in *Cogewea* not in differences of diction but in differences of content. Wilson identifies McWhorter in the novel with "the ethnological philosophy of the late nineteenth and early twentieth century, which sees Indian cultures as either pure or impure, with change as a debasement."[100] In opposition, he identifies Mourning Dove with a discourse that represents "the oral tradition" as a dynamic cultural mode of "those who embody the changing conditions of life—namely, the mixed-bloods who live on the ranch," the novel's setting.[101] Unlike Penn, Wilson understands the different registers of language in the novel not as necessarily identifying the difference between McWhorter and Mourning Dove but as representing Cogewea's mixed-blood education in both the oral and Western traditions (the tradition of European letters):

> On the one hand, Cogewea experienced a traditional Okanogan upbringing under the tutelage of the Stemteemä; on the other hand, she underwent a formal education at the Carlisle Indian School

in Pennsylvania. Thus, Cogewea is able to speak the language of the Okanogan (she sometimes serves as a translator for her grandmother); the language of her formal education; and a third language—that of the Horseshoe Bend Ranch, the area "between two fires," where the novel takes place. Her multilingual abilities are not lost on other people at the ranch, nor is she unaware of her multiple voice.[102]

Such multilingual abilities were certainly a part of Mourning Dove's repertoire. Thus, while both Penn and Wilson identify Mourning Dove with the oral tradition and McWhorter with the written, their ideas of the oral tradition are opposed in such a way that the style of Penn's McWhorter blends into the style of Wilson's Mourning Dove. Is there any reason not to believe that Mourning Dove herself, whose education in both Western and Indian cultures provides a model for Cogewea, did not "read too many bad novels," and so produced the kind of mixed style that Wilson finds characteristic of the oral tradition?

This question is meant to emphasize the difficulty, if not the impossibility, of distinguishing Mourning Dove from McWhorter in the text. I find this quest futile, generated as it is by supposed evidence that tempts as it foils. In a letter to McWhorter that Fisher cites in her introduction to the novel, Mourning Dove remarks of McWhorter's editorial job: "I felt like it was someone else's book and not mine at all"—though after stating, "The changes that you made [. . .] are fine [. . .] a tasty dressing like a cook would do with a fine meal."[103] The metaphor suggests that Mourning Dove's text (the meal) and McWhorter's rewriting (the dressing) can be distinguished, while Mourning Dove's feeling that her book had become "someone else's" in the process of revision suggests a wholly transformed original, where the two writers are indistinguishable. Fisher also quotes a letter from Martha McKelvie to McWhorter stating that "you practically wrote *Cogewea*."[104] Perhaps the question ought not be, where is McWhorter and where is Mourning Dove in the text, but why should such a question be asked in the first place? My answer would be that the question is generated by the colonial politics that asks, who is an Indian? It is these politics and the historical question of identity they pose that, in revising the philosophical or theoretical theme of mixed-blood between two worlds (two identities), ground a reading of *Cogewea* and by extension of the American Indian novel in an understanding of the history of U.S. federal Indian law.

Cogewea's author, Mourning Dove (Hum-ishu-ma, or Christine Quintasket), was born, by her own estimation, in 1888, a year after the general allotment act, and died in 1936, two years after its repeal by the IRA: "She was born in a canoe while her mother was crossing the Kootenay River near Bonner's Ferry, Idaho, but she grew up in the lands of her people, members of Interior Salishan tribes along the upper Columbia River. Her father, Joseph, was from the Okanagans, and her mother, Lucy (née Stuikin), was from the chiefly family of the Colvilles at the important fishery of Kettle Falls."[105]

In his introduction to her autobiography, Jay Miller remarks: "Mourning Dove claimed [her paternal grandfather] was a Scot, but his other children and the census records deny this. Evidently Christine provided a white ancestor to appeal to her readers."[106] In his introduction ("To The Reader") to *Cogewea*, McWhorter notes that Mourning Dove only "bears a remote strain of good *Celtic* blood, dating back to the earlier advent of the Hudson Bay Company into the Northwest."[107] McWhorter also identifies her with the Okanagans, "whose language she speaks."[108] She married Hector McLeod, a Flathead, in 1909, which would account for her placing the action of *Cogewea* on the Flathead reservation, which was opened to allotment in 1905[109] and where she "witnessed the 1908 roundup of the last free-ranging bison herd,"[110] an event that Cogewea laments in the novel (143). Mourning Dove locates the action on the Horseshoe Bend Ranch, carved out of the reservation and owned by the Euramerican cattleman John Carter, who is married to Julia, Cogewea's oldest sister. Mourning Dove's marriage to McLeod lasted only a few years. "By 1912 Christine was living in Portland, where she began her novel and took Mourning Dove as her pen name."[111] The novel appears to be set around this time. She met McWhorter in 1915. Fisher notes that they had finished the "collaboration" on *Cogewea* by 1916, though it would not be published until 1927.[112]

In contrast to her main character, then, Mourning Dove, who appears to have fantasized her mixed-bloodedness, was full-blood by blood quantum standards, and an enrolled member of the Colville Confederated Tribes and Reservation of Washington State.[113] Cogewea is the child of an Okanogan mother, who, like Mourning Dove's own mother, dies early in her life, and a white father of Scots descent, Bertram Macdonald, who abandons her and her two sisters, Mary and Julia, to prospect for gold in Alaska. At the end of the novel, a legal error, "a technical flaw in daddy's will," will allow the girls "a share in some of his fortune, amounting to a quarter million dollars each" (284). While Mourning Dove and Cogewea are not identical in terms of blood quantum, what they do share in common is an allotment: they are both beneficiaries (in the strictly legal sense) of the Dawes Act. On March 14, 1921, Mourning Dove "was approved for a patent in fee simple for her allotted land" on the Colville Reservation.[114] In order to receive this allotment in fee, she would have had to be judged by BIA authorities legally competent to manage her affairs. Under the BIA administration of Cato Sells, who served as commissioner of Indian Affairs during Woodrow Wilson's two terms as president (1913–21), "persons who were less than one-half Indian or who had graduated from a government school would receive fee patents immediately."[115] Because she was more than half Indian, it would appear that in order to support her competency claim, Mourning Dove "listed her school as Colville Mission, four years; Fort Spokane, one year; Fort Shaw, three years; and Calgary College, two years"—certainly enough Western education to have learned to read the bad novels and perhaps write in the Latinate style that Penn and others attribute solely to McWhorter.[116] Because it is not clear from the Miller introduction to her autobiography that she graduated from either of the two government schools she attended, the judgment of competency may have needed the support of the Colville superintendent O. C. Upchurch, who wrote, "She is intelligent and industrious, and as capable of handling her affairs as the average white woman in the community."[117] The competency standard here—"the average white woman in the community"—is thoroughly racialized.

Unlike her creator, Cogewea, presumably because she has half white blood, could have been judged competent on that standard alone to receive her "allotment of eighty acres" in fee (162, 262).[118] The question of Cogewea's legal competency comes up near the end of the novel, when she goes to the bank to withdraw a thousand dollars, conned from her by marriage promises of her white Eastern suitor, Alfred Densmore—who, the reader knows long before Cogewea catches on, is only after what he believes, wrongly, to be her wealth in land and livestock. A bank cashier tries to talk her out of the withdrawal and into an investment in "preferred stock." The cashier implores her to "recall" the recommendation of her former official guardian "the Indian Agent, [who advised her] to draw only small amounts as [she] might need for immediate wants; and if [she] contemplated an investment to advise with the bank." Cogewea gives this "retort": "Yes, I do recall but who recommends the Agent? I know what a time I had getting this money pried loose from the grasp of the Bureau, and I now intend handling it without an assistance from that bunch. I am no longer an 'incompetent' and in the present instance I believe that I can determine my own affairs" (256). The "Bureau" referred to here is, of course, the Bureau of Indian Affairs (BIA); modern, informed readers cannot help but hear an ironic resonance in Cogewea's insistence that she will manage her money "without any assistance from that bunch"; for, in recognizing the corruption in the BIA's handling of Indian trust accounts at the time of the novel, her rejoinder to the advice of the Indian Agent uncannily looks forward to the *Cobell* suit and suggests the historical and fictional intimacy of Washburn's *The Sacred White Turkey* with Cogewea, whether or not Washburn read the latter, which I suspect she has. In the immediate context of the conversation, Cogewea's mention of her former incompetency references her coming "of age," her status as a legal minor and her subsequent attainment of her majority (255). But the scare quotes around "incompetent" and the larger context of the novel cannot help but invoke the competency commissions of the allotment period, which, as noted, came into being in the wake of the Burke Act in 1906.[119]

The subject of allotment is referenced throughout the novel; in fact, the plot is driven by the politics of allotment, which is to say the Euramerican legalized theft of Indian land, which includes as an integral part of its grand larceny the theft of Indian identity. The subtitle of the novel, *A Depiction of the Great Montana Cattle Range,* references the theft of Indian land on the Great Plains, which was converted from buffalo to cattle range by Euramerican settlers, just as the title of the novel, *Cogewea, the Half-Blood,* references the theft of Indian identity by BIA regulations. When Cogewea laments "the invader['s]" destruction of the buffalo ("Colleague of my race, with him went our hopes, our ambition, and our life"), Densmore dismisses her elegy by invoking allotment: "The Government is working hard for his ('the Indian') betterment, and he should respond with a willingness to advance by adjusting himself to the new order of things. The opening of this reservation to settlement, tends to mingle him with his white brother, leading to an inter-marriage of the two races"—an intermarriage, Densmore might have added, voicing the explicit ideology of allotment, that envisioned the eventual disappearance of Indians through assimilation (143–44). In the novel, these integral thefts of land and identity are figured by Densmore's plot to marry Cogewea so he can possess what, taken in by the playful exaggerations of the ranch hands, he thinks is her vast allotment and herds (207–8). As in the Osage murders of the early 1920s, where a group of whites conspired to marry and then murder Osage men and women for their oil wealth gained through allotment, Densmore fantasizes about marrying and then murdering Cogewea for what he imagines to be her wealth (254). In the end, though, when Cogewea finally realizes what he is up to, his violence is limited to beating her and robbing her of the thousand dollars (262–63).[120]

Densmore's plot to dispossess Cogewea of what he imagines to be her land and its products takes on a representative status generated not only by the historical context of allotment but also by the context of the European invasion of the Americas in which allotment finds its ultimate rationale. Having already invoked "the just laws of our land" to justify his plot, Densmore gives a cynical rejoinder to Cogewea, when she protests his robbing her, that could well stand as the epigraph of this book: "The law—," she begins, only to be interrupted by Densmore: "—is absolutely helpless to help you! [. . .] The law is of the white man's make, interpreted by the white man, made to talk by the white man's money" (264). Within the colonial contexts that generated *Cogewea*, Densmore is a figure of the archetypal settler, Columbus, haunted by his hallucinations of Indian gold, always receding before him, always over the next horizon:

> The touch of sadness in Cogewea's voice as she spoke of her parents, was lost on the Easterner. But the mention of "gold in the Yukon" had aroused to new life his latent passion for wealth. It was the one god of his ambition to go back home a rich man. For this, he had left the city and society. He must make good; he was not so particular how, but in some way. He had struck a rough, strange people and was gaining an exuberant experience with which to regale his associates upon his return to his old haunts. There must be wealth somewhere in this new country—mines of it among the Indians— requiring only brains and strategy to possess. (84)

This description of Densmore's consciousness is the stuff of colonial romance, the epitome of which are Columbus's journals, or the narratives of Coronado's trek north from Mexico into the land of the

Zunis in 1540 to find the Seven Cities of Cíbola: the adventure of the younger son (excluded from Old World wealth by primogeniture or class) into new worlds, where he seeks his fortune among a "rough, strange people," who seem to offer both captivating narratives and vast wealth, fabled but never found—at least not in the infantilized form of instant gratification. Early in the novel, before Densmore's arrival, while in conversation with her future husband, James LaGrinder, the mixed-blood foreman of her white brother-in-law's ranch, Cogewea invokes "Columbus [. . .] honored by all nations for the correctness of his ideas" (34). Her honoring of the first Euramerican invader of Native America rings with irony by the end of the novel, in light of Densmore's Columbian rapacity.

In *Cogewea,* race matters are matters of the law. This situation is focused in what is the most analyzed scene in the novel: the two racially divided Fourth of July horse races, one for the "squaws" and one for the "ladies," both of which Cogewea enters and wins, asserting her Indian blood to enter the former and her white blood to enter the latter. Critics have noted the pun on "race."[121] What also needs to be noted is the connection between race and law that the scene makes explicit. "Squaws" and "ladies," though apparently intended in the chapter to distinguish Indians from whites through the biologic or essentialist reasoning of race (though class is also implicit in the term "ladies"), are logically not mutually exclusive categories, and the fact that both terms are placed in quotation marks in the chapter's title suggests an ironic consciousness at work. Outside the polemical purposes of the context, each category could be included in the other: a squaw can be a lady logically (in terms of sex/gender if one erases the socially constructed racial divide) and a lady, a squaw—a point Cogewea seems intent on making by her participation in both races. She makes the point explicitly when, in response to her white competitor's racist query, "Why is this *squaw* permitted to ride?" Cogewea responds: "Perhaps I am allowed because no '*ladies*' of the silvery-hue have entered" (63). On the one hand, in the Algonquian language of the Narragansett Indians, "*sunksquaw* meant 'queen' or 'lady.'"[122] Although the "literal meaning of the word *squaw* is obscure,"[123] its meaning did not become derogatory until taken over by non-Natives and applied to all Indian women, which is the way the white community in the novel is using it. On the other hand, Cogewea seems intent on restoring the Algonquian term to its proper usage. When Jim compliments her on winning the ladies' race, referring to her as my "tiny squaw," Cogewea's "eyes sparkled at the compliment, for 'squaw' had not been intended as epithetical" (64). Whatever the intended biologic of the terms "ladies" and "squaws" in the novel, cultural logic keeps subverting them.

When Cogewea enters the "squaw" race, she changes from her Western riding habit into "native costume," so that even the ranch hands who know her "recognized her only by the horse" (64–65). "Proceeding to the grandstand, Cogewea paid her entrance fee of two and a half dollars. Supposing that the Indian girl did not understand English, the judge turned to his companion" with some comments disrespectful of Indian women ("Some swell looker for a Kootenai squaw, eh? Mighty good pickin' for a young feller like you") and gets a reply "of like sinister import" before the two of them begin "conversing in lowered tones." This dialogue necessarily jolts Cogewea: "The girl's eyes filled with tears, as she turned away; brooding over the constantly light spoken words of the 'higher' race regarding her people of the incessant insults offered Indian women by the 'gentleman' whites" (65). The quotes around "higher" and "gentleman" reinforce the cultural logic that identifies "lady" with "squaw" and thus deconstructs the biologic of racial definition, which seeks to decouple the two terms.

This is a deconstruction that Cogewea performs at every turn, asserting the importance of behavior and, crucially, community recognition of such behavior over biological appearance in identity formation. This deconstruction is one of the primary functions of Native American literatures. At the very least, in Cogewea, the dismantling of essentialized identities has the effect of problematizing the melodramatic rhetoric in the novel that seems to insist that the theme of the mixed-blood caught between two worlds be taken at face value. This kind of rhetoric comes into play after Cogewea is rebuffed by one of the contestants in the squaw race with, "This is a race for Indians and not for breeds!" "Cogewea made no reply, but she was overwhelmed with the soul-yearning for sympathy. For her class—the maligned outcast half-blood—there seemed no welcome on the face of all God's creation. Denied social standing with either of the parent races, she felt that the world was crying out against her" (66). One wonders if those critics who identify the Latinate style solely with McWhorter would also identify such Latinate passages with him as well. This characterization of Cogewea's extreme social isolation is contradicted by her actual position in the narrative. After she wins the squaw race, she is welcomed at an Indian dance by the traditional figure of the "Chief of the Pend d'Oreille," the husband of the woman whom she beat in the race, with these words: "To this maiden of another tribe, I give, as a token of my good will to her and her people, one of my best horses. It is the pinto, ridden by my wife and which took second prize in today's race. My gift!" (77). Cogewea also finds constant community with her grandmother, another traditional figure, the Stemteemä, for whom behavior, even when couched in the language of blood, seems much more important than blood quantum in determining who is an Indian. "You are an Indian," the Stemteemä tells mixed-blood Jim LeGranger, hoping to enlist him in convincing Cogewea not to believe in Densmore, although she (the Stemteemä) is "in doubt about confiding to this strong, determined man—a stranger. But the blood-tie was there, strengthened by the mutual knowledge of language and her need was sore" (216). "If you were not of my own kind, I would not talk," the Stemteemä tells Jim. "Although the white blood has made fairer your skin, I like you and I trust you" (217). Grounded in important cultural attributes (Jim speaks Okanogan) and trusted by the community, a mixed- blood can be a full-blood—an unqualified Indian, she seems to imply.

This culturally driven definition of Jim, and more generally of who is an Indian, is strengthened in an encounter between Jim and Mary, the youngest sister and the closest of the three to the Stemteemä and traditional Okanogan life, when the two join in building a traditional "sweat house" in which the Stemteemä can "commune [. . .] with the Great Spirit" (238). "For the first time since their acquaintance, he seemed near to her. She now regarded him as one of her own kind. He had not scorned the sweat house! He had not thrown aside the beliefs of his Indian forefathers, as had so many of the educated halfbloods. The books of the white man had not destroyed the earlier training of his mind" (241–42).

Like Cogewea and Julia (the most assimilated of the three sisters), Mary is mixed-blood, and with her fair skin and deep blue eyes (43), she is biologically the whitest of the three; yet as her place in the narrative and this passage suggests, she thinks of herself, and is thought of by the traditional community, represented by the Stemteemä, as a fullblood because of her adherence to traditional Okanogan cultural practices. When she thinks of Jim "as one of her own kind," then, we are to assume that she thinks of him as a full-blood because, though biologically mixed-blood like herself, he also conforms to a traditional cultural logic, represented by figures such as the Stemteemä and the chief of the Pend d'Oreille. We are reminded here of the culturally logical identity criteria that Silko attributes to the pre–World War I Laguna generation as opposed to the biological criteria of subsequent generations, influenced by the European biologization of race; for the former, behavior rather than biological appearance is crucial. The logic of *Cogewea* indicates that while some degree of Indian blood is necessary for Indian identity, blood itself is not sufficient without the cultural logic of behavior and its recognition by the Native community. The novel also suggests repeatedly that the difference between full-blood and mixed-blood is not biological but cultural.

As progenitor of a major theme in the U.S. Native novel, *Cogewea* folds the mixed-blood caught between two worlds into the conflict and imbrication of two cultural logics of identity, one Native, the other Western. The Western identity logic finds its apotheosis in federal Indian law. After Cogewea wins the two races, she and Jim approach the judge so that she can collect the prize money. The judge, "surprise[d]" at the "perfect English" of "this breed girl [. . .] direct[s] his assistant to pay her the prize money" for winning the squaw race, not realizing (because of Cogewea's changes of costume, her cultural cross-dressing) that the winner of the squaws' race is also the winner of the ladies'—that the "squaw" is also the "lady" (67). Cogewea is quick to inform him that she is indeed the winner of both races and so can claim both prizes, which the judge finds an "effrontery" (67). At first he supports his judgment by telling Cogewea that a "protest has already been filed against you in this race, in behalf of Miss Webster, to whom the first prize money will be paid. You never would have led coming in had you not quirted her horse over the head" (67)—a move the reader knows was provoked by Miss Webster's use of the quirt against Cogewea. At this point, Jim intervenes, explaining, "Every one who saw the race know how the quirt fightin' come 'bout," and appealing to the judge for a "fair" decision (68). But the judge refuses to change his decision (Cogewea will only get the money for winning the squaw race) and adds: "No Injun can come around here and dictate to me in regard to judging these races. Do you savey that?" (68). This rejoinder is at once gratuitous and revealing. Simply put, the judge's response tells us unequivocally that the law is racially based. Jim's instant response makes this fact explicit: "'The white man's rulin' is law,' rejoined Jim calmly, [']but maybe you'll tell the little gal just why she's not to have this here prize she won so fairly in the ladies' race.'" "'Because,' sneered the now irate judge, 'she is a *squaw* and had no right to ride in the *ladies'* race'" (68). The judge's opinion in the case—his absolute separation of the categories "squaw" and "lady"—is affirmed and backed up with the threat of violence by a crowd of white men (68–69). But Jim coolly seeks a clarification of the logic, and in doing so, he spells it out: "I take it that little gal bein' a *squaw,* she can't be a *lady!* Is that it?" (69).

Enraged at "the brazen effrontery of the breed" for challenging his authority, the judge orders Jim arrested for "malicious interference with an honest distribution of *race* awards" (69, 70; italics added). The force of the pun is certainly lost on the judge, but it is not lost on Cogewea, who returns the "tainted money" for the "*racial* prizes" with disgust (70). This judgment of the two races with a law that is imperiously race-based epitomizes the history of federal Indian law, and the allotment period in particular.[124] Just as Cogewea works to expose the social construction of race along with its political valences, U.S. law (both inside and outside the novel) works to construct race biologically in order to assert the essential separateness of the terms "squaw" and "lady," "mixed-blood" and "full-blood," "Indian" and "white."

In *Cogewea,* we are confronted once again with the legal and literary question, what is an Indian? We are confronted with this question, as we have been in the other literary collaborations discussed previously, in which the structure of authorship raises the question. We are also confronted with this question in the plot of the novel, which deconstructs the biologic of race on which Native identity within the provenance of federal Indian law is based. It performs this deconstruction in the cases of both Jim and Mary, who are biologically mixed-bloods but culturally full-bloods. Centrally, the deconstruction is performed in the case of Cogewea who can be both a squaw and a lady, depending on her choice of costume—that is, her choice of cultures.

As I have noted previously, within the provenance of federal Indian law we have two major decisions on Native identity: *U.S. v. Rogers* (1846), which has become the legal rationale to define Indians as a biological group; and *Morton v. Mancari* (1974), which defines them as "quasi-sovereign tribal entities"—that is, as political communities, with the proviso (almost an afterthought) that in terms of hiring for the BIA, the applicant must also have one-fourth Indian blood and be a member of a federally recognized tribe. For general recognition as an Indian by the BIA, the person must have some degree of Indian blood and be a member of a federally recognized tribe. Federal Indian law, then, in one definition of Indian or another, is grounded in biologic. In response to a proposed definition of "Indian" in 1986, which stipulated that an Indian is "a person who is a member of a federally recognized tribe, or eligible to be a member, lives on or near a reservation, and has at least one-quarter Indian blood," Patricia Nelson Limerick wrote with some irony: "Set the blood quantum at one-quarter, hold to it as a rigid definition of Indianness, let intermarriage proceed as it had for centuries and eventually Indians will be defined out of existence. When that happens the federal government will be free of its persistent 'Indian problem.'"[125] While the current BIA definition of "Indian" has left open the blood quantum requirements that each tribe formalizes for membership, it has not relinquished them, and some tribes have kept between a quarter and a half blood quantum requirement. It is important to emphasize here that before the European invasion there were no Indians, only members of thousands of Indigenous kinship groups, each of which used its own names to reference larger groupings. Membership in these groups depended not on blood (for which there was no category in these communities) but on the social category of behavior. In an important sense, the definition of Indians as a political group in *Morton v. Mancari* corresponds to their preinvasion status and points to a contradiction with *Rogers*. Is the answer to the question "what is an Indian?" biological or political? Federal Indian law combines the two (both *Rogers* and *Mancari* stand). However, rather than resolving the contradiction, the standing of the two cases only places the contradiction in relief. After invasion and until the federal identity regime was imposed, a European like Mary Jemison could become a member of a particular kinship group—in this case because Jemison's adoptive clan needed to replace members killed in the French and Indian War. Echoing the Indigenous method of adoption but with revolutionary political intent, the National Indigenous Congress of Mexico completely erases the Indigenous identity borders of biologic and genealogy: "The basic element of the notion of indigenous peoples determined by the National Indigenous Congress (CNI) [. . .] is that indigenous are those who self-proclaim themselves indigenous, who self-identify as indigenous. There's no DNA test, no blood test, no test of cultural roots; to be indigenous it is enough to say so. And that's how we recognize ourselves, the CNI says."[126] This radical opening of Indigenous identity (presumably for those who adopt Indigenous values) serves the goal of revolutionary political organizing against global capitalism and for Indigenous communalism. But it can also serve as a model, a way to think about what and who the identity structure of federal Indian law serves and how reformulating that structure in the terms of *Buen Vivir,* for example, would serve a decolonial movement. Whatever answer one arrives at to the question "what is an Indian?" posed by *Cogewea* and the other texts I have been reviewing, the quote from Limerick, along with the identity model of traditional Indigenous adoption, which Black Elk followed in the case of Neihardt, and the model of the CNI, argues the point that following biologic in the matter of Indian identity will only inevitably lead to the elimination of the Native—the goal of settler colonialism, the topic I turn to next.

SETTLER COLONIALISM AND THE TYRANNY OF BORDERS

> Borders are those invented lines drawn with ash on maps and sewn into the ground by bullets.
>
> Mosab Abu Toha, *Things You May Find Hidden in My Ear*

Beginning with the 2006 publication in the *Journal of Genocide Research* of Patrick Wolfe's generative essay "Settler Colonialism and the Elimination of the Native," the field of (post)colonial studies began to articulate a variation within the domain of colonialism.[1] The variation of settler colonialism within colonialism lies precisely in the word "elimination." Colonialism, as practiced, for example, in India, exploits the human and material resources of the colonized country, principally the land and its yield, but does not seek the elimination of the Indigenous population precisely because it needs that population to do its work. Colonialism can encourage settlement (South Africa) or not, as the case may be, but whatever the case, the Indigenous population is retained as a necessary workforce. In settler colonialism, however, the end, as the title of Wolfe's essay specifies, is the *elimination* of the native in order for the colonizer to possess the land and work it. As Wolfe notes, this elimination takes the form of genocide in the strictest sense: that of the U.N. Convention of 1948, which emphasizes the physical elimination of the Indigenous population or its attempt, though the convention is not without its ambiguities.[2] But, Wolfe elaborates, elimination has other modalities: "The positive outcomes of the logic of elimination [positive from the settler standpoint in that they avoid physical genocide] can include officially encouraged miscegenation, the breaking-down of native title into alienable individual freeholds, native citizenship, child abduction, religious conversion, resocialization in total institutions such as missions or boarding schools, and a whole range of cognate biocultural assimilations. All these strategies, including frontier homicide, are characteristic of settler colonialism. Some of them are more controversial in genocide studies than others."[3] That is, while the debate leading up to the U.N. Convention rejected the notion of "cultural genocide," there are arguments for its inclusion. In the United States and Canada, conventional genocide and the corollaries that Wolfe lists, with the exception of "of *officially* encouraged miscegenation," obtain. By the end of the nineteenth century, from an Indigenous population that was five-plus million within what would become the boundaries of the continental United States, there remained 250,000 Native individuals, the result primarily of conventional genocide, including thousands of deaths on forced marches of ethnic cleansing, exemplified by the Cherokee, Choctaw, Seminole, Muscogee (Creek), and Chickasaw Trail of Tears in the 1830s and the Navajo (Diné) Long Walk in 1864.[4]

From the end of the nineteenth century to the present, the other modalities of elimination that Wolfe lists have been dominant. I have reviewed, for example, the Dawes Act, which, until it was revoked in 1934, enabled the legalized theft of an additional 90 million acres of Indian land. The act exemplifies what Wolfe terms "the breaking-down of native title into alienable individual freeholds," destroying Indigenous communal economies and forcing Indian communities into ever deepening poverty. In conjunction with the assimilationist force of the Dawes Act, this era and well beyond saw the institution of the Indian boarding school system, exemplified by the creation of the Carlisle Indian School in 1879, whose founder and director, Richard Henry Pratt, framed its brutal, assimilationist motto: "Kill the Indian, save the man." In 1924, Congress passed the Indian Citizenship Act, which was a further attempt, met with Native resistance,[5] to assimilate American Indians into U.S. culture and society. Woven into the fabric of these eliminatory institutions, I have emphasized the era of termination of over a hundred Indian tribes and the relocation of their inhabitants to urban areas, which lasted from the mid-1940s to 1960; the sterilization of Indian women without their permission in the 1970s;[6] the forced transfer by way of adoption of Indian children from their homes and communities until 1978, with the passage of the Indian Child Welfare Act;[7] and the continued disproportionate rape and murder of Indian women and the murder of Indian men by non-Native assailants (a continuation of "frontier homicide"), a result in significant part of the federal government's lax enforcement of major crimes in Indian Country, where it has usurped jurisdiction.[8] Overall, as noted previously, Indian Country, and Native America more generally, is the poorest part of the United States as a result of federal neglect of its health, education, and welfare. Such neglect is a form of elimination, as the disproportionate impact of the Covid-19 pandemic on Indian Country emphatically demonstrates.[9]

As noted in the introduction, I originally placed the *post-* of "postcolonial" in parentheses in the title of the original version of this book to indicate that despite the fact of the Indian Citizenship Act (ICA), which could be read as initiating postcolonialism in Native America in 1924, Native America was still a colonized country. Indeed, as read from the perspective of settler colonialism, the ICA does not mark the beginning of postcolonialism—or (post)colonialism—in the United States but is part of the ongoing settler colonization of Native America, a form of the elimination of the Native in which there is no "post." Wolfe puts it succinctly: "The logic of elimination not only refers to the summary liquidation of Indigenous people. [. . .] In common with genocide [. . .] settler colonialism has both negative and positive dimensions. Negatively, it strives for the dissolution of native societies. Positively, it erects a new colonial society on the expropriated land base—as I put it, settlers come to stay: *invasion is a structure not an event.*"[10] That is, the logic of invasion drives the settler society continually after the physical invasion takes place. U.S. federal Indian law is the engine of that logic, which American Indian literatures detail.

However, as a way of continuing to analyze that detail within the context of settler colonialism, I want to open one Native novel in particular, Anishinaabe novelist Louise Erdrich's *The Round House* (2012), because its plot, originally, is centered on a detailed critique of U.S. federal Indian law, after which I will open an influential contemporary scholarly work on federal Indian law, Kevin Bruyneel's *The Third Space of Sovereignty*. Although Bruyneel certainly acknowledges federal Indian law's colonial underpinnings and offers insights into its process, he also argues that the engine may be retooled to make it function positively for Native people in certain respects. My contention—and, I argue, the contention of American Indian literatures—is the opposite: the engine cannot be retooled to serve Native nations precisely because it is the motor of settler colonialism; it can only be junked with no usable parts. Erdrich's *Round House* argues this forcefully.

The novel's action takes place in 1988. Because of the lines that federal Indian law draws between federal, state, and tribal jurisdictions, Linden Lark, a non-Native rapist of one Native woman, Geraldine

Coutts (the narrator's mother), and murderer of another, Mayla Wolfskin, is able to escape Western justice when the jurisdiction of his crimes remains indeterminate. Remembering the time of the rape when he was a thirteen-year-old, the son of the raped woman, Antone Bazil Coutts Jr., who is the adult narrator of the novel, feels compelled to take justice into his own hands, aided by his closest friend, Virgil "Cappy" Lafournais, shooting dead the perpetrator of these crimes.[11] The boys (the narrator named himself Joe "when [he] was six" because he'd "fight anyone who put a junior in back of my name" [4]), who were barely teenagers at the time of the rape and murder, deem the perpetrator a "wiindigoo," an Anishinaabe embodied evil spirit, subject to execution under traditional tribal law, which requires community consensus. But as it moved across the continent, settler colonialism usurped tribal law with federal Indian law. This insured the abrogation of justice in Indian Country—not simply under the circumstances that the novel depicts but, by extension, to the thousands of victims of overwhelmingly white violence, both Native women and men, effectively ignored by federal law enforcement. In his Executive Order of November 15, 2021, on Improving Public Safety and Criminal Justice for Native Americans and Addressing the Crisis of Missing or Murdered Indigenous People, President Joe Biden stated the crisis accurately, only to mince words in addressing federal responsibility for the crisis:

> Generations of Native Americans have experienced violence or mourned a missing or murdered family member or loved one, and the lasting impacts of such tragedies are felt throughout the country. Native Americans face unacceptably high levels of violence, and are victims of violent crime at a rate much higher than the national average. Native American women, in particular, are disproportionately the victims of sexual and gender-based violence, including intimate partner homicide. Research shows that approximately half of Native American women have experienced sexual violence and that approximately half have experienced physical violence by an intimate partner. LGBTQ+ Native Americans and people who identify as "Two-Spirit" people within Tribal communities are also often the targets of violence. And the vast majority of Native American survivors report being victimized by a non-Native American individual.
>
> For far too long, justice has been elusive for many Native American victims, survivors, and families. Criminal jurisdiction

complexities and resource constraints have left many injustices unaddressed.

"Complexities" and "resource restraints" constitute the bureaucratic jargon that euphemizes the draconian legal and economic limits imposed by the federal government on Indian Country. Here are the facts underlying these "criminal jurisdiction complexities and resource constraints." As early as the Trade and Intercourse Acts (1790–1834), the federal government asserted virtual control of crimes committed in Indian Country by or against non-Native persons, and then in the Major Crimes Act of 1885 assumed control of Indian-on-Indian major felonies as well.[12] By the end of the nineteenth century, when the federal government had extended its reach from coast to coast (and the virtual became actual), it simultaneously limited the resources needed to bring justice to the Native victims—and thus, through lack of enforcement, enforcing "genocide by other means."[13] As the narrator of *The Round House* notes: "The problem with most Indian rape cases was that even after there was an indictment the U.S. attorney often declined to take the case to trial for one reason or another. Usually a raft of bigger cases" (41). What is implicit in this matter of fact statement is the devalued status of Indian lives, particularly the lives of Indian women and girls, in U.S. society.[14]

In a telling scene in *The Round House*, Joe confronts his father, Antone Bazil Coutts Sr., a tribal judge, about the truncated reach of tribal legal authority (no longer traditional tribal law but an offshoot of U.S. law sometimes integrated with tribal law[15]): "All you catch are drunks and hog thieves," Joe—who, ironically, will become a tribal judge himself—says accusatorily after Lark is released from custody because jurisdiction cannot be established, even though all the evidence for rape and murder points at him (226). Joe gets to the point quickly: "You said yourself. You've got zero authority, Dad, one big zero, nothing you can do. Why do it anyway?" (226). To begin his answer, the judge takes "one of Clemence's uneaten casseroles" out of the refrigerator and places it on a table. (Clemence is Joe's maternal aunt, who has been feeding father and son while Joe's mom has been incapacitated by her trauma.) The casserole's "noodles had turned black, but stashed near enough to the cold refrigeration coils that it had frozen and so didn't stink yet. [. . .] With a savage thump [the judge] turned the casserole over onto the table. He lifted off the pan. The thing was shot through with white fuzz but held its oblong shape." Next the judge builds a "weird sculpture" with "a large carving knife [. . .] on top of the frozen casserole," while "all around it [he] proceeded to stack one fork, another fork [. . .] adding a spoon here, a butter knife, a ladle, a spatula." Finally, "he balanced [four steel butcher knives] precariously on top of the other silverware." "That's Indian Law," the judge says, and proceeds to enumerate five Supreme Court cases that represent this "weird sculpture" with a metal superstructure on a rotten base that, once it thaws, will collapse (227–28).

The five cases the judge focuses on are these: *Johnson v. M'Intosh* (1823), *Lone Wolf v. Hitchcock* (1903), *Tee-Hit-Ton Indians v. United States* (1955), *Worcester v. Georgia* (1832), and *Oliphant v. Suquamish* (1978). This is the order in which the judge takes them up, though without supplying the dates except for *Johnson*, the first case in the Marshall Trilogy, which includes *Cherokee Nation v. Georgia* (1831) and *Worcester*. Named after Chief Justice John Marshall, who wrote the opinions in all three cases, the Marshall Trilogy forms the core of U.S. federal Indian law; and as the judge notes of *Johnson*,

> Justice Marshall went out of his way to strip away all Indian title to all lands viewed—i.e., "discovered"—by Europeans. He basically upheld the medieval doctrine of discovery for a government that was supposedly based on the rights and freedoms of the individual. Marshall vested absolute title to the land in the government and gave Indians nothing more than the right of occupancy, a right that could be taken away at any time. Even to this day, his words are used to continue the dispossession of our lands. But what particularly galls the intelligent person is that the language he used survives in the law, that we are savages living off the forest, and to leave our land to us was to leave it useless wilderness, that our character and religion is so inferior a stamp that the superior genius of Europe must certainly claim ascendancy and on and on. (228–29)

Joe responds: "I got it then. I pointed at the bottom of the mess." The judge replies: "I suppose that's *Lone Wolf v. Hitchcock*. [. . .] And *Tee-Hit-Ton*." But he gives no explanation of either case, and Joe does not ask for one; rather, "I asked Dad about the first knife he laid on the casserole, stabilizing it." The judge responds, "*Worcester v. Georgia*. Now that would be a better foundation" (229). But as with the other two cases, he gives no explanation for his opinion, instead continuing to place the last case: "But this one—my father teased a particularly disgusting bit of sludge from the pile with the edge of his fork—this one is the one I'd abolish right this minute if I had the power of a movie shaman. *Oliphant v. Suquamish*. He shook the fork and the stink wafted at me. Took from us the right to prosecute non-Indians who commit crimes on our land" (229).

After marking *Oliphant* as the rottenest part of the whole rotten edifice of federal Indian law, the judge immediately begins the next sentence with, "So even if . . . ," a trailing-off he does not finish, it would seem, because *Oliphant* has erased the possibility of "even if." A moment later, he resumes the unfinished sentence: "So even if I could prosecute Lark . . ." Again, he can't finish it, suggesting the finality of *Oliphant*, which prompts Joe to ask: "Okay, Dad. [. . .] How come you do it? How come you stay here?" At this point, "[t]he casserole was starting to ooze and thaw. My father arranged the odd bit of cutlery and knives so they made an edifice that stood by itself. He had suspended Mom's good knives carefully. He nodded at the knives" (229). Having separated the metal superstructure from the rotten base, although without explaining what composed the superstructure in terms of cases or how a superstructure can stand on its own in the world beyond the cutlery on a kitchen table, the judge proceeds to explain why he remains on the job, upholding what the narrator has referred to as "our toothless sovereignty" (142):

> These are the decisions that I and many other tribal judges try to make. Solid decisions with no scattershot opinions attached. Everything we do, no matter how trivial, must be crafted keenly. We are trying to build a solid base here for our sovereignty. We try to press against the boundaries of what we are allowed, walk a step past the edge. Our records will be scrutinized by Congress one day and decisions on whether to enlarge our jurisdiction will be made. Some day. *We want the right to prosecute criminals of all races on all lands within our original boundaries.* Which is why I try to run a tight courtroom, Joe. What I am doing now is for the future, though it may seem small, or trivial, or boring, to you. (229–30)

Joe does not respond in the 1988 of the novel; nor does the narrator from his position many years in an indeterminate future. The narrative simply stops, then proceeds to another part of the story. Why the silence? We can only speculate.

The narrative silence at the close of the judge's explanation for his staying on the job in the face of the "toothless sovereignty" of Native nations is suggestive. Joe does not respond, perhaps because he cannot, at thirteen, engage his father in a debate about federal Indian law even though he is aware of its limits and evinces a considerable interest in it. Indeed, at the beginning of the novel, we find Joe, "having slipped into my father's study," trying to read "the law book my father called the Bible, Felix S. Cohen's *Handbook of Federal Indian Law*" (2). But despite his interest, Joe does not, for example, ask for an explanation of *Lone Wolf v. Hitchcock*, which solidifies the plenary power of Congress in Indian affairs; or *Tee-Hit-Ton Indian v. United States*, which in effect denied tribal ownership of traditional lands on which the United States had taken timber without payment to the tribe; or *Worcester v. Georgia*, in which the Court recognized that although federal sovereignty was absolute in Indian affairs, the Cherokees—and eventually, by extension, all Native nations—retained a sovereignty within the borders of their lands that could not be breached by the states, though this has now been done in a 5–4 decision in *Oklahoma v. Castro-Huerta* (June 29, 2022) by a right wing–dominated Supreme Court that appears intent on abrogating the doctrine of stare decisis.

The adult Joe as narrator does not respond—perhaps because, voicing Erdrich, the future, our present, in which he is now a tribal judge, he himself has not altered the "toothless sovereignty" of 1988. That is, to quote the judge, Native nations still do not have "the right to prosecute criminals of all races on all lands within our original boundaries," the right to which would indicate a significant step forward to actual sovereignty. Biden's executive order, cited above, bears implicit witness to the legal status quo, which only Congress with its plenary power or the Supreme Court can change, but as Lumbee legal theorist David Wilkins has pointed out, "the judiciary has never voided a single congressional act that diminished or abrogated any inherent or aboriginal tribal rights."[16] There is simply no judicial review in U.S. federal Indian law. That is, until now, as *Oklahoma v. Castro-Huerta* demonstrates, the direction here is regressive, an attack on what is left of tribal sovereignty. Where Congress has the power to legislate progressively, it allows the Court to legislate regressively, which simply maintains U.S. federal Indian law as the engine—or, following Erdrich, the rotten casserole—at the basis of U.S. settler colonialism.

The judge's hopeful look to a virtual future in which Native nations have "the right to prosecute criminals of all races on all lands within our original boundaries" seems at best wishful thinking because it rests on the possibility of a revolution that will overturn settler colonialism—a future that, given the state of the union, what I have termed elsewhere "the collapse of liberal democracy in the United States," seems utopian.[17] This collapse is characterized by a two-party system that masks, with less and less effectiveness, a one-party corporate state in which Democrats and Republicans are polarized in paralysis over domestic policy—a paralysis that guarantees the continuation of a status quo marked by gross income inequality even as they agree on ever-increasingly militarized, imperial foreign policy that consumes 60 percent of federal discretionary spending. Within this agenda, which has no horizon, and in which climate collapse, lacking effective address, threatens apocalypse, Judge Coutts's projection of a future in which Native nations will actually have sovereignty, in which federal Indian law will somehow accommodate this future, seems perpetually virtual. Judge Coutts's projection of a future in which federal Indian law will accommodate itself to Native sovereignty not in name but in substance raises the question of the limits of that law. In addressing that question, I want to open *The Third Space of Sovereignty* by scholar Kevin Bruyneel.

Published in 2007, Kevin Bruyneel's *The Third Space of Sovereignty: The Postcolonial Politics of U.S. Indigenous Relations* is one of the most influential books in the field of Native studies in the last fifteen years. Bruyneel's take on federal Indian law is essentially equivocal, by which I mean that the "third space" his title references is constructed by a dynamic he terms American colonial ambivalence, by which he understands federal Indian law as situating Native nations simultaneously within and outside the borders of the United States—that is, as being neither entirely domestic nor foreign but both at once spatially, or alternating in emphasis temporally according to the federal agenda:

> *American colonial ambivalence* refers to the inconsistencies in the application of colonial rule, and it is the product of both institutional and cultural dynamics. The most recognizable consequences of colonial ambivalence are the persistent shifts in U.S. Indian policy, reflecting what Thomas Biolsi has referred to as the "tension between *uniqueness* and *uniformity*" in federal Indian law, whereby an "imaginary Indian policy pendulum" swings between eras that

emphasize recognition of tribal governments (uniqueness) and eras that emphasize the assimilation of indigenous individuals (uniformity). This ambivalence in policymaking is colonial because it stems from the privileged position of the United States, from which it can unilaterally shift the terms of its relationship to indigenous people. But colonial ambivalence is also a form of American uncertainty, which indigenous political actors can provoke and exploit to their own ends.[18]

Taking a Native perspective, then, Bruyneel understands the third space as a space of resistance, a "refusal of the imperial binary," domestic/foreign and inside/outside. It is "a location inassimilable to the liberal democratic settler-state, and as such it problematizes the boundaries of colonial rule but does not seek to capture or erase these boundaries."[19] One may sense in this formulation a paradox in the idea of problematizing but not erasing. That is, working within the legal framework of the settler state Native nations can somehow resist, even transform, this framework; they can "provoke and exploit" it to their own ends, but they cannot end it: "The indigenous political effort to construct and maintain the coherence of community is premised on straddling and thus re-marking the boundaries that purport to secure the coherence of American community. This does not mean that indigenous political actors can deny the real power inequity between their communities and the American nation. Rather, the lesson here is that in generating political claims indigenous people do not simply adhere to the options set out by the American political framework."[20] It is one thing to "generat[e] political claims" but quite another to have them recognized officially—or, more importantly, to achieve them, which has not happened, as we read in *The Round House*. Bruyneel's "not simply adhere," then, like Judge Coutts's vision of the future, seems to point only to a virtual time and space beyond the border of U.S. federal Indian law.

In his book's conclusion, Bruyneel lays out two approaches, each by a separate group of scholars, to resolving the issue of American Indian sovereignty.[21] The first states, "There can be no equal standing for indigenous peoples until they are acknowledged as equal sovereigns within a postcolonial constitutional arrangement." The second group notes, "It is the very nature of the sovereign state that must be rethought." While it seems to me that the first resolution is necessarily dependent on the second, and while Bruyneel, in a roundabout way, appears to concur, he nevertheless finds that "missing from these formulations [...] is a precise concept as well as vocabulary that can pin down the alternatives represented in this 'postcolonial arrangement' and/or 'rethinking of the sovereign state.'" For Bruyneel, the "precise concept" is "the third space," which "may well provide the vocabulary that both captures and helps us constitute a viable, increasingly sought-after location of indigenous postcolonial political autonomy that refuses the choices set out by settler-society." But "one of the first steps toward moving in this direction will involve refusing the false choice set out by the settler-state."[22] To define this "false choice," Bruyneel references the work of legal scholar Julie Cassidy: "The false choice here is that either indigenous tribes and nations must become sovereign states, thereby destroying the settler-states within which they reside, or their citizens must accept unambiguous inclusion in the settler polity, thereby denying their collective claim to sovereignty."[23]

Bruyneel thus implies, contradictorily, that it is possible for Indigenous sovereignty to be achieved within the settler state, even though it is the settler state that has subordinated Indigenous sovereignty, as expressed in the oxymoronic phrase formulated by Chief Justice Marshall in *Cherokee Nation v. Georgia* (1831): "domestic dependent nations." Settler colonialism, Patrick Wolfe reminds us, is a structure, not an event, and as I have been arguing, U.S. federal Indian law is that structure, with the result that imagining sovereignty for Native nations within that structure—the very structure that denies them sovereignty—becomes the kind of wishful thinking, whistling past the graveyard, in which Judge Coutts and Kevin Bruyneel indulge. As my usage here suggests, I consider the phrase "subordinate sovereignty" an oxymoron. The sovereign that is subordinate is not by definition a sovereign. Justice Clarence Thomas in *United States v. Lara* (2004) articulates the paradox of a sovereign that is not in effect a sovereign: "In my view, the tribes either are or are not separate sovereigns and our federal Indian law cases untenably hold both positions simultaneously."[24] Nevertheless, Thomas makes this statement in a concurring opinion that upholds the dual sovereignty doctrine in federal Indian law. But near the end of his opinion, he doubles down on his skepticism of dual sovereignty as articulated in *U.S. v. Wheeler* (1978): "I find it difficult to reconcile the result in *Wheeler* with Congress' 1871 prospective prohibition on the making of treaties with the Indian tribes.

The Federal Government cannot simultaneously claim power to regulate virtually every aspect of the tribes through ordinary domestic legislation and also maintain that the tribes possess anything resembling 'sovereignty.'"[25]

Thomas concludes his opinion by calling into question the plenary power of Congress, in Indian affairs, located in the Commerce Clause, which he understands as justifying Congress's regulation of Indian sovereignty:

> The Court should admit that it has failed in its quest to find a source of congressional power to adjust tribal sovereignty. Such an acknowledgment might allow the Court to ask the logically antecedent question *whether* Congress (as opposed to the President) has this power. A cogent answer would serve as a foundation for the analysis of the sovereignty issues posed by this case. We might find that the Federal Government cannot regulate the tribes through ordinary domestic legislation and simultaneously maintain that the tribes are sovereigns in any meaningful sense. But until we begin to analyze these questions honestly and rigorously, the confusion that I have identified will continue to haunt our cases.[26]

Thomas's position on sovereignty can be read as a call to foreclose the separate sovereignty of Indian nations, and the protections it provides, which is constantly under attack. I quote it, then, not to endorse it but to point to the inherent contradiction it identifies at the heart of federal Indian law—the contradiction implicit in the phrase "subordinate sovereignty, or domestic dependent nations." Although Bruyneel's notion of colonial ambivalence touches on this contradiction, it does not fully confront it. His idea of a third space does no more than try to escape it but is inevitably caught within it.

It is inevitably caught because of the contradiction I am pointing out. Considering Native sovereignty within the settler state, Bruyneel's strongest suit is when he considers the third space of sovereignty as a theoretical construct for rethinking the concept of sovereignty itself: "The 'imagining' of alternative 'political geographies' is a fundamental part of the effort to see viable alternatives to the statist or colonialist conceptions of sovereignty. To be sure, this antistatist or anticolonial effort does not exist in a vacuum, relevant only to indigenous political concerns, but is connected and possible even constitutive of the effort to reimagine the role and meaning of sovereignty in the political world generally."[27] To this end of "reimagin[ing] [. . .] sovereignty," Bruyneel references the work of Kanien'kehaka (Mohawk) scholar Taiaiake Alfred, who has critiqued the theory and practice of sovereignty as a Western hierarchical form of governance incompatible with traditional Indigenous forms.[28] In his book *Peace, Power, Righteousness: An Indigenous Manifesto*, which Bruyneel cites, Alfred quotes Menno Bolt and Tony Long as saying, "By adopting the European-Western ideology of sovereignty, the current generation of Indian leaders is buttressing the imposed alien authority structures within its communities, and is legitimizing the associated hierarchy comprised of indigenous political and bureaucratic elites. This endorsement of hierarchical authority and a ruling entity constitutes a complete rupture with traditional indigenous principles."[29] Alfred continues to contrast these principles, which I have cited, with those of Western sovereignty:

> Traditional indigenous nationhood stands in sharp contrast to the dominant understanding of "the state": there is no absolute authority, no coercive enforcement of decisions, no hierarchy, and no separate ruling entity. In accepting the idea that progress is attainable within the framework of the state, therefore, indigenous people are moving towards acceptance of forms of government that more closely resemble the state than traditional systems. Is it possible to accomplish good in a system designed to promote harm? Yes, on the margins. But eventually the grinding engine of discord and deprivation will obliterate the marginal good. The real goal should be to stop the engine.[30]

At this moment in his work, Bruyneel appears to suggest that the third space of sovereignty indeed cannot exist within the settler state, the "political geographies" of which must themselves be reimagined—not simply to accommodate traditional Indigenous governance but also to accommodate a regime of social justice more generally, which would, in the first place, make it compatible with traditional Indigenous governance. But the example he gives at this point of the possibility of the third space's functioning within the settler state is no more than a minor concession envisioned within the framework of federal Indian law, not a transformation of or end to it. The example comes from the person who was at the time the chief justice of the supreme court of the Sac and Fox Nation of Kansas and Missouri, Robert Porter, who argues "for a form of decolonization that I deem postcolonial in nature because it is based on an understanding that 'a decolonized relationship does not mean that there is no relationship at all. The United States remains committed by treaty and legal obligations.' To this end, he proposes specific forms of decolonization that directly reshape the boundaries of U.S.–indigenous legal jurisdiction, such as a change in 'federal law to recognize the power of Indian nations over misdemeanors committed by non-Indians within tribal borders.'"[31]

Such a proposal would roll back *Oliphant*, the "disgusting bit of sludge" in Judge Coutts's federal Indian law casserole, but it does not touch the Major Crimes Act, thus not realizing what Judge Coutts's sees as the mark of Native sovereignty: "the right to prosecute criminals of all races on all lands within our original boundaries," which implicitly includes the right to prosecute all crimes, major and minor, within tribal boundaries. From the perspective of settler colonialism, the Porter proposal, which remains virtual in any event, could only ever be a partial act of decolonization, if one can even call it that, which essentially would not stop the engine of federal Indian law but would only slow it a tad. As Alfred notes in the passage cited above: "But eventually the grinding engine of discord and deprivation will obliterate the marginal good. The real goal should be to stop the engine."

In the first place, the "engine" of Western sovereignty was imposed on Indian communities by the Marshall Court in *Worcester v. Georgia*, where, in a passage previously cited in his opinion, Marshall states: "The words 'treaty' and 'nation' are words of our own language, selected in our diplomatic and legislative proceedings by ourselves, having each a definite and well understood meaning. We have applied them to Indians as we have applied them to the other nations of the earth. They are applied to all in the same sense,"[32] but with the key exception that they are applied to Indian communities as, oxymoronically, subordinate sovereigns. Marshall's words here make clear the process of translation by which Indian communities were translated into Western law, by which kinship societies, grounded in reciprocal responsibilities, were translated into the key words of U.S. and international law: "treaty" and "nation," forms that are grounded in systems of rights, which are the offspring of sovereignty. One requires rights to protect one against the transgressions of the sovereign, the state of exception, whereas, to quote Alfred in a passage cited previously, in Indigenous governance, there is "no separate ruling entity"—no sovereign. Indian treaties, like all treaties, do indeed outline the responsibilities of the signatories (rights to a certain extent imply responsibilities), but these responsibilities are based in a vertical system of authority (the treaties were forced on Native communities through an asymmetry of material power in the course of a genocide), not in a horizontal system of kinship, where the intrinsic equality of the participants obviates the need for rights. Translated through treaties into the term "nation" (treaties are by definition signed between foreign nations), kinship communities were translated into the regime of sovereignty, in which they were recognized by the sovereign as sovereign only in the sense that, as I have analyzed previously, Coulthard has elaborated in *Red Skin, White Masks.*

When Alfred cites Bolt and Long referring to the present generation of Native leaders as "adopting the European-Western ideology of sovereignty," what comes to mind is Coulthard's "colonial politics of recognition": "behavior that implicitly or explicitly commit the colonized to the types of practices and subject positions that are required for their continued domination"[33]—that is, the position of subordinate sovereigns. When in his colloquy with Joe about the rotten casserole of federal Indian law, the judge notes of *Worcester,* "now that would be a better foundation," we might want to think of him as under the spell of federal Indian law and its bible, Cohen's *Handbook,* but with the understanding that, as Erdrich portrays him, the judge is not simply a colonized subject but to the very end of the novel is conflicted about the limits of that law in its inability to deliver justice.

As for sovereignty, third space or otherwise, Alfred puts it succinctly: "'sovereignty' is inappropriate as a political objective for indigenous peoples."[34] Nevertheless, there is a moment in the essay where Alfred suggests an Indigenous appropriation of the word: "The challenge for indigenous peoples in building appropriate postcolonial governing systems is to disconnect the notion of sovereignty from its Western legal roots and to transform it."[35] This work of transformation is the focus of Anishinaabe novelist, poet, and essayist Gerald Vizenor, who, against the Western legal grain, defines, "the essence of sovereignty" as "imaginative, an original tribal trope, communal and spiritual, an idea that is more than metes and bounds in treaties."[36] What this quote suggests is that Western sovereignty is about creating and maintaining borders, which is the heart of federal Indian law, the core of which is the treaty.

I have begun to analyze how federal Indian law establishes and enforces those borders, and in what follows, taking *The Round House* as prelude, I will continue this analysis as I analyze the way American Indian literatures resist the establishment and enforcement of borders, calling their legality into question. This resistance is epitomized in Vizenor's *Bearheart: The Heirship Chronicles*, first published in 1978 at the end of a decade of generative American Indian fiction that begins with Kiowa author N. Scott Momaday's Pulitzer Prize–winning novel *House Made of Dawn*, followed by Blackfeet author James Welch's *Winter in the Blood* (1974) and Laguna Pueblo author Leslie Marmon Silko's *Ceremony* (1977). Each of these novels interrogates the borders established by federal Indian law. But before analyzing Vizenor's books—which interrogate borders in a cosmic, comic mode: the mode of the trickster—I want to briefly analyze these generative works of American Indian fiction to suggest a common theme in the field. This theme is the resistance to the borders established by U.S. federal Indian law intertwined with the imagining of an Indigenous space beyond the limits of settler colonialism. This space is not the third space of sovereignty, which is an accommodation to the status quo, but the end of sovereignty in the Western sense of the word.

In Momaday's novel, which is set during the post–World War II period of termination and relocation, Momaday's Jemez Pueblo protagonist, Abel, a returning veteran, represents the tradition of Indian resistance to Western law. Abel kills an albino member of the tribe, known in the novel as "the white man," whom, within the context of Pueblo traditions, he believes to be a witch, which corresponds to the windigo of Anishinaabe tradition. Momaday makes a point of noting that Abel's killing of "the white man" (his understanding of the albino as a witch) cannot be contained within the terms, which are the borders, of Western law. "Homicide," says the Catholic priest of Jemez during Abel's trial, "is a legal term, but the law is not my context; and certainly it isn't his."[37] Thus, as if to mark the radically different contexts of Jemez culture and Western law, under which Abel is being tried, the narrator comments: "When he had told his story once, simply, Abel refused to speak. [. . .] for he should not have known what more to say. Word by word by word these men were disposing of him in language, *their* language, and they were making a bad job of it."[38] Linguistic difference here implicitly points to a cultural difference to which the court is not granting legitimacy. That is, the court is erasing the national border of Jemez Pueblo in order to incorporate the Jemez nation within the borders the United States, thereby effectively erasing its language or, rather, the efficacy of its language, which constructs another reality, another set of borders, within which Abel is acting. Though Momaday does not state it explicitly, the informed reader understands that Abel is being tried in Western rather than Jemez terms of law because under the provisions of the Major Crimes Act of 1885, Congress subordinated tribal sovereignty in matters of Indian-on-Indian crime to federal jurisdiction over all major felonies taking place within the borders of an Indian reservation.

The nameless Blackfeet narrator of Welch's novel, who at the beginning is "as distant from myself as a hawk from the moon,"[39] finds himself by crossing the border between his present alienation and his heretofore hidden ancestral past of "survivance," which in *Manifest Manners* Vizenor defines as "an active sense of presence, the continuation of native stories, not a mere reaction, or a survivable name. Native survivance stories are renunciations of dominance, tragedy, and victimry. Survivance means the right of succession or reversion of an estate, and in that sense, the estate of Native survivancy."[40] The narrator's survivance comes through "the continuation of native stories," which put him in touch with his history—in this case, a story of survivance told to him by Yellow Calf, an old Native man who lives near his mother's home and whom the narrator as a child visited with his father, now deceased, never knowing who the old man was, until it becomes clear in the story that Yellow Calf is the narrator's maternal grandfather.

The story Yellow Calf tells takes place in the starvation winter (1883–84) of the Blackfeet,[41] when the United States had decimated the buffalo, which had provided the primary material and nutritional resources of all the Plains nations. The government, which had not provided adequate provisions, as stipulated in treaties, left the Blackfeet and other tribes to starve in the ongoing genocide, of which the wanton slaughter of the buffalo is a central component. Contemporary Blackfeet writer Stephen Graham Jones, in his speculative historical novel *Ledfeather* (2008), details the genocidal effects of this winter, along with the federal corruption that enabled it, and their ongoing aftermath in the present.

Welch's Yellow Calf tells how the narrator's grandmother, recently deceased, survived the winter as a young woman when abandoned by the rest of her "desperate" group, who, suffering under the spell of settler-colonial violence, blamed her "bad medicine" for their condition.[42] But Yellow Calf, with apparent cultural reticence, refuses to speak the means of her survival. The narrator must do it for him: "'You . . . you're the one.' I laughed, as the secret unfolded itself. 'The only one . . . you, her hunter . . .' And the wave behind my eyes broke."[43] It is at precisely this moment that the narrator realizes that Yellow Calf is his grandfather, his tears washing away a taboo boundary.[44] The border washed away here reveals an officially repressed history: the history of U.S. Native genocide and Native resistance to it, cut off from official U.S. history of "property, profit, production, and progress,"[45] with a "no trespassing" sign prominently displayed. In none of its Supreme Court decisions does federal Indian law reference this genocidal history. Lumbee legal scholar Robert A. Williams Jr. catches the force of *Johnson v. M'Intosh* (1823), the primal case in federal Indian law, at the time it was enacted: "While the tasks of conquest and colonization had not yet been fully actualized on the entire American continent, the original legal rules and principles of federal Indian law set down by Marshall in *Johnson v. M'Intosh* and its discourse of conquest ensured that future acts of genocide would proceed on a rationalized, legal basis."[46] "Rationalized" here means, in effect, erased. In fact, the U.S. government has never acknowledged that the United States is founded on stolen Native land (Indian, Alaska Native, and Native Hawaiian) in the course of a national genocide. This erased fact and its articulation forms a central movement in Lakota poet Layli Long Soldier's book of poems *Whereas*. In her introduction to the second part of the book, entitled "Whereas," Long Soldier states the following matter-of-factly:

> On Saturday, December 19, 2009, U.S. President Barack Obama signed the Congressional Resolution of Apology to Native Americans. No tribal leaders or official representatives were invited to witness and receive the Apology on behalf of tribal nations. President Obama never read the Apology aloud, publicly—although for the record, Senator Sam Brownback five months later read the Apology to a gathering of five tribal leaders, though there are some 560 federally recognized tribes [in the lower forty-eight states and Alaska] in the U.S. The Apology was then folded into a large, unrelated piece of legislation called the 2010 Defense Appropriations Act.[47]

The poem moves fluidly streaming the personal, the historical, and the political, all in a format implicitly satirizing the "whereas" statement, which is the form of the apology. As the speaker of the poem reminds us, "Whatever comes after the word 'Whereas' and before the semicolon in a Congressional document falls short of legal grounds, is never cause to sue the Government, the Government's courts say."[48] In another moment, having left a "discussion" of the apology without speaking, she writes among a number of "whereas" clauses: "Whereas I could've but didn't broach the subject of 'genocide' the absence of this term from the Apology and its rephrasing as 'conflict' for example."[49] This clause emphasizes the erasure "of this term" in U.S. federal Indian law and official U.S. history. Indeed, federal Indian law is the structure that erases the term and thereby naturalizes the borders of the sovereign nation-state and its "domestic dependent nations," compelled to be domestic and dependent by the history of the term "genocide," about which "we, the people" promise not to say a word.

In *Ceremony*, the supremacy of settler power that naturalizes the borders of the nation-state is denaturalized in a generative scene. In this scene, the protagonist, Tayo, a World War II veteran with posttraumatic stress syndrome exacerbated by white racism, expresses feelings of helplessness in the face of settler power: "I wonder what good Indian ceremonies can do against the sickness which comes from their wars, their bombs, their lies?" Betonie, the unconventional Navajo healer conducting the ceremony, replies with:

> That is the trickery of the witchcraft. [. . .] They want us to believe all evil resides with white people. Then we will look no further to see what is really happening. They want us to separate ourselves from white people, to be ignorant and helpless as we watch our own destruction. But white people are only tools that the witchery manipulates; and I will tell you, we can deal with white people, with their machines and their beliefs. We can because we invented white people; it was Indian witchery that made white people in the first place.[50]

That we cannot read Betonie's claim within a Western epistemology is the point of the statement. Tayo is sick because he accepts that epistemology, the foundation of federal Indian law. His healing requires that he inhabit a Laguna epistemology in which settler power is not autonomous; rather "in the beginning / there were no white people in the world / there was nothing European. / And this world might have gone on like that / except for one thing: / witchery. / This world was already complete / even without white people. / There was everything / including witchery" (132–33). Then, so the story goes, the witches from all nations, Native and non-Native, assembled and held a competition to see who could create the greatest evil. After all the witches had displayed their skills, "finally there was only one / who hadn't shown off charms or powers. / The witch stood in the shadows beyond the fire / and no one ever knew where this witch came from / which tribe / or if it was a woman or a man. / But the important thing was / this witch didn't show off any dark thunder charcoals / or red ant-hill beads. / This witch told them to listen: / 'What I have is a story'" (134–35). The other witches laugh at the idea that a story can surpass the evil they have demonstrated. The witch from nowhere replies: "Okay / go ahead / laugh if you want to / but as I tell the story / it will begin to happen" (135). The story the witch tells is the story of European imperialism and its progeny, colonialism and settler colonialism; she tells the story of "white skin people / like the belly of a fish / covered with hair," who "see no life / When they look / they see only objects. / The world is a dead thing for them. [. . .] / They fear the world. / They destroy what they fear. / They fear themselves" (135). We know the rest of the story. We also know that unless we start to tell a different one, "they will take this world from ocean to ocean / they will turn on each other / they will destroy each other. [. . .] and explode everything" (137).

In *Ceremony*, as in *Fight Back* and *Almanac of the Dead*, this explosion is linked to uranium in the form of the atomic bomb. As Tayo travels to complete his ceremony on Laguna land, he recalls his grandmother telling him about seeing the flash of an A-bomb test while Tayo was, ironically, overseas serving in Japan, the ultimate target for which that test was preparing:

> He had been so close to it, caught up in it for so long that its simplicity struck him deep inside his chest: Trinity site, where they exploded the first atomic bomb was only three hundred miles to the southeast at White Sands. And the top-secret laboratories where the bomb had been created were deep in the Jemez Mountains, on land the Government took from Cochiti Pueblo: Los Alamos, only a hundred miles northeast of him now. [. . . .] There was no end to it; it knew no boundaries; and he had arrived at the point of convergence where the fate of all living things, and even the earth, had been laid. (245–46)

For Tayo to complete the ceremony, he must round up the cattle, a "new breed [. . .] that could live in spite of drought and hard weather," which his deceased uncle, Josiah, had bought, and which, after Josiah's death and Tayo's absence during the war, had shown up on the fenced land of a white rancher, Floyd Lee: "The Texans who had bought the land fenced it and posted signs in English and Spanish warning trespassers to keep out. But the people from the land grants and the people from Laguna and Acoma ignored the signs and hunted deer" (187). To bring the cattle back home, Tayo must cut the fence that marks the border between Lee's land and the Laguna reservation:

> But something inside him made him hesitate to say [that Lee had stolen the cattle] now that the cattle were on a white man's ranch. He had a crazy desire to believe that there had been some mistake, that Floyd Lee had gotten them innocently. [. . .] Why did he hesitate to accuse a white man of stealing but not a Mexican or an Indian? [. . .] He knew that he had learned the lie by heart—the lie which they had wanted him to learn: only brown-skinned people were thieves; white people didn't steal because they always had the money to buy whatever they wanted. [. . .] The lie. He cut into the wire as if cutting away at the lie inside himself. The liars had fooled everyone, white people and Indians alike. [. . .] He stood back and looked at the gaping cut in the wire. If the white people never looked beyond the lie, to see that theirs was a nation built on stolen land, then they would never be able to understand how they had been used by the witchery; they would never know that they were still being manipulated by those who knew how to stir the ingredients together: white thievery and injustice boiling up the anger and hatred that would finally destroy the world: the starving against the fat, the colored against the white [. . .] the lies devoured white hearts, and for more than two hundred years white people had worked to fill their emptiness; they tried to gut the hollowness with patriotic wars and with great technology and the wealth it brought. And always they had been fooling themselves and they knew it. (190–91)

As this passage makes clear, *Ceremony* focuses on the denaturalization (the politicization) of borders, literal and figurative, that have been naturalized by settler colonialism. The lie is the naturalization that legitimizes the borders of "a nation built on stolen land," that legitimizes the moral hierarchy of white over "brown-skinned people," so that the latter are seen as natural thieves in the eyes of the law, and that naturalizes the law that enforces these borders. The "gaping cut in the wire," which Tayo has made, points to the "white" construction of this law, as well as to the fact that it can be reconstructed without borders.

TRICKSTER LOGIC

The Transgression of Borders

In chapter 6, we will read Gerald Vizenor's deconstruction of borders through trickster logic in his novel *Bearheart*. However, in order to analyze *Bearheart*, we need to look first at the way trickster logic functions across Indigenous cultures.

Ubiquitous in the stories of Native oral cultures, moving fluidly between what the West categorizes as human and animal forms, as well as between what the West categorizes as genders, trickster is a consummate figure of the transgression of boundaries, be they political, social, or physical. In traditional kinship societies, where there were boundaries of rank but no boundaries of class (in the sense of one group exploiting another for the products of its labor), every person's contribution was equally valuable to the sustenance of the group, and there were no systems of incarceration.[1] Thus, solutions to intragroup conflict (the transgression of social boundaries) were conceived primarily in terms of restoring balance to social relations (reestablishing social boundaries) rather than, as in Western societies, isolating transgressors in confinement. The trickster figure is always both losing and regaining balance in extreme social situations, but is never apart from the social—that is, isolated from the community. Indeed, trickster represents community.

Vizenor contrasts the comedic Anishinaabe trickster figure Naanabozho to the Western tragic hero in that trickster is a figure of community (nature). The tragic hero is a figure of isolation from community—a prototype of the alien, or alienated, "individual." Here we might consider the kinds of boundaries that construct the Western individual, a category of personhood foreign to traditional Indigenous societies:

The trickster is related to plants and animals and trees; he [she/they/it] is a teacher and healer in various personalities who, as numerous stories reveal, explains the values of healing plants, wild rice, maple sugar, basswood, and birch bark to woodland tribal people. More than a magnanimous teacher and transformer, the trickster is capable of violence, deceptions, and cruelties: the realities of human imperfections. The woodland trickster is an existential shaman in the comic mode, not an isolated and sentimental tragic hero in conflict with nature.

The trickster is comic in the sense that he does not reclaim idealistic ethics, but survives as a part of the natural world; he represents a spiritual balance in a comic drama rather than the romantic elimination of human contradictions and evil.[2]

"Stand up, fall, regain balance, and stumble again; such was the pattern of Nana'b'oozoo's life," remarks Anishinaabe scholar Basil Johnston in his recounting of some Nana'b'oozoo narratives.[3]

In his generative English compilation of Winnebago (Ho-Chunk) trickster narratives, a collaboration with tribal members Sam Blowsnake, John Baptiste, and Oliver Lamere, anthropologist Paul Radin has read in trickster a combination of "benefactor and buffoon."[4] Arnold Krupat speculates on the origin of the term "trickster" itself and suggests the multiple local manifestations of this figure across Native communities:

> It has again and again been said in print that the term *trickster* first appeared in Daniel G. Brinton's *The Myths of the New World*, published in 1868. But Lewis Hyde, in an important study of the trickster, states that he has not been able to find the word in any one of the three editions of Brinton's book! Hyde suggests that it is in Franz Boas's introduction to James Teit's *Traditions of the Thompson River Indians* (1898) that the term first appears in English (Hyde 1998, 355). In any case, since the late nineteenth century, the term *trickster* has been used to describe a character who [. . .] is a wandering, bawdy, and gluttonous figure, typically male but able to alter his sex at will. [. . .] Here it should be noted that the trickster, as he is generally called, has no such generic name among the various tribal nations themselves. Rather, all these peoples have very specific and concrete names for trickster. In California, Oregon, the inland plateau, the Great Basin, the southern Plains, and the

Southwest, the trickster figure is most commonly called Coyote. In the Southeast, trickster is Rabbit or Hare; Raven or Crow in the Arctic and sub-Arctic; Jay or Wolverine in parts of Canada. Among the Lakota of the plains, whose people we call the Sioux, the trickster [. . .] is Iktomi or Ikto, a word translated as "spider." Among the Hochank, or Winnebago, the trickster is named Wakjankaga, although Wacdjungega, Hare, is also a Hochank trickster. For the Anishinaabe or Chippewa, the trickster is Nenabos, or Manabozho, in a number of variant pronunciations and spellings, and also Hare. For the Gros Ventre of Montana, Nixant is the trickster's name, as it is Veeho for the Cheyenne, Sitconski for the Assiniboine, Istinike for the Ponca and, and Napi for the Blackfeet. In the northeast we find [. . .] Kluskap, Glous'gap or Gluskabe. Among the Cree peoples of Canada, the trickster is known as Wesucechak, or Wisahketchahk, anglicized to "Whiskey Jack." Among the Modoc of California, there is someone called Tusasas or Joker. Northern neighbors of the Modoc, the Klamath people tell tales in which Skunk sometimes acts the role of the trickster, but there are also stories told of Mink and his younger brother Weasel in which they also behave in trickster-like fashion. And there are yet other names for Native American tricksters. New England Algonquian-speaking nations have Lox, who seems to combine characteristics of the beaver, the badger, and the wolverine, along with a figure known as Ableegumooch, who appears to be Rabbit by another name.[5]

Trickster therefore has no fixed form, either from Native community to community or within any given community, where, as Krupat notes, in line with precedent scholarship, trickster combines attributes of "human, animal, and divine nature."[6] But Barre Toelken has cautioned against inferring from these local figures "a universal macrotradition of 'The Trickster,' a concept that has become not only a handy carrying bag for anthropologists, but a passionately faddish focal point for Jungian analysts, literary critics, and New Age gurus."[7] Citing the comments of Native storytellers themselves, Krupat notes that the function of trickster narratives across Native communities is twofold: it is both philosophical, prompting the listeners to think about the world, and pedagogical, teaching the listeners what it means, by example, to be a good and a bad community member.[8] To this I would add teaching about the reciprocal responsibilities of kinship, which entail recognizing the specific boundaries that kin relations establish. For example, among the Navajo, one is born *into* one's mother's clan but *for* one's father's clan. The former entails relations of "sharing or giving" to other clan members; the latter entails relations of "exchange and reciprocity" between mother's and father's clans. Both relationships are based in "bonds of solidarity." However, the patrilineal bonds "are weaker than those of the matrilineal categories, because the descent category on which this category is based (father–child) is a weaker one than that on which matrilineal categories are based (mother–child)."[9]

Thus, in the Radin/Blowsnake/Baptiste/Lamere Winnebago narratives, trickster is the very principle of kinship and its antithesis. Trickster is related to everyone and everything by kinship terms—even, amusingly, parts of its own body. "He ambled along calling all the objects in the world younger brothers when speaking to them. He and all the objects in the world understood one another, understood, indeed, one another's language" (§ 3). Trickster is usually "older brother," even to its anus and penis (§§ 14 and 16). Trickster is "First-Born" (§ 16) and "old man" (§ 25). But he is also "grandson" to grandmother skunk, who digs a hole for trickster in the hill, which trickster uses to lure its raccoon kin into a trap, then roasting them for a meal. But as usual in this world of tricks and countertricks, trickster is in turn tricked out of the meal by a tree and some wolves (§ 28–30). At the same time, trickster is continually prevailing on kinship relations, principally for food (trickster is always hungry), then continually violating them by refusing reciprocity, often in the most violent of ways. The importance of kinship, the very fabric of Native societies, is highlighted through its comic violation by trickster. Trickster kills a buffalo, and there ensues a battle between trickster's right and left arm for the carcass (§ 5). Trickster fools some ducks into dancing with their eyes closed, and then, hungry as usual, wrings their necks one by one, putting its anus on guard to watch the cooking ducks while trickster sleeps. But trickster's anus, even though it farts continually, cannot repel the foxes who come to eat the food. So, upon waking, to punish its anus, trickster burns it and later eats it roasted, not remembering at first in either case that trickster is burning and then eating the nether parts of trickster (§§ 12–14). In another narrative, trickster's detachable penis, which it carries in a box, swims through the water to have intercourse with the chief's daughter (§ 16). Thus, trickster violates the boundaries of the unitary, organic human body, suggesting that all boundaries are constructed and thus can be deconstructed.

Tulalip storyteller Johnny Moses, in a taped bilingual performance made for me by my brother, tells the story of the trickster figure Crow, who, visiting members of its community in turn, makes itself unwelcome by displaying the kind of arrogant behavior that violates the boundaries of Native etiquette.[10] Whenever anyone tries to give advice of any kind at all, this trickster replies in a nasal, scratchy whine, "I know everything; nobody can tell me anything"—an assertion tellingly close to the Western style of competitive individualism, which is the opposite of Native kinship behavior. Moving from family to family in the village of "animal people," Crow is warned first by "Deer Woman" and then by the "Bear People" not to visit "Octopus Lady" when the tide is out. But at each warning, Crow repeats in an annoying whine the refrain "I know," until all the people in village no longer want to entertain Crow. So Crow, with what approximates settler behavior, aggressively intoning, "Nothing can bother me; I'll go wherever I want to go," ventures down to the beach at low tide, where Octopus Lady appears, "with the biggest head [Crow] had ever seen in the world." Octopus Lady welcomes Crow. But "he'd never seen Octopus Lady before *because he never listened to the people;* he knew everything."

"Every night, every day, there was always stories," Johnny Moses tells his audience about his childhood in a Native community, "always stories being born every day as well as the old-time stories . . . so this is the way we memorized our way of life; the stories was a way of life; this is how we survived in the forest; how we survived, knowing what kind of plants to use and what kind of animals to relate to for our healing." Born in local experience, Native stories *are* that experience. But having never listened to the stories of the people, Crow, who thinks he knows everything, is unprepared for the deadly charms of Octopus Lady, when in her gurgling voice she welcomes him into her multiple arms: "Come a little closer; it is nice to see you, Crow." To which Crow whines characteristically, "I know," and moves closer. "Oh, you are handsome, Crow," gurgles Octopus Lady. To which Crow whines, "I know," as she puts another arm around him. "Where do you live; do you know a lot of things?" "I know everything," Crow whines again, as she puts still another arm around him. "One arm after the other as they talked longer and longer. He was getting hungry; he was getting very hungry," so he demands: "I'm hungry. When are we going to eat?" Gurglingly, Octopus Lady replies, "'We're going to eat pretty soon, Crow.' And then she got down to her last arm. And then, you know, when they were talking away, talking away, the water began to rise, began to rise, and the water was way up to his neck now. When it was up to his neck, he demands of her again: 'What is for dinner? I'm hungry right now. I want to eat something. What is for dinner?'" As she wraps her last arm around him, she gurgles, "You are the dinner, Crow." Crow, of course, replies, "I know." Knowledge, the narrative suggests, if not communally based, which is to say proceeding from reciprocity, is not only useless but potentially fatal. Crow inhabits his fatal lack of knowledge because of the rigid boundary he has maintained between himself and the community. Further, the story is a lesson against arrogance, which also sets up a boundary between individuals and community.[11]

Trickster narratives, like all oral productions, are not frozen in time but are repeated in ongoing and changing contexts, so they gather new meanings. The Crow narrative, which certainly has pedagogical relevance in a preinvasion setting, takes on new meaning in a postsettler world. As Miwok/Pomo scholar and fiction writer Greg Sarris reminds us: "Naturally stories are told differently in different situations, and tellers often do not suggest much about the situation in which they are told or invite further discourse about the stories or the world of the stories."[12] We should be aware, then, that among its multiple contexts, this Crow story, which exists actually and potentially in a range of contexts, moved from entirely Native contexts located in what is now the state of Washington to the time and place of its tape recording in Detroit, Michigan, before a non-Native audience, where it not only had different meanings for its audience but also commented on them in different ways. "More and more," Sarris notes, "scholars of oral literatures are looking to the broader contexts in which these literatures live. Specifically, they are considering what lies beyond the spoken word, beyond their perceptual range as listeners and readers, and what that larger context says about their position as literate speakers and writers for and about oral traditions. Concerns regarding context become particularly significant in cross-cultural situations."[13] The cross-cultural situation that concerns us here is the translation of Native oral production into alphabetic writing, about which Sarris remarks: "Writing recreates oral experience in given ways. The transcriptions of American Indian oral literatures, for example, sometimes provide nothing about the context in which the literatures were told and recorded or the manner in which they were translated. In the end we have a story as an object devoid of the context that might suggest something about the story beyond our interaction with it as an independent text."[14]

While the figure of the trickster originated in preinvasion times and thus refers to cultural contexts that are not answerable to the European invasion, trickster nevertheless later expanded to include responses to the effects of European imperialism and its colonial forms on Native communities. Thus, without getting into problems of intention or origin, in one of its possible meanings, we can understand a narrative like Crow's as offering a particular critique of Western epistemology in contrast to Native modes of knowing, which implies a boundary exists between the two. Indeed, for all we know, this particular narrative may have originated within the colonial context as a direct response to the egocentric arrogance of the colonizers. As Krupat notes, trickster logic blurs the boundaries between identities that the West has come to think of

> not merely [as] differences but oppositions, and the Western way of doing philosophy has, historically, involved reasoning by means of an abstract logic that analytically constructs perceived differences and dualities as *oppositions*. This logic developed and, indeed, became fixed in Western thought as the internalization of the habits of alphabetic literacy slowly gained sway. [. . .] But the traditional philosophy of an oral culture constructs its pairings not in *oppositional* but, rather, in *conjunctural* or *complementary* fashion, and it conducts its philosophical and pedagogical work of thinking through difference and duality not by means of an abstract, and analytical discourse but, rather, by means of highly concrete narratives.[15]

Citing the work of Daniel Heath Justice on dualisms in the Cherokee worldview, Krupat notes that "such apparent oppositions, Justice argues, are mediated by 'the concept of balance.'" "'To acknowledge these dualistic pairings,' Justice writes, 'is not to presume an antagonistic relationship of supremacy between them. The emphasis, rather, is balance and complementarity.'" "With reference to the work of Mary Churchill, Justice affirms that to understand 'Cherokee dualism is to understand its necessary *complementarity*,' its 'dynamic and relational perspective.'"[16] Thus, Krupat notes, "storytelling is the primary means of gaining and conveying knowledge, or doing philosophy."[17]

In his book of stories *Dead Voices,* Vizenor remarks on the dynamism of storytelling. Speaking of "Bagese. . . . the same tribal woman who was haunted by stones and mirrors," Vizenor notes that

> she was a bear and teased me in mirrors as she did the children, and at the same time she said that tribal stories must be told not recorded, told to listeners but not readers, and she insisted that stories be heard through the ear not the eye. [. . .] "Printed books are the habits of dead voices," she said and turned a mirror in my direction to distract me. "The ear not the eye sees the stories."[18]

I want to emphasize that in referencing American Indian literatures, I am using "literature" in the strictest sense of the word to denote what is formed by letters—that is, written. Native cultures in what Europeans were to name the Americas were predominantly oral.[19] Until the European invasion, beginning in 1492, alphabetic writing was not a part of Native technological repertoires; and even after learning about it, Native societies, if not geographically removed from its influence (and by the second half of the nineteenth century, such distance would come to an end for all the U.S. Native communities), were divided over its adoption, so that, for example, in the United States, which is the terrain of this volume, Native writing in English did not become visible until the end of the eighteenth century, in the sermons and letters of Mohegan Christian convert Samson Occom, who also wrote an ethnography of the Montauk Indians, which was published after his death in 1809. While the oral tradition forms an important ongoing part of the social and cultural life of Native communities, where it always contributes form, content, and ideological energy to Native writing, I have chosen to distinguish it from Native American literatures per se for a number of political, historical, and cultural reasons that have to do with its strategic positions in relation to alphabetic writing, which in this context is a distinct product of colonialism via Indian boarding school indoctrination and U.S. federal Indian law. These oral strategies, inevitably strategies of resistance, are embodied in the complicated word "traditional," which I have defined previously as a dynamic historical force.

In *Native American Renaissance* (1983), Kenneth Lincoln develops an opposition between Native and Western relationships to language that is virtually ubiquitous in contemporary Native writing and that threatens to become a cliché in its unquestioned—that is, its unhistoricized—repetition. Lincoln quotes Sioux medicine man Lame Deer, whose statement epitomizes the opposition: "We Indians live in a world of symbols and images where the spiritual and the commonplace are one. To you symbols are just words, spoken or written in a book."[20] Westerners are alienated from language, and writing is the vehicle of that alienation, whereas for Indians, words "are part of nature, part of ourselves. . . . We try to understand them not with the head but with the heart."[21] The opposition idealizes as it romanticizes a history of Native American resistance to European invasion in which the primal negotiation is the apocalyptic, discontinuous movement from preinvasion to invasion, from orality to writing. Writing a literary history, I have no choice but to narrativize this negotiation, which, because of the discontinuities between the oral and the written, cannot simply be written.

Nevertheless, here is the outline of the story, which I will attempt to complicate. Before contact with European cultures, there was no Native American literature because the word "literature," which derives from the Latin word for "letter" and thereby implies the technology of alphabetic writing, cannot translate a preinvasion Native oral relationship with language, however we (Natives and non-Natives alike) may imagine such a relationship. It has been one of the major drives of Native American literatures of the United States (by which I mean alphabetic writing by Natives) to imagine this precontact relationship, what Lincoln terms "tribal poetics": "the song-poet lives an individual for the sake of the tribe; his singing is a matter of life or death for the people. He does not celebrate himself separately, his vision apart from the natural world, but sings of kinship in the tribal circle."[22] Imagination in this context performs the crucial political work, as Lincoln puts it, of "resisting Euro-American literary conceptions."[23] The assertion of tradition by Native Americans has been historically a crucial mode of resistance to European colonialism. It is within the context of this resistance that statements about language like Lame Deer's must be understood. When we remove them from this history, they become clichés, figurations of the noble savage.

The resistances to the translation of land into property and of orality into alphabetic writing are linked. At its introduction in the Americas, this writing was destructive of the traditional Native relationship to land. When the Spanish, following Columbus, invaded, they brought with them a legal document known as the Requirimiento, declaring, with a boundless imperial narcissism intent in establishing boundaries, the virtual dispossession of Indian land and culture.[24] The first act of invasion was to read this law aloud to Indigenous communities, which could no more be expected to understand the language of its global imperatives than the invaders could be expected to understand the local Native languages for which they expressed such contempt as to deem them virtually nonexistent. Four hundred years later, U.S. agents, as a part of federal policy tied to the ideology of allotment, were kidnapping Indian children and sending them to boarding schools where they were forbidden to speak their Native languages on pain of punishment and were forced to learn to speak, read, and write English. In her book of interwoven stories, *The Dance Boots,* focused on Anishinaabe survivance of the brutal boarding schools, Anishinaabe writer Linda Legarde Grover sets the stage for her narrative in the first story with a story told to the narrator, Artense, by her Aunt Shirley:

> The story she told me is a multigenerational one of Indian boarding schools, home sickness and cruelty, racism, and most of all, the hopes broken and revived in the survival of an extended family. From the beginning of her story, when my grandmother was sent to a Catholic mission school in Canada, to the heyday of boarding schools in the 1910s and 1920s, through the 1930s when the Indian Reorganization Act provided money incentives for local school districts to admit Indian children, I experienced through Shirley my family's role as participants in and witnesses to a vast experiment in the breaking of a culture through the education of its young.[25]

In her painfully vivid, empathetic historical recreation and personal memoir *Fort Marion Prisoners and the Trauma of Native Education,* and indeed her meditation on the writing of history as a perpetual presence, Cherokee novelist, poet, and teacher Diane Glancy traces the founding of the boarding school movement to the education of Plains Indian captives at Fort Marion prison in St. Augustine, Florida, from 1875 to 1878. The commandant of the military prison and their teacher was Captain Richard Henry Pratt, who in 1879 would found the Carlisle Indian Industrial School, the first government-run Indian boarding school in the United States and a model for Native boarding school education. Glancy's focus in her narrative is the interlocking relationship between Native captivity and Native education not only in the militarized boarding school system but in the reverberations of that system in her own education. At the beginning of her narrative, which traces the journey of the prisoners, shackled in boxcars, from Oklahoma to Florida, Glancy notes at the Fort Still, Oklahoma, military reservation,

> there was a museum on the army base. It must have been where the departure of the Plains Indian prisoners first registered. Somehow there was a residue of voices. A visage of the story. Not simplistic but elemental. Plain as the southwestern Oklahoma landscape. It was the kind of *voices* I picked up as *overlay* when I traveled. I think it was where I began to recognize the dislocation at the heart of education, especially Native education.[26]

Of this dislocation in her own education, Glancy remarks: "This I know. I was at school. I stayed out of the way. I was relegated to invisibility. I could not speak. Once I ran from the class when I had to say something. I left no evidence of my having been there. I was a reminder of what people didn't want to be reminded of—the stories in America's history that they wouldn't look at."[27] Among these stories is that of Fort Marion, where, among other subjects, the prisoners were taught (which is to say forced) to write in English. Writing, then, was a form of punishment, or worse: "The letters in the words [. . .] were traitors, those letters. They were Indian scouts for the U.S. cavalry."[28] The lesson of *Fort Marion*/Fort Marion is the alienation of education for both Natives and non-Natives (for whom that alienation is their alienation from the genocidal truth of U.S. history): "To live in this world, I had to be educated, but to become educated, I had to be separated from a part of myself—that was the catch. Self was the distance I had to travel from. That was the first lesson for the Fort Marion prisoners. That was the lesson with which I struggled. It was my focus for the prisoners—the beginning of Native education and the upheaval there."[29]

In a 1999 letter to Hopi tribal chairman Wayne Taylor, which represents her refusal to sign a rental agreement (known as the Accommodation Agreement, or AA) for traditional Navajo land taken in the name of the Hopi tribe by the U.S. government, Navajo elder Katherine Smith, who suffered during her boarding school experience in the 1920s and whose life (she died in 2017) since then was, as she puts it, lived within the "prison" of Western law, draws a familiar distinction between the Native relationship to land and that law:

> Here I sit on the East side of Big Mountain. My prayers, my songs, that I communicate with the stars, the rain, the Earth, and all the

living beings here on this land. Those are my laws of understanding. If you put upon me the White Man's laws your so-called AA's, how can we both live in harmony? For these reasons, I have never signed anything that comes from the gov't.[30]

At the end of her short story "Keyo," about an alienated Indian boy desperately resisting literacy at school, Glancy has her narrator remark, "He was angry he was born in a world that required books. He was angry at words that swarmed like insects in the creek bottoms, forever out of reach, forever spelling their own secret language that left him a stranger in their world."[31] We should remember, then, that alphabetic writing has a history—or more precisely, histories. Its history within Native America is at best ambivalent because of its advent and continuance in the form of (federal) laws of dispossession and exclusion. Writing would eventually become a tool of resistance to this law as well, beginning in the late 1820s with the antiremoval writings of Elias Boudinot,[32] editor of the first Indian newspaper, the *Cherokee Phoenix*; and Pequot activist William Apess, whose *Indian Nullification of the Unconstitutional Law of Massachusetts* (1835) is the first detailed critique of federal Indian law and whose public address, "Eulogy on King Phillip" (1836), is the first thoroughgoing revision of Western colonial history from a Native point of view.

By emphasizing the distinction between oral tradition and literature as strategic, I emphasize that whether a given culture developed or did not develop writing has nothing to do with the perceived sophistication or complexity of that culture—that is, its value. Plato, whom the West claims as a generative thinker, viewed the innovation of writing as a distinct threat to the integrity of intimate human discourse and the function of memory.[33] This view is compatible with a strain of Native thinking, as N. Scott Momaday makes clear through his character and *porte-parole* Tosamah in *House Made of Dawn*, the generative text for the development of the Native novel that has followed its publication. Tosamah, self-styled "Priest of the Sun" and founder of the "Pan-Indian Rescue Mission" (a figure in the novel for the Native American Church, incorporated in 1918[34]), delivers Momaday's famous set piece, a sermon on the "Word," focusing the difference between what Tosamah understands as the white man's deceptive use of language, in effect the secularization of it through writing, and Indian storytelling, the oral tradition, which for Tosamah retains its sacred force: "The white man takes such things as words and literatures for granted, as indeed he must, for nothing in his world is so commonplace. [. . .] He has diluted and multiplied the Word, and words have begun to close in upon him. He is sated and insensitive; his regard for language—for the Word itself—as an instrument of creation has diminished nearly to the point of no return."[35] In contrast to this diminished white use of language, in which the "multiplied" word would appear to refer to the technology of writing translated into print culture, Tosamah offers the example of his Kiowa grandmother's relation to the oral tradition: "Consider for a moment that old Kiowa woman, my grandmother, whose use of language was confined to speech. And be assured that her regard for words was always keen in proportion as she depended upon them. You see, for her words were medicine; they were magic and invisible. They came from nothing into sound and meaning. They were beyond price; they could neither be bought nor sold. And she never threw words away."[36]

Tosamah's grandmother's relation to language is implicitly intertwined here with the Native relation to land, which, like language, is not a commodity to be bought and sold but a precious resource to be husbanded and shared with the kin group. Thus, the force of the oral tradition, of storytelling itself, becomes a nodal point of resistance to U.S. colonialism, as this passage from *House Made of Dawn* suggests:

> The people of the town have little need. They do not hanker after progress and have never changed their essential way of life. Their invaders were a long time in conquering them; and now, after four centuries of Christianity, they still pray in Tanoan to the old deities of the earth and sky and make their living from the things that are and have always been within their reach; while in the discrimination of pride they acquire from their conquerors only the luxury of example. They have assumed the names and gestures of their enemies but have held on to their own, secret souls; and in this there is a resistance and an overcoming, a long outwaiting.[37]

This epistemological privileging of oral storytelling is articulated by a range of contemporary Native writers. Remember that Silko left law school because she "decided the only way to seek justice was through the power of stories."[38] The power of stories is always communal. Here, Silko tells us, it relies on the power of kinship: "The stories are always bringing us together, keeping this whole together, keeping this family together, keeping this clan together. And so there is this constant pulling together to resist the tendency to run or hide or separate oneself during a traumatic emotional experience. This separation not only endangers the group but the individual as well—one does not recover by oneself."[39] Ultimately, Native storytelling, which reinforces kinship, is land based, tied to the local sites of communities that narrate their origins as autochthonous. In the Southwest, this typically takes the form of emergence narratives, where, unlike the Judeo-Christian narrative of a grand fall into alienated separation, community is formed and constantly tested as it rises through a series of worlds to its present home. "Human identity, imagination and storytelling were inextricably linked to the land," Silko tells us, "to Mother earth, just as the strands of the spider's web radiate from the center of the web."[40]

We might *read* Native *oral* narratives, then (cognizant of the paradox that constrains us[41]), and specifically trickster narratives, as, through their centering the social value of kinship/land, inherently resistant to the Western narrative of the fall. Following Krupat, we can understand that narrative as grounded in the epistemology of alphabetic writing, of "opposition, hierarchy, and exclusion"—that is, the epistemology of alienation, which creates what the West will come to valorize as the individual, the I-centered person. This is also the epistemology of tragedy, of the fall of the singular figure, separated from community, the prototype for which is Sophocles's Oedipus.

Vizenor contrasts this tragic epistemology to the comic/communal, or we-centered, epistemology of trickster. In Silko's *Ceremony*, her Puebloan protagonist, Tayo, returning to the hegemonic white world of the United States from the trauma of World War II, struggles to free himself from the disease of a Western I-centered narrative through the acting out of a Native we-centered story. In the following passage, we hear Tayo struggling with the issue of health, his return to balance, exemplified by the Navajo singer (healer) Betonie:

> "We all have been waiting for help a long time. But it never has been easy. The people must do it. You must do it." Betonie sounded as if he were explaining something simple but important to a small child. But Tayo's stomach clenched around the words like knives stuck into his guts. There was something large and terrifying in the old man's words. He wanted to yell at the medicine man, to yell the things the white doctors had yelled at him—that he had to think only of himself, and not about the others, that he would never get

well as long as he used words like "we" and "us." But he had known the answer all along, even while the doctors were telling him he could get well and he was trying to believe them: medicine didn't work that way, because the world didn't work that way. His sickness was only part of something larger, and his cure would be found only in something great and inclusive of everything.[42]

In one of the Winnebago trickster narratives, trickster, traveling alone, meets his "younger brother," fox, who tells him, "The world is going to be a difficult place to live in." Trickster replies: "'Oh, oh, my younger brother, what you have said is very true. I, too, was thinking of the very same thing. I have always wanted to have a companion, so let us live together.' Trickster consented and so they went on to look for a place in which to dwell" (§ 19), ultimately joining with other companions to found a community. This is one of the few narratives that Radin reproduces in the Winnebago trickster cycle in which the community is not fractured by tricks and countertricks. By putting the comic antics of trickster in parentheses for a moment, the story stresses the necessity of kinship for survival in a difficult world. This is *Ceremony*'s insight as well. To the extent that Tayo, until the very end of the novel, struggles with himself and other figures he meets along the way, we can read him as a trickster, affirming kinship, though often through showing us the disasters of its subversion. In one way or another, this trickster dialectic of kinship is the central dynamic of Native writing from William Apess to the present.

Kenneth Lincoln remarks, "Silko's novel is a word ceremony. It tells Tayo's story as a curative act."[43] Formally, this "curative act" is committed to the representation of oral narrative in writing as Silko notes: "I began to think more about the written word as a picture of the spoken word."[44] In this respect, *Ceremony*'s protagonist, Tayo, seems to be the written counterpart of Tiyo, a cultural hero figure appearing in the oral narratives of the Hopi, who, with the help of Spider Grandmother, retraces the path of emergence in order to obtain the spiritual power that will bring an end to a drought that is threatening the community.[45] In terms of content, the curative act of contemporary Native American writing is committed to the communal, or kinship, logic of trickster narratives. While these narratives, as a social formation, precede the European invasion of the Americas, the trickster logic of these narratives is inherently positioned, thanks to its commitment to kinship as the driving principle of social life, to resist the Western oppositional logics that came to buttress and be buttressed by the logic of capitalism: individualism, commodification, and acquisitive competition because whenever trickster asserts his acquisitive self, his acquisitiveness is subverted by countertricks. Chief among these oppositional logics is the logic of law. In its agonistic structure, written law forms a zero-sum game founded in an exclusionary idea of property—an idea that is the very antithesis of the communal ethos of Native oral narratives, which trickster narratives exemplify.

BEARHEART

The End of Borders

Gerald Vizenor's *Bearheart: The Heirship Chronicles* is an Indigenous *Canterbury Tales,* narrating the journey of "a caravan of tribal circus ['mixedblood'] pilgrims" in a postapocalyptic United States across the country to the ceremonial space of Pueblo Bonito in Chaco Canyon, "our new world paradise in New Mexico."[1] The novel performs the trickster tradition in a postmodern, written form that envisions the obliteration of the boundaries that U.S. federal Indian law enforces. I use the term postmodern in the sense that, as one of the pilgrim tricksters remarks, "words are the meaning of living now. [. . .] The word is where the world is at now" (170–71). As in trickster tales, which might be categorized paradoxically as prepostmodern, there are no characters and no plot in any conventional sense in *Bearheart,* only the play of words narrating the play of forces at work in the conflict between kinship and capitalist cultures. Language here is not referential but a world unto itself. Alan Velie summarizes, citing Vizenor's essay "Trickster Discourse":

> However one might categorize *Bearheart,* it is first and foremost a trickster novel. [. . .] To Vizenor trickster is first and foremost a sign in the semiotic sense, a sign in a language game, a comic holotrope. This means that Vizenor conceives of trickster as a product of language, who must be seen in a linguistic context; trickster is not a reified social urge, fitting neatly into the model of a social scientist.
> By "holotrope" Vizenor means whole, freestanding, both signified and signifier. Quoting Bakhtin, Vizenor describes the comic holotrope as a "dialogism," meaning that trickster can only be understood as part of a greater whole, the "collection of 'utterances' in oral traditions." [. . .] To Vizenor the tribal world view is comic and communal; the comic spirit is centered in trickster, a figure created

by the tribe as a whole, not an individual author. Vizenor argues that, "The opposite of a comic discourse is a monologue, an utterance in isolation, which comes closer to the tragic mode in literature [the soliloquy] and not a comic tribal world view."[2]

Coincident with the boundary-obliterating vision, *Bearheart* implicitly asks whether the nation-state can deliver social justice. The answer is decidedly "no." Vizenor wants us to think beyond the boundaries of the nation-state and its institutions. To that end, *Bearheart* takes place in a postapocalyptic time that is simultaneously the present, where the United States is devastated by an energy crisis. "The nation ran out of gasoline and fuel oil. [. . .] Economic power had become the religion of the nation; when it failed people turned to their own violence and bizarre terminal creeds for comfort and meaning" (23). "Terminal creeds" is a key phrase in the novel, where it signifies unquestionable dogma of a religious or a legal kind. *Bearheart* points to federal Indian law as the terminal creed of settler colonialism.

Evoking the context of federal Indian law, before the narrative proper commences—that is, before we read *Bearheart*—there is a "Letter to the Reader" (the whole of which is in italics in the original text) by the fictional author of the book, a trickster bear. It begins:

> The bear is in me now.
> Not since the darkness of the federal boarding school and the writing of this book, the heirship chronicles on the wicked road to the fourth world, has the blood and deep voice of the bear moved me with such power.
> Listen, ha ha ha haaaa. (vii)

The references to federal boarding school and heirship locate the author's history at its origin in the allotment era, when the federal government devised a system of determining the heirs to allotments, a process that eventuated in the fractioning of allotment ownership, with the resulting dispossession of generations of allottees:[3]

> The voices of the bear spoke through me for the first time when the boarding school superintendent cornered me in a dark narrow closet on the reservation. [. . .] We were twelve years old then and had run from that federal school four times, once in winter. The moons were wild, and the government agents were waiting, waiting, waiting for the heirs at the treelines, waiting for the defeated

tribes to stop running from the uniforms and closets. The agents, colonial hunters hired by the government, captured me once as me, three time as a crow, and ran me back four times from dreams in the sacred cedar. [. . .] We survived as crows and bears because we were never known as humans. [. . .] The fourth time back to the boarding school we were chained and bruised, the last time as a crow, and we learned to outwit the government in the darkness. We were pushed and punched, cornered in a narrow closet by the superintendent. We were the heirs he would never tame, and the promotions were measured by our assimilation, our tribal death. (viii–ix)

The description of the boarding school—which were developed, as I have noted in my reading of Diane Glancy's *Fort Marion Prisoners and the Trauma of Native Education,* by Colonel Pratt at the Fort Marion prison for captives of the Plains wars—as a place of colonial imprisonment, torture, and sexual violence is made literal here. Even as the passage focuses on the crimes of the boarding school regime, it also focuses resistance to that regime by its Native "students," who are tricksters, "the heirs he would never tame," taking the form of bears and crows able "to outwit the government in the darkness." This resistance is specifically noted as resistance to "assimilation" and "tribal death," the achievement of which is the basis for "promotions" in the system. The system, then, is specifically marked as one of what we now recognize as settler colonialism, the goal of which, as noted previously, is elimination of the Native. The heirs here are thus not simply heirs to fractionated Native land but heirs of survivance as Native peoples, able to resist and persist because the colonizers can neither imagine them as human (that is to say, as capable human beings) nor understand their kinship with animals, which dissolves the boundary between nature and culture, thus expanding the domain of the social world and with that expansion the knowledge of survivance.

From the boarding school era, the letter skips forward to a time when, its author tells us, "The Bureau of Indian Affairs hired me to dance in the darkness on the cabinets and to remember the heirship documents, the crossblood tricksters at the treelines. We laughed, no one in the cities would believe that we were related to animals, that we were bears in these stories" (ix). The job description clearly contradicts the bureaucratic function of the Bureau of Indian Affairs (BIA), suggesting that trickster bears have taken over the Bureau: "we are bears in the Bureau of Indian Affairs. [...] The others are outside, lost memories in the word wars and we are here with the bears" (xii). At this moment, "someone beats on the door" (ix), and time shifts to November 3–9, 1972, when the American Indian Movement (AIM) occupies the BIA.[4] The person beating on the door is a female activist, Songidee, from AIM, whose first words are, "Stand against the wall, old man" (ix).

The rest of the letter represents the confrontation between Songidee, who "has little white chickens in her heart," and the bear, whom she refers to as a "White Indian" (xii). The confrontation concerns the question of liberation from colonial rule: "We took this building for tribal people, for our past and future on the reservations, says the bare chicken. We are the new warriors out for tribal freedom, but you old fuckers sold out to the white man too long ago to understand the real movement" (xiii). The bear's rejoinder is simply an invitation to "touch me" and a reference to the book *Bearheart*: "we are word bears in our book." Songidee responds, "What book?" The bear provides a précis of *Bearheart*: "One word at a time, the heirship documents and bears on the road to the fourth world. Proude Cedarfair, the old shaman, our bearheart on the winter solstice. We are there now, in our own documents." In sum, as the bear notes, the book is about "Trickster liberation," which is his alternative, a virtual utopian present, to the confrontational politics of AIM: "We are there now, in our own documents" (xiii).

When Songidee in turn asks the bear, "What is your book about?," he responds, "Sex and violence," which certainly comprise the unadulterated medium of trickster tales. Yet within this medium, the message of these tales is the complex relationship to boundaries I have been analyzing, a deconstruction since 1492 of the settler-colonial borders between nature and culture. While implementing this deconstruction, these tales maintain the preinvasion focus on the ethics of kinship, in which the whole world is one of reciprocal social relations. Initially, Songidee denies the existence of the book. "You never wrote no heirship book on bears," she accuses, conflating, as she has done since the beginning of the conversation, "heir" with "hair," suggesting either a failure on her part to distinguish the pronunciation of the two words ("air" from "hair") or a failure of the bear's pronunciation (xiv). But then "she rises, opens the cabinet in the closet, opens the bound manuscript, and reads out loud sections in the heirship documents" (xiv), choosing a passage of comic sexual intercourse between two federal agents, identified only as the "federal woman" and the "federal man," who have come to dispossess the cedar-circus Natives of their trees but forget their mission in the throes of fumbling ecstasy:

> The federal man leaned over and touched her muscular calves. . . . She stumbled out of her clothes. His short blunt penis was wobbling like the neck of a dead sparrow. She leaned back on her elbows over the cedar fronds and spread her legs open to the federal man. . . . He missed more than half his frantic earthbound thrusts, leaving her spread and moaning, falling through cloudless space, out of time and green paper, plastic flowers, part thunder, and poison rain. (xiv)[5]

Here the "Letter to the Reader" ends with the bear having the last laugh because, apparently, Songidee's denial of the book has been proven wrong, and the AIM activist is engrossed in it: "Bearheart, ha ha ha haaaa" (xiv).

Bearheart proper begins when, facing the energy crisis, the federal government, echoing the *Tee-Hit-Ton* case, appropriates the trees on reservations without compensation to the tribes (23). The Native resistance to this taking in the novel is figured in the generations of four Proude Cedarfairs, who "celebrated the sacred cedar trees" that the federal government would reduce to a commodity. In trickster tradition, the first Proude Cedarfair assumes animal form as a "ceremonial bear. He dreams in sudden moods and soars through stone windows on the solstice sunrise. The clown crows trail his luminous breath and thunder voice ha ha ha haaaa from his magical directions into the fourth world" (5). Following the first Proude, all Cedarfairs exist between bear and human.

The "Morning Prelude" to *Bearheart* mixes elements of both the Anishinaabe creation story, an earth-diver narrative, where Muskrat dives into the waters of a global flood, brought about by the creator to punish the violence of humans, and returns with a piece of earth that will grow on Turtle's back into North America (Turtle Island); and Southwestern emergence narratives, where Indigenous peoples transform, after numerous transgressions, into their present human forms in the course of emerging through four or five worlds (depending on the particular version of the story):

> The earth turtles emerge from the great flood of the first world. In the second world the earth is alive in the magical voices and ceremonial words of birds and the healing energies of plants. The

white otter is the carrier of animal dreams in the new hearts of humans. The third world turns evil with contempt for living and fear of death. [...] In the fourth world evil spirits are outwitted in the secret languages of animals and birds. Bears and crows choose the new singers. The crows crow in their blackness. Ha ha ha haaaa the bears call from sunrise. (5)

The Bears' laughter ("ha ha ha haaaa") signals the comic mode of Vizenor's trickster tale in which we find, as I have noted in traditional trickster stories, the blurring of boundaries between animal and human, interspecies sexuality, and violence in all its forms.

"Four Proude Cedarfairs," the narrative continues, "have celebrated the sacred cedar trees"; and "Three Proude Cedarfairs have defended their sovereign circle ['circus'] from national and state and tribal governments, from missionaries, treekillers and evil tribal leaders" (7). The Cedarfairs' battle is against settler-colonialism, which has co-opted "tribal governments" as part and parcel of its agenda: "Nineteenth century frontier politics favored the interests of the railroads and treekillers and agrarian settlers who were promised ownership of the earth" (7).

"First Proude Cedarfair was at war with the federal government and the treekillers. [...] Proude [...] won the cedar war and preserved his sovereign nation in the circus." But "the cedar trees at the edge of the circus had turned brown and died from the violence." In the aftermath of the war, Proude is honored as "a warrior, praised for his visions. Tribal people came to visit him, to share his courage and to tell him stories about the summer bears and thunderbirds from the mountains and deserts and plains." But "the federal government ignored him, treekillers no longer needed him and politicians honored his courage and pride, telling the new voters of the state that he was a true patriot, a true and honest man defending his rights" (9–10). Although Proude had "won the cedar war and preserved his sovereign nation in the circus," settler colonialism had established itself, the sign of which is the idealization of Proude as an icon of liberal democracy—that is, the noble savage.

What remained was a fight for circus autonomy with the federal reservation hierarchy:

> Tribal leaders on the new federal reservation surrounding the circus, coveted the power of the cedar and the man who spoke and acted

from his heart. Proude told the leaders that he would recognize no government but his own, no nation but the cedar, and no families but his own blood. We are sovereign from all tribal and religious and national governments, he told the leaders, and we will listen to nothing more about the future. [. . .] When new trees began to grow over the stumps surrounding the cedar circus other tribal families following the example of Cedarfair declared themselves sovereign circuses. [. . .] He and other families exposed the evil of tribal governments and taught people to control themselves and not to fear the political witching of shamans from the evil underworld. (10)

Vizenor's use of "blood" may seem contradictory in light of his deconstruction of the term later in the novel in the scene with the hunters and breeders at Orion, which I have noted previously. But his main point here is, first, to mark the historic resistance of grass roots Native peoples against the federally imposed tribal leadership of reservations, examples of which I have noted in the conflict generating the *Crow Dog* case, the Second Wounded Knee, the Navajo–Hopi land dispute, the division in the Dakota Access Pipeline (DAPL) pipeline resistance, and, not previously noted, the resistance of the traditional Gayogo̱hó:nǫ' (Cayuga) to the federally imposed leadership of the Clint Halftown faction.[6] Second, Vizenor's narrative here begins to redraw the federal boundaries that recognize the absolute sovereignty of the federal government in Indian affairs and the subordinate sovereignty of federal reservations. In this context, I recall the definition of sovereignty in Vizenor's *Heirs of Columbus:* "The essence of sovereignty is imaginative, an original tribal trope, communal and spiritual, an idea that is more than metes and bounds in treaties."[7] In *Bearheart,* the first Proude Cedarfair imagines and enacts a definition of sovereignty that reconfigures national borders in refusing subordination to the federal sovereign. The circus is the figure of this reconfiguration—not only in its invocation of the circle, a sacred figure across Indigenous communities, as opposed to the straight lines of borders, but also in its invocation of the comic performance of clowns, those tricksters who play a central part in Indigenous Southwestern ceremonies.

The "Second Proude. [. . .] was moved [. . .] to defend the values and beliefs of his father and the creation of the cedar circus." He "organized the circuses surrounding the cedar nation into a common defense league" and "declared war on evil and corruption in tribal government

[. . .] that considered the circuses to be within the original colonial boundaries of the reservation, the boundaries created in treaties with the federal government, which meant that that the tribal circus families were in violation of the orders wherever they lived on the circuses" (12). The struggle, then, is manifestly a struggle over borders imposed by the colonial governments, federal and tribal. "The war ended when the president of the reservation government and two council representatives were kidnapped by circus warriors. The tribal government collapsed and the allied circuses declared themselves the provisional reservation tribal government," which lasted "for the next two decades. Second Proud Cedarfair retained his title as allied circus commander, but bestowed responsibilities for the cedar nation on his son, Third Proude" (13–14). Weaving together history and fiction—legal history with speculative fiction—Vizenor has Second Proude die at the Second Wounded Knee, "where the American Indian Movement had declared a new pantribal political nation." There,

> in sight of the radical encampment [. . .] the second old man of the cedar was stopped by a tribal government policeman. When he began singing in the deep voice of bears and continued walking toward Wounded Knee the policeman shot him in the face and chest with a shotgun. The blast knocked him down but the old man, blinded with his own blood, lifted himself to his feet and started walking again. The policeman shot him a second and third time in the back of the head. Second Proude fell forward on the stiff prairie grass and moaned his last vision of the bear into death. [. . .] When Third Proude questioned the policeman about the death of his father he was told that the old man would not stop walking toward Wounded Knee. It took three shotgun blasts to stop the old fool, the policeman said. Third Proude told the policeman that he had killed a powerful tribal shaman. The bones of the allied circus commander were returned to the cedar circus and dropped in the red cedar water near the head of his father First Proude. (14)

Second Proude's murder recalls the murder of Crazy Horse and Sitting Bull by colonial tribal police in the wake of the Battle of the Greasy Grass (Little Bighorn). It recalls the routine violence enacted historically against Indigenous peoples of the Americas in the course of an international genocide that continues today. However, the refusal of Second Proude to stop walking to Wounded Knee even after being shot represents the continuing resistance of Indigenous peoples to settler colonialism.

"The women taught [Third Proude] to seek peace and avoid conflicts." His motto: "Outwit but never kill evil . . . evil revenge is blind and cannot be appeased by the living. The tricksters and warrior clowns have stopped more evil and violence with their wit than have lovers with their lusts and fools with the power and rage" (14–15). Third Proude was killed by lightning. Over the course of his career, Vizenor appears ambivalent about the politics of AIM, as the difference between the "Letter to the Reader" and this passage, which emphasizes trickster resistance, suggests. But *Bearheart*'s approbation of AIM's declaration of a "new pantribal political nation" points to at least a partial affirmation of the movement.

Following in the steps of his father, "Fourth Proude Cedarfair, the last leader of the cedar nation, avoided word wars and terminal creeds. [. . .] The sense of peace at the cedar nation endured for more than a decade" before the federal government, supported by Jordan Coward, the federally recognized tribal president, came to claim the cedar trees for fuel in the energy crisis: "When federal officials arrived with an executive order reserving half of all the timber on the reservations, Coward attached the cedar nation to meet the demands of the government" (15, 23). Thus, the federal government, with the reservation's backing, reasserts its national boundaries. Coward, addressing Proude as a "stinking bear," makes the end of cedar sovereignty explicit: "'This cedar nation shit is done,' Coward hollered in a febrile rage. 'Pack up your goddamn circus crusade and leave our reservation. You have never been welcome here. The government is going to split this goddamn circus into little sticks and burn it for paperwork. [. . .] The laws have changed and you will never find a crusader to help you in a hundred miles'" (24). Here utopian time (the sovereignty of the cedar nation) collapses into the real time ("the laws have changed") of federal Indian law: "The federals opened a plain green federal envelope . . . and recited the executive order attaching the cedar circus trees" (25).

Proude responds by asserting cedar national sovereignty: "This is a sovereign nation. [. . .] These trees were the first to grow here, the first to speak of living on this earth. . . . These trees are sovereign. We are cedar and we are not your citizens. . . . We are the cedar and the guardians of the sacred directions into the fourth world. . . . Can you see and feel how we shun your indifference to our lives" (26). These words echo the declaration of Tuscarora leader Clinton Rickard, who, in repudiating the Indian Citizenship Act, "articulated a political identity that explicitly stood for defying and crossing the boundaries of settler-states such as the United States and Canada."[8] While Bruyneel, from whom I am citing, understands Rickard's position as carving out a third space of sovereignty within the federal system, I read the position in conjunction with Vizenor as proclaiming that there is no space within the system for Indigenous sovereignty—and I mean full sovereignty, with Indigenous autonomy linked to self-determination, not the subordinate sovereignty of federal Indian law—precisely because Indigenous sovereignty is thinking from a different place than Western sovereignty. It thinks from a place where the trees are living beings that can speak and assert their sovereignty, which implicitly erases the boundaries between human and nonhuman, asserting, as I have noted, the kinship relation between these realms that federal Indian law in cases like *Lyng* denies but that Native literature asserts in resistance to settler colonialism.

Explaining the historical precedence of the cedar nation's sovereignty, Proude continues his address to the federal representatives:

> Our families have lived in this circus with these cedar trees for more than a hundred years. People in our families have died defending the rights of these sovereign trees and now you come to tell me from green paper about citizenship and government responsibilities. [. . .] You speak in the language of newspapers and false pictures. Your speech has nothing but words to see what you have said. I did not read or listen to the words that spoke to you from that green paper. [. . .] We will not listen to your possessive voices. We will not bring harm to our visions and dreams with your word wars . . . if you choose to speak with me alone in your personal voices then I will listen. (26)

What is articulated in this passage is the opposition between the written and the oral, between the rhetoric of government documents ("green paper"), the "possessive voices" of property, and the "personal *voices*" of "visions and dreams" that assert precedence on the land. But this is Proude's last colloquy with the feds. Faced, it seems, with the combined force of federal and tribal colonial power, Proude and his wife, Rosina Parent, decide to leave the cedar circus. At this moment, Vizenor stresses the permeable boundary between bear and human: "Rosina was awakened by the sound of his roaring bear voice. [. . .]

The sound of his roaring voice echoed across the lake and up the river past the boundaries of the cedar nation. Standing naked on the *migis* he roared ha ha ha haaaa and roared until the eastern night turned deep blue. Proude dressed, waved to the seven crows and walked with his wife back to the cabin," which Jordan Coward prepares to burn down, believing the two are sleeping inside because, in trickster style, "they stuffed their bed with shadowless shapes," deceiving Coward and his cohort (32). But Fourth Proude and Rosina were gone: "Fourth Proude, the last old man of the cedar circus, listened until evil and the fire had died in peace. Tribal leaders were not honest enough to bear the dreams, he said, and then he turned the past under when he passed through the brown cedar ghosts on the border of the circus. The cedar would be alone for the first time in four generations" (33).

Having been forced out of the cedar circus by the feds in league with the reservation government, Proude and Rosina begin a trip, a trickster trajectory, across the country, crossing boundaries of all kinds, emblematized by the crossing of boundaries between species, the nature/culture divide. Vizenor uses this trajectory to point to this divide, the separation of nature from culture, which is at the heart of the human and environmental catastrophe we call the West.

The life at their first stop, the "scapehouse," where they are greeted by trickster Benito (Bigfoot) Saint Plumero, represents this trajectory:

> There was a circular parade of humans and animals and birds in conversations from the kitchen to the scapehouse dining room. Sparrows and bluebirds and crows fled down the halls between rooms and rode back on the heads and shoulders of the humans bearing food to the tables. Birds sang in the parade, humans hummed, crows crowed, the animals barked and moaned, hissed and sniffed from the food pens. The scapehouse smelled of chicken and kitten and fish, nettles and yams, dumplings, carrots and greens, and several shapes and colors of breads. (43)

Just as the odors of the scapehouse are blended, so are the sounds of humans and animals, who exist at one moment, harmoniously and communally, in the same space. This harmony is not contradicted but intensified by a certain violence: "Cannibalism was practical in the scapehouse of the weirds and sensitives [the thirteen women poets who founded the scapehouse]. The women agreed that their bodies would be their food. The women eat what is known, what and who is part of their lives in the scapehouse, the plants and animals, and so their lives are continued in the cellular consciousness of the living energies in the scapehouse" (37).

Writing in *The Poetics of Imperialism* of Montaigne's essay "Of Cannibals," I argue that Montaigne projected Indigenous cannibalism, the consuming of one's enemies after death, alleged by Europeans among the Indigenous Tupi, as a figure of kinship, a way of taking the other into one's self, of erasing the border between the self and the other. I understand the passage cited here as focusing the same figure, one of intimacy that erases the boundary between nature and culture. Such an intimacy is experienced by traditional Indigenous cultures, as a matter of fact: "'Death is death and food is food,' said Sister Caprice. 'The cells of kittens [stuffed kittens are one of the dishes served at dinner] are poised no more from fear of the chopping block than from games on the kitchen floor'" (45). Or the sister might have said "food requires death," which is plain enough in subsistence societies, where one hunts for one's food, but nevertheless where one is bound by kinship to the animals who supply that food. Anishinaabe scholar Basil Johnston writes of the intimate connection between subsistence and the spirit and intellect: "It has long been assumed that people who were preoccupied with material needs and wants would have little interest in matters of the spirit and the mind. On the contrary, it was this very mode of life, this simple way of meeting simple needs, that awakened in man and woman a consciousness that there were realities and presences in life other than the corporeal and the material."[9] In fact, in the world that capitalism made and sustains, the world of factory farms, alienation from the source of food is alienation from the spirit through the instrumentalization of the intellect. What Montaigne knew was that what the West termed "savage" was civilized in relation to Western savagery. In this respect, Vizenor makes a distinction between the cannibalism of the scapehouse and the cannibalism of "whitecannibals," whom the tribal pilgrims encounter on the road. When offered a heart left over from one of the murdered victims of a whitecannibal, the hungry pilgrims are tempted, but Proude says: "We cannot eat this human heart. [...] We cannot take the vision of violence and the violence of the flesh without rituals together in our bodies.... That heart has no power but evil to live in our bodies.... The animals will choose for themselves" (175). The specificity is crucial here. It isn't that we cannot eat a human heart. Rather, we cannot eat "*this* human heart," because of how it was taken: with "evil" intent and "without rituals together in our bodies"—that is, without a communal, ceremonial context of the kind practiced by the women of the scapehouse. In contrast, these whitecannibals are termed "food fascists" (176) whose prey are served, fittingly, at a capitalist enterprise: the "Ponca Witch Hunt Restaurant and Fast Foods" (175).

As in trickster narratives, the scene in the scapehouse shifts without transition from food and death to sex (the three foundations of life). The meal ends in an orgy, described graphically by Vizenor:

> Sister Flame, who had been licking her bright lips, drew Bigfoot into her crotch under the table. Then he rubbed his nose in the soft hair and brushed the stubble on her legs with his hands. The dogs were nudging him under the arms. [...] The women of the scapehouse were moaning under the lips and tongue and fingers of the clown. [...] The women were moaning and touching each other. Bigfoot climbed out from under the table and was standing over three women on the floor. The women were unwrapping the red velvet leg bands and pulling down his leather trousers. When the leather fell from his buttocks his penis lifted like a proud president [jackson, the name of his penis]. Sister Flame whistled hail to the chief as he kneeled between her legs and pumped her until she trembled in deep orgasm. Then president jackson penetrated the other women in turn in a circle on the floor around the table. While the president ducked through slick lips and hair and other sensitives sucked his tight testicles until the president throbbed and spurted. [...] "These are survivors," said Proude. (45)

Vizenor is trying to achieve something in passages of uncensored sexuality like this, which are repeated throughout the novel, that is perhaps impossible: the creation in a modern—or indeed postmodern—idiom of trickster transgressions. Vizenor's purpose is not to shock; we can only imagine that traditional Indigenous audiences were/are not shocked by narratives that were/are an integral part of the culture. Rather, what we have here is matter-of-factly comic. It offers a burlesque of our ordinary drives and desires—a burlesque to remind us of who we are, including the genocidal drive represented in the erect, rapacious penis, president andrew jackson, the notorious Indian killer, who signed the Indian Removal Act that instituted the Trail of Tears, the deadly ethnic cleansing of the so-called Five Civilized Tribes:

Choctaw, Seminole, Chickasaw, Muscogee (Creek), and Cherokee. The burlesque of "president jackson," reduced in print from upper- to lowercase letters and from a whole body to a penis, suggests that part of the genocidal drive comes from a sexual drive thwarted and sublimated into a drive for power. In the after-dinner orgy, sexuality is clearly not sublimated. It is allowed to express itself as such, so President Andrew Jackson can become president jackson, an ordinary (lowercase)—that is, sexual—human being (the part standing for the whole) seeking pleasure rather than power (though certainly pleasure is a kind of power) in killing Indians and enforcing the genocidal legal act of removal.[10] As Proude notes, "These are survivors." Survival here, it is suggested, has to do with transgressing the borders of law and life established by settler-colonial regimes of containment, of which U.S. federal Indian law is paramount.

Vizenor's trickster pilgrimage, like all trickster tales, is orgiastic and violent. As noted, there are in *Bearheart* life-affirming orgasmic and violent forces. But the boundary between what is life affirming and what is death dealing is permeable. In the novel, that boundary is transgressed by the hordes of murderous "whitepeople" that the thirteen tribal pilgrims encounter on their pilgrimage, so that by the end of their journey, only five of them are left, with four of the eight who do not make it murdered by whitepeople. The representative transgressor of this boundary between life and death is "the evil gambler," Sir Cecil Staples, whose "culture is death," the culture of the nation-state: "'What holds us together now is what held the nation together for two centuries,' wheezed the evil gambler. [. . .] 'The constitutional government and the political organizations were deceptive games of evil. . . . Personal games became public programs. National games that preserved and protected the causes of evil'" (101, 132).

In "Sacred Chance: Gambling and the Contemporary Native American Indian Novel," Paul Pasquaretta notes that

> traditional gambling stories and their attendant practices provide a ritual site where the forces of assimilation are contested. In each, a good gambler is pitted against an evil opponent. The evil opponent is associated with both European American culture and the evil gamblers of Native American tradition. In this way, gambling stories provide a framework to assign value and difference. Because these values and differences are imagined within an indigenous paradigm

that "anthropologizes" European American culture, the gambling ritual also provides a means to theorize about the role traditional belief systems might play in resisting, if not defeating, the demands of a colonial occupation. [...] Despite centuries of cultural assault, ritual gambling has remained among the most important of native traditions. In modern times, the gambling story is important both as a feature of traditional culture and myth and as a theory of present conditions and possibility. [...] Native North American gambling stories are usually related to gambling practices, and, by extension, to a particularly indigenous manner of negotiating chance and uncertainty. The stories often recall a time of crisis, feature a hero and his evil opponent, and include a high-stakes game of chance. This game is eventually won by the hero; he defeats his powerful opponent through the exercise of wisdom, courage and self-sacrifice.[11]

In the three novels he is analyzing—Silko's *Ceremony,* Erdrich's *Love Medicine,* and Vizenor's *Bearheart*—Pasquaretta notes the relationship between gambling and Indian identity: "In each case, traditional gambling referents inform a particular attitude towards 'Indianness,' an orientation that distinguishes the Indian from the non-Indian, the indigenous from the alien and the tribal from the non-tribal."[12] The relationship to identity is thus not biological (blood) but cultural, with the relationship to a particular practice stemming from a particular narrative. In the case of *Bearheart,* as Pasquaretta remarks, the underlying narrative involves the trickster Manabozo (Nana'b'oozoo), who "contests the gambler during a time of crisis, and the stakes of the game are extremely high; the destiny of Manabozho and the salvation of the Anishinaabe people depend upon a single chance. With courage and good humor Manabozho confronts his opponent. He consents to stake his life on the outcome of the game and agrees to the Nita Ataged's [the evil gambler's] terms."[13]

At this point in *Bearheart,* the tribal pilgrims are traveling in a commandeered "postal truck" and as such are looking for gasoline, of which the evil gambler, "the monarch of unleaded gasoline," with his "heinous horde" of "mixedblood mercenaries," is the sole possessor (102, 109–10). The figure of the capitalist in a seller's market is clear enough, and the title "monarch" denotes imperialism. But in this case, the seller will only release his commodity if the buyer gambles for five gallons of gasoline, putting up his, her, or their life as the bet. The presence of mixedblood mercenaries on the gambler's side signals the situation to be colonial, where a certain segment of the colonized side with the colonizer in the interest of survival and/or gain. The game to be played is modeled on the Anishinaabe "dish game" (110).

The pilgrims play a number game to decide which of them will gamble with the evil gambler. The winner is Lilith Mae Ferrier, who forms an interspecies love triangle with her two boxer dogs. But Lilith Mae loses to the gambler. Winning, then, can be losing as the boundary between the two blurs: "The problem was in the meaning of chance. Chance did not have a chance. 'Nothing is chance,' said Proude. 'There is no chance in chance. [. . .] Chances are terminal creeds'" (110–11). The powers that be—the evil gamblers—would like the masses to think that the terminal creed of capitalism gives everyone a chance, when in fact the rules of the game are fixed in favor of the house. Within the bounds of federal Indian law—represented in *Bearheart* by white people and mixedblood mercenaries like Jordan Coward—the Indians don't have a chance. In her book *Journeying Forward: Dreaming First Nations Independence,* Canadian Mohawk legal scholar Patricia Monture-Angus notes "that law contains no answers but is in fact a very large and very real part of the problem Aboriginal people continue to face. Law is one of the instruments through which colonialism continues to flow."[14]

After Lilith Mae gambles her life away—which Proude will redeem, only to find that Lilith Mae has self-immolated, along with her boxers (135)—Proude enters the game room: "Proude Cedarfair could smell ammonia when he entered the trailer. He waited near the door. It was warm from bodies. The trailer smelled of chance and loss, of promises and failures. The pungent odor of false civilizations, foolish terminal creeds and the bare visions of death. Living smells sweet and gives other lives breath. Death has the smell of cities and machines and plastics. There was death and evil in the altar trailer" (120). What Proude smells is capitalism—the culture of death, profit over people, profit at any cost. It is important to emphasize again here that U.S. federal Indian law, like the U.S. Constitution, is grounded in the logic of property law, which is the foundation of capitalism. The ur-case in federal Indian law, *Johnson v. M'Intosh* (1823), which I have already discussed, makes this clear in that its decision to confer title to the Native land in question is grounded in the translation of all Native land, which is traditionally a nonfungible living part of the community, into property—

that is, land bounded by strict borders and *titled* to individuals or corporations, so that as a commodity, it is fit for the market, exactly like the gasoline the evil gambler is offering to trade in the market of life and death. Fittingly, as an implied figure of capitalism, the evil gambler readily, even proudly, admits that his "*business* has been to bring people to their death" (my italics) but that

> killing people now has lost the excitement it once had. . . . Why? Because, I suppose, killing is just too easy now, thousands of people do it everyday to others and themselves. Nothing new. No surprises. That thin plastic film known as social control hanging over the savage urge to kill was dissolved when the government failed and the economic world collapsed. What reason was there not to kill when money no longer worked? The government and private business, the business bigger than government, started this indifference toward death with their pollution and industrial poisons. [. . .] Thousands of people have died the slow death from disfiguring cancers because the government failed to protect the public. The government tortured people and sanctioned killing. [. . .] The worst part of the government killing people is the indifference. [. . .] When the values of material possessions were useless without petroleum, when all the motors and gears stopped, when the coin returns no longer returned, there were no common values to bind people together and hold down their needs for violence and the experience of death. [. . .] Death was too simple then. [. . .] What does it mean to know evil power when love and the power to do good has died in the hands of indifferent bureaucrats? (126–27)

Published in 1978, *Bearheart* both represents the status quo and predicts what has come to pass; we are now in an era of endless war and climate collapse, of growing poverty and income inequality, which was just beginning its meteoric rise at the time. In the world of *Bearheart*, the only "common values" for society at large are economic ones, so when those "material values were useless [. . .] there were no common values to bind people together." The boundary between the pre- and postapocalyptic worlds is effectively erased in the evil gambler's assessment of the world, which is the world the trickster pilgrims are traversing and trying to escape.

Following the trajectory of the Nana'b'oozoo and the gambler narrative, Proude must gamble with the evil gambler, who asserts, "'We are equals at the game of good and evil mister proud. Nothing is lost between equals.' [...] 'But we are not equals,' Proude responded. 'We are not bound in common experiences. . . . We do not share a common vision. Your values and language come from evil. Your power is adverse to living. Your culture is death'" (132). Within the context of capitalist exploitation, Proude makes a clear distinction between Indigenous and capitalist values—a distinction that cannot be collapsed the way, as I have noted, the hunters and breeders collapse the distinction Belladonna will try to make between tribal and Western values in asserting Indian identity at Orion, precisely because Belladonna posits her argument as being outside of the two opposed economic contexts, where the clear border between kinship and capitalist economic values cannot be erased, even as settler colonialism strives to erase it in its struggle to eliminate the Native.

As the game proceeds, to Proude's assertion about values, the evil gambler responds: "And so we are equal opposites." Proude replies: "Death is not the opposite of living, but you are the opposite of living. . . . Your evil is malignant. The energies to live are never malignant" (132). What Proude asserts here implicitly is, as I have noted, that in Indigenous epistemologies, there is no border between nature and culture; death and living are integral. In contrast, in the evil gambler's epistemology, which is to say the epitome of the West's way of thinking, death and living are alienated, antagonistic, so if we are attuned to this conversation, we understand that the basis of the culture of death is the nature/culture divide. Put on the defensive by Proude's assertions, the evil gambler "wheeze[s]": "Splendid words. [...] Your kindness overwhelms me. [...] You are not in a good place to make tribal pronunciamentos" (132). But Proude does not respond because he is psychically elsewhere, immersed in the dish game's ceremony: "Proude raised the dish in ceremonial gestures to the four directions while he voiced an honoring message to the morning and the circle of magical dreams" (132). Clearly for Proude, gaming is ceremonial. The dish game in the novel entails dropping the dish, which contains four figures representing the four directions, so that the four figures remain upright (in balance) when the dish is dropped. For the evil gambler, in contrast, gambling is the glue of the capitalist system, which is collapsing:

> "What holds us together now is what held the nation together for two centuries," wheezed the evil gambler as he knocked down the

four directions. "The constitutional government and the political organizations were deceptive games of evil. . . . Personal games became public programs. National games that preserved and protected the causes of evil. . . . What happens between us when the game ends is what happened to the government when the political games were exposed . . . nothing! Nothing but the loss of faith among gambling fools. Nothing but chance. Fools and the games with their fantasies that living is more than death and evil is less than goodness. . . . Winning is losing." (132)

The evil gambler raises the question of what happens to the capitalist system when there is a "loss of faith among gambling fools," when the "fantasies that living is more than death and evil is less than goodness" (132) no longer command the belief of the masses—that is, when the ideology that makes sense of the narrative of the nation no longer commands the allegiance of the people. Capitalism, the culture of death, functions on the denial of death, whereas in traditional Indigenous thought, living is not more than death; death is an integral part of living. As I have noted, trickster tales tell us that evil and goodness are integral as well; they are not opposites but complements. "Winning is losing" in a system where the world is not integrated through extended kinship but divided into winners and losers, because ultimately, the world that *Bearheart* represents resonates with W. B. Yeats's famous words: "Things fall apart; the centre cannot hold; / Mere anarchy is loosed upon the world." These lines, from the poem "The Second Coming," were published in 1920, during the Irish war of independence from Britain, an anticolonial war. In *Bearheart*, the evil gambler is a colonial figure, and the tribal pilgrims from Proude's resistance in the cedar circus to governmental and reservation authority are anticolonial fighters in the form of tricksters. As such, Proude, following the narrative trajectory of Nana'b'oozoo, defeats the evil gambler: "Sir Cecil Staples, picked up the dish for his third and last toss of the game. When he pitched the four directions and brought the burnished dish down in a sudden movement, confident good and evil were in a strange balance, Proude made a teasing whistle on the wind. . . . The dish cracked against the cabinet and the four directions wobbled and fell. All four directions fell forward into the dish" (132).

As opposites within Western ideology, good and evil cannot be balanced, because "evil is less than goodness." It is only within trickster epistemology, as complementary forces, that good and evil achieve balance, so that in the last toss of the evil gambler, who is the antithesis of the trickster, the four directions collapse. Proude comments, "You have lost the power and the balance of evil. [. . .] Our game has ended and the pilgrims have not lost their spirit to death and the evil hands of your darkness" (133). But the evil gambler, seeking to have the last play, replies: "You are still a fool . . . There is no gasoline. Your own selfish needs have brought you here with fantasies of winning gasoline. Do you think I would still be alive with a secret reservoir of gasoline? [. . .] You are still losers. . . . Terminal believers in your own goodness" (133). For the evil gambler, the world is still the capitalist-colonial world of winners and losers and of terminal creeds. But "Fourth Proude Cedarfair smiled and picked up the four directions from the dish and walked out of the altar trailer of evil" (133). For Proude, the game was not fundamentally about winning or losing but about resistance to the evil gambler's world.

In *Bearheart,* the resistance of tricksters is located in language: "Second Proude has won his war, he had fought in the word wars of the whiteman and for the sacred dominion in the cedar" (14). Trickster resistance, then, obtains in what I have termed "thinking from a different place"[15]—a place, as noted previously, not of semantic oppositions but of complementarities, so that the notion of winner versus loser, for example, which is the fundamental opposition of Western law grounded in capitalism, does not exist in systems of restorative justice, which I have reviewed. In this context, Proude's gambling with the evil gambler takes the form of a Western trial, within which Proude is the winner at the same time that he is thinking of the contest in different terms so that when at the end of the game the gambler insists on using oppositional terms ("You are still losers"), Proude's response is to smile, perhaps at his victory, perhaps at the absurdity of the gambler's oppositional language, and "walk [. . .] out of the altar trailer of evil."

Western trials, which are all trial by combat, are a form of gambling within a set of rules where chance (whose narrative, after evidence has been submitted, will the judge or jury believe?) plays a significant role. The Western trial is a zero-sum game where, unlike restorative justice, balance (justice) may be the stated concern but as the trial of poor, minoritized people demonstrate is unevenly applied and too often geared to the ability to afford effective counsel. In the case of U.S. federal

Indian law—a law whose clear concern is not even justice but the containment of Native sovereignty—the rules of the game are insurmountably stacked in favor of the house. *Bearheart* begins with resistance to this law, the containment of the cedar circus within the confines of a federal reservation, and in the tricksters' pilgrimage, they encounter manifestations of the law, both explicitly, as in the case of the hunters and breeders' subversion of the definition of "Indian," and implicitly, in the form of the evil gambler, who represents a game stacked against all comers with the loser doomed to die—until Proude turns the tables on the house. Pasquaretta explains this turn as resistance to the colonization of language I have been analyzing:

> Here Proude disallows the hegemonic binaries that inform Sir Cecil's terminal creed. Assuming an all inclusive world view, this evil gambler, attempting to speak for Proude, fails to recognize fundamental questions of difference. His cultural narcissism is illustrated during the game. Throwing against Proude his figures fall into the cracked center of the dish. Proude's figures, however, stand back to back, facing out toward the world beyond the self. He wins the contest because he does not gamble for sheer amusement, power, or gain. [. . .] Proude also gambles to defeat linguistic colonization.[16]

In *Bearheart*, then, "survival on the interstate was more verbal than spiritual" (161). The world returned to one grounded in oral culture:

> Oral traditions were honored. Families welcomed the good tellers of stories, the wandering historians of follies and tragedies. Readers and writers were seldom praised but the travelling raconteurs were one form of the new shamans on the interstates. Facts and the need for facts had died with newspapers and politics. Nonfacts were more believable. The listeners traveled with the tellers through the same frames of time and space. The telling was in the listening. [. . .] Stories were told about fools and tricksters and human animals. Myth became the center of meaning again. (162)

In his memoir of his fieldwork among the oral cultures of Brazilian Indians in the 1930s, *Tristes Tropiques,* journeying with the Nambikwara, anthropologist Claude Lévi-Strauss hypothesizes that the origin of writing is "concomitant" not with the preservation and expansion of knowledge but with the creation of cities and empires, that is the integration of large numbers of individuals into a political system, and their grading into castes or classes. [...] It seems to have favoured the exploitation of human beings rather than their enlightenment. [...] The fight against illiteracy is therefore connected with an increase in governmental authority over the citizens. Everyone must be able to read, so the government can say: ignorance of the law is no excuse. [...] Through gaining access to knowledge stored in libraries, these people have also become vulnerable to the still greater proportion of lies propagated in printed documents.[17]

Envisioning as it does the dissolution of print culture, the passage cited above from *Bearheart*—indeed the thrust of the whole novel—intersects with this passage from *Tristes Tropiques*. As noted, *Bearheart*'s project is "linguistic decolonization," the final step of which is the return to the storytelling traditions of oral cultures, where the hierarchy of author and reader is dissolved and the two become one: "The telling was in the listening." In this borderless "time and place," one is freed from "the need for facts," which "had died with newspapers and politics" (162). In *Bearheart*, the death of politics is marked by the collapse of government bureaucracies and their system of federal laws based in "facts"— the "fact" of conquest, for example, which grounds federal Indian law. In a passage cited previously, Taiaiake Alfred suggests that the "fact" of conquest is in fact a "myth of conquest" supporting "the maintenance of state dominance over indigenous peoples."[18] The passage from *Bearheart* implicitly points to the necessarily cultural context of what are determined to be facts in its linking of facts to Western print culture. That is, in oral cultures, the facts are myths (stories), but these myths are not myths in the Western sense. In his 2008 collection *Survivance*, Vizenor gives us a telling example of the strategic necessity of cultural context in the court testimony of Anishinaabe Charles Aubid:

> This inspired storier was a sworn witness in federal court that autumn more than thirty years ago in Minneapolis, Minnesota. He raised his hand, listened to the oath for the first time in the language of the Anishinaabe, Chippewa, or Ojibwe, and then waved, an ironic gesture of the oath, at United States District Judge Miles Lord. [...]
> Aubid was a witness in a dispute with the federal government over the right to regulate the manoomin, wild rice, harvest on Rice Lake National Wildlife Refuge in Minnesota. Federal agents had as-

sumed the authority to determine the wild rice season and to regulate the harvest, a bureaucratic action that decried a native sense of survivance and sovereignty.

Aubid, who was eighty-six years old at the time, testified through translators that he was present as a young man when the federal agents told old John Squirrel that the Anishinaabe would always have control of the manoomin harvest. Aubid told the judge that the Anishinaabe always understood their rights by stories. John Squirrel was there in memories, a storied presence of native survivance. The court could have heard the testimony in a visual trace of a parol agreement, a function of discourse, both relevant and necessary.

Justice Lord agreed with the objection of the federal attorney that the testimony was hearsay and therefore not admissible and explained that the court could not hear as evidence what a dead man said, only the actual experiences of the witness. "John Squirrel is dead," said the judge. "And you can't say what a dead man said."

Aubid turned brusquely in the witness chair, bothered by what the judge had said about John Squirrel. Aubid pointed at the legal books on the bench, and then in English, his second language, he shouted that those books contained stories of dead white men. "Why should I believe what a white man says, when you don't believe John Squirrel?" Judge Lord was deferential, amused by the analogy of native stories to court testimony, judicial decisions, precedent, and hearsay. "You've got me there," he said, and then considered the testimony of other Anishinaabe witnesses.[19]

I emphasize that Judge Lord is an anomaly in the annals of U.S. federal Indian law, where oral testimony has typically not been admitted in the courts or has not been accorded the same validity as written documents. Aubid points to the irony governing the disciplinary separation of law and literature, which is that Western law is itself nothing but a set of stories, distinguishing itself from literature by function more than form. That is, on the one hand, when the West speaks of literature today, it tends to mean nonfunctional, in the sense of aesthetic, fictions of one kind or another: novels, poems, plays, short stories, belles lettres, and other texts that have no immediate practical force in the world. On the other hand, legal fictions have a function; they are instrumental in the criminal and civil justice system.[20] In the West, law is not understood as literature—that is to say, as stories—unless, of course, one studies it as such, concentrating on narrative structure, rhetorical agendas, and evasions and contradictions—that is, as fictions in a literary, not legal, sense. Put another way, today in the West, the law and its fictions have a particular political or juridical force that literature does not possess because of the way the West has increasingly compartmentalized knowledge over time. This contrasts with traditional Indigenous life, in which, both philosophically and practically, stories have what the West might understand as juridical force, which is to say they prescribe behavior.[21] Colonialism has skewed traditional thought, not thwarted it, precisely because the traditional is dynamic, adopting without necessarily adapting. Within an Indigenous cultural context, we can understand U.S. federal Indian law as the myth of Native conquest and Native literatures as the deconstruction of that myth.[22]

NOTES

INTRODUCTION

1. Linda Hogan, *Solar Storms* (New York: Simon & Schuster, 1995), 325.
2. See William Apess, *On Our Own Ground: The Complete Writings of William Apess, a Pequot*, ed. Barry O'Connell (Amherst: University of Massachusetts Press, 1992).
3. See Chadwick Allen, "Productive Tensions: Trans/national, Trans/Indigenous," in *The World, the Text, and the Indian: Global Dimensions of Native American Literature*, ed. Scott Richard Lyons (Albany: State University of New York Press, 2017), 239–56.
4. Elizabeth Cook-Lynn, "Editor's Commentary," *Wicazo Sa Review* 12 (1997): 7.
5. Abraham Chapman, ed., *Literature of the American Indians: Views and Interpretations* (New York: New American Library, 1975). In this volume are Constance Rourke, "The Indian Background of American Theatricals" (1942; 256–65); and Lawrence C. Wroth, "The Indian Treaty as Literature" (1928; 324–37).
6. Rourke, "Indian Background," 259, 258.
7. Wroth, "Indian Treaty," 324, 337.
8. Wroth, "Indian Treaty," 327.
9. Michael Leroy Oberg, *Peacemakers: The Iroquois, the United States, and the Treaty of Canadaigua, 1794* (Oxford: Oxford University Press, 2016), 1.
10. Wroth, "Indian Treaty," 327.
11. Wroth, "Indian Treaty," 327.
12. Wroth, "Indian Treaty," 326.
13. Joseph Bruchac, "Contemporary Native American Writing: An Overview," in *Handbook of Native American Literature*, ed. Andrew Wiget (New York: Garland, 1996), 322.
14. Wroth, "Indian Treaty," 327.
15. Chief Justice Marshall refers to tribes as "domestic dependent nations" in *Cherokee Nation v. Georgia*, 30 U.S. 1 (1831) at 17.

1. THE COLONIAL CONSTRUCTION OF INDIAN COUNTRY

1. There are 227 federally recognized Alaska Native villages, which, along with the 347 federally recognized tribes in the lower forty-eight states, total 574 federally recognized Native communities in the United States. There is also one federally recognized Indian tribe in Alaska: the Metlakatla Indian Community of the Annette Island Reserve in southeastern Alaska. See the Bureau of Indian Affairs website at https://www.bia.gov/bia (accessed April 8, 2023).
2. See Roy M. Huhndorf and Shari M. Huhndorf, "Alaska Native Politics since the Alaska Native Claims Settlement Act," in "Sovereignty, Indigeneity, and the Law," ed. Eric Cheyfitz, N. Bruce Duthu, and Shari M. Huhndorf,

special issue, *South Atlantic Quarterly* 110, no. 2 (2011): 385–401; Cecily Hilleary, "Native Hawaiians Divided on Federal Recognition," *VOA (Voice of America),* February 7, 2019, https://www.voanews.com/a/native-hawaiians-divided-on-federal-recognition/4775275.html (accessed April 10, 2023). For a detailed account of settler colonialism in Hawaii, see Haunani-Kay Trask, *From a Native Daughter: Colonialism and Sovereignty in Hawai'i,* rev. ed. (Honolulu: University of Hawai'i Press, 1999). Trask writes the following about the current state of Native Hawaiian lands: "The Hawaiian Monarchy provided for future generations by bequeathing their personal entitlements to land in trust for the Hawaiian people.... These private trust lands and assets are currently managed pursuant to State and Federal law, despite the fact that they are entitlements of Hawaiians.... Hawaiian beneficiaries have never had any opportunity to set policy for the administration of these assets" (230–31).

3. Joanne Barker, *Native Acts: Law, Recognition, and Cultural Authenticity* (Durham, N.C.: Duke University Press, 2011), Kindle.

4. Keynote remarks of Kevin Gover, Assistant Secretary–Indian Affairs, delivered September 8, 2000, on the 175th anniversary of the establishment of the Bureau of Indian Affairs. Gover's remarks can be found by searching for this title on the BIA website.

5. Diane Glancy, *Pushing the Bear: A Novel of the Trail of Tears* (New York: Harcourt Brace, 1996). Glancy also published a sequel, *Pushing the Bear: After the Trail of Tears* (Norman: University of Oklahoma Press, 2009).

6. See Francis Paul Prucha, *Documents of United States Indian Policy,* 3rd ed. (Lincoln: University of Nebraska Press, 2000), docs. 33, 49, 54, 56. This is an indispensable volume for anyone seeking to familiarize themselves with the history of federal Indian law and thus is indispensable as a reference for anyone reading U.S. Native literatures.

7. Prucha, *Documents,* doc. 104.

8. Prucha, *Documents,* doc. 141.

9. Felix Cohen, *Felix Cohen's Handbook of Federal Indian Law* (1942; reprint, Albuquerque: University of New Mexico Press, n.d.), 216. This edition is a reprint of the original 1942 edition.

10. Cohen, *Felix Cohen's Handbook,* 216.

11. Keith Richotte Jr., *Federal Indian Law and Policy: An Introduction* (St. Paul, Minn.: West Academic, 2020 [Falmouth Institute, January 1, 1994]), 99.

12. A comprehensive history of allotment is available at the Indian Land Tenure Foundation's website, https://iltf.org/land-issues/history/ (accessed April 10, 2023).

13. See George Russell, *The American Indian Digest* (Falmouth Institue, January 1, 1994), 33. I have found it difficult to locate the amount of trust allotment land, but in 1993, Russell gives the amount of federally recognized reservation trust land at 55 million acres, which has not increased substantially in 2022. He lists 44 million acres of that land as "tribal trust lands" and the remaining 11 million acres as "individually owned." I am assuming that the land that is "individually owned" is trust allotment land because it is included in the total amount of Native trust land but is "owned" (that is, held by) individuals for whom the

government remains the trustee. A search of the BIA website did not yield information on this subject.

14. *Cobell v. Babbitt*, 52 F. Supp. 2d 11 (D.D.C. 1999) at 18 lists the number of beneficiaries as 300,000.

15. John Ahni Schertow, "*Cobell v. Norton*: Overview and Chronology," https://intercontinentalcry.org/cobell-v-norton-overview-and-chronology/ (accessed April 10, 2023). The named defendant in the suit changed in accord with succeeding secretaries of the Interior over the thirteen-year duration of the litigation, which began when Bruce Babbitt was secretary, succeeded by Gale Norton, then Dirk Kempthorne, and finally Ken Salazar.

16. "Cobell v. Salazar," Wikipedia, https://en.wikipedia.org/wiki/Cobell_v._Salazar (accessed April 10, 2023).

17. Quoted in Richotte, *Federal Indian Law and Policy*, 304. Richotte is quoting from *Cobell v. Norton*, 229 F.R.D. 5, 7 (D.D.C. 2005).

18. Brendan Tobin, *Indigenous Peoples, Customary Law, and Human Rights—Why Living Law Matters* (New York: Routledge, 2014), Kindle.

19. "Plenary power" gives Congress the absolute legislative power to rule in Indian matters. Richotte, *Federal Indian Law and Policy*, 305.

20. James Warren, "A Victory for Native Americans?" *Atlantic*, June 7, 2010, https://www.theatlantic.com/national/archive/2010/06/a-victory-for-native-americans/57769/.

21. Frances Washburn, *The Sacred White Turkey* (Lincoln: University of Nebraska Press, 2010), 34.

22. Washburn, *Sacred White Turkey*, 80.

23. Washburn, *Sacred White Turkey*, 80–81.

24. For a discussion of the trust relationship, see David E. Wilkins and K. Tsianina Lomawaima, *Uneven Ground: American Indian Sovereignty and Federal Law* (Norman: University of Oklahoma Press, 2001). Among other legal scholars, Wilkins and Lomawaima cite the work of Vine Deloria Jr.: "Deloria and others decry the fact that there is no agreed-upon definition of the federal-tribal 'trust relationship.' The contest over the trust doctrine's meaning puts tribes at risk. They cannot be assured that their rights will be protected by—or from—their 'trustee'" (67).

25. Leslie Marmon Silko, *Ceremony* (New York: Penguin, 1977), 125.

26. Quoted in Cohen, *Felix Cohen's Handbook*, 154.

27. Francis Paul Prucha, *The Great Father: The United States Government and the American Indians* (Lincoln: University of Nebraska Press, 1984), 2: 673–76.

28. Alan Macfarlane, *The Origin of English Individualism: The Family, Property, and Social Transition* (Cambridge: Cambridge University Press, 1978).

29. Trask, *From a Native Daughter*, 107.

30. Linda Hogan, *Solar Storms* (New York: Simon & Schuster, 1995), 96.

31. Linda Hogan, *Dwellings: A Spiritual History of the Living World* (New York: Simon & Schuster, 1995), 89.

32. *Lyng v. Norwest Indian Cemetery Protective Association*, 485 U.S. 439 (1988).

33. *Lyng*, 485 U.S. 439 at 441–42.
34. *Lyng*, 485 U.S. 439 at 459–60; internal references omitted.
35. *Lyng*, 485 U.S. 439 at 460; internal references omitted.
36. *Lyng*, 485 U.S. 439 at 461; internal references omitted. Brennan cites Edward H. Spicer, *Cycles of Conquest: The Impact of Spain, Mexico, and the United States on the Indians of the Southwest, 1533–1960* (Tucson: University of Arizona Press, 1962), 576.
37. Quoted in Arnold Krupat, *Red Matters: Native American Studies* (Philadelphia: University of Pennsylvania Press, 2002), 21 (my italics).
38. Krupat, *Red Matters*, 60.
39. For a history of the translation of the Native relationship to land into the Western relationship of property, see Eric Cheyfitz, *The Poetics of Imperialism: Translation and Colonization from "The Tempest" to "Tarzan"* (1991; reprint, Philadelphia: University of Pennsylvania Press, 1997).
40. *United States v. Sioux Nation of Indians*, 448 U.S. 371 (1980).
41. David E. Wilkins, *American Indian Sovereignty and the U.S. Supreme Court: The Masking of Justice* (Austin: University of Texas Press, 1997), 233–34.
42. "United States v. Sioux Nation of Indians," Wikipedia, https://en.wikipedia.org/wiki/United_States_v._Sioux_Nation_of_Indians (accessed April 10, 2023).
43. Nora Marks Dauenhauer, *Life Woven with Song* (Tucson: University of Arizona Press, 2000), 4.
44. Dauenhauer, *Life Woven with Song*, 5.
45. Donald L. Fixico, *Termination and Relocation: Federal Indian Policy, 1945–1960* (Albuquerque: University of New Mexico Press, 1986), 97.
46. Louise Erdrich, *The Night Watchman* (New York: Harper Collins, 2020), 447.
47. Joe Whittle, "Most Native Americans Live in Cities, Not Reservations. Here Are Their Stories," *Guardian*, September 4, 2007, https://www.theguardian.com/us-news/2017/sep/04/native-americans-stories-california (accessed April 10, 2023).
48. David Getches, Charles F. Wilkinson, and Robert A. Williams, *Cases and Materials on Federal Indian Law*, 4th ed. (St. Paul, Minn.: West Group, 1998), 209; note the slight discrepancy with Erdrich's figure.
49. Getches, *Cases and Materials*, 208.
50. Getches, *Cases and Materials*, 207.
51. Getches, *Cases and Materials*. 204.
52. Erdrich, *Night Watchman*, 18.
53. Erdrich, *Night Watchman*, 79; italics Erdrich's.
54. Erdrich, *Night Watchman*, 23.
55. Tommy Orange, *There There* (New York: Knopf, 2018), 11.
56. Orange, *There There*, 290.
57. Patricia Nelson Limerick, *The Legacy of Conquest: The Unbroken Past of the American West* (New York: Norton, 1987), 204.
58. For a discussion of Hopi resistance to the tribal council, see Indian Law Resource Center, *Report to the Hopi Kikmongwis and Other Traditional Hopi*

Leaders on Docket 196 and the Continuing Threat to Hopi Land and Sovereignty (Washington, D.C.: Indian Law Resource Center, 1979), 55–69. Oglala Lakota resistance to its IRA-constituted tribal council is focused in the second Wounded Knee conflict on the Pine Ridge Reservation. For a history of this conflict, see Peter Matthiessen, *In the Spirit of Crazy Horse* (1983; reprint, New York: Viking, 1991), particularly chap. 6. For a history of contemporary resistance in 2000–2001, see http://members.tripod.com/GrassRootsOyate/Poem3.htm (accessed April 11, 2023). See also Eric Cheyfitz, "The Colonial Double Bind: Sovereignty and Civil Rights in Indian Country," *University of Pennsylvania Journal of Constitutional Law* 2 (2003): 226.

59. Nick Estes, *Our History Is the Future: Standing Rock versus the Dakota Access Pipeline, and the Long Tradition of Indigenous Resistance* (London: Verso, 2019), Kindle.

60. Prucha, *Great Father*, 2:793.

61. *Santa Clara Pueblo v. Martinez*, 436 U.S. 49 (1978).

62. *Santa Clara Pueblo v. Martinez*, 436 U.S. 49 at 51.

63. Cheyfitz, "Colonial Double Bind," 225.

64. *Winton v. Amos*, 255 U.S. 373 (1921) at 391–92; my emphasis.

65. Jonathan B. Taylor and Joseph P. Kalt, *American Indians on Reservations: A Databook of Socioeconomic Change between the 1990 and 2000 Census* (Cambridge, Mass.: Harvard Project on American Indian Economic Development, 2005), xii.

66. Dedrick Asante-Muhammad, Esha Kamra, Connor Sanchez, Kathy Ramirez, and Rogelio Tec, "Racial Wealth Snapshot: Native Americans," National Community Reinvestment Coalition (NCRC), February 14, 2022, https://ncrc.org/racial-wealth-snapshot-native-americans/ (accessed April 11, 2023).

67. Northwestern Institute for Policy Research, "What Drives Native American Poverty?," February 24, 2020, https://www.ipr.northwestern.edu/news/2020/redbird-what-drives-native-american-poverty.html (accessed April 11, 2023).

68. Eric Cheyfitz, "The Navajo–Hopi Land Dispute: A Brief History," *Interventions* 2 (2000): 248–75.

69. On the first voyage, Columbus kidnapped seven Indians and took them back to Spain so that they could be displayed as proof of his voyage and so that they could learn Spanish and act as interpreters on subsequent voyages. The letter by Dr. Chanca, which is a report of the second trip, tells us that of the seven, two survived to return to Hispaniola. How effective they were as interpreters cannot be assessed because the Spanish were at that point relatively unconcerned with the problems of translation. For an extended discussion of these problems in the European conquest of the Americas, see Cheyfitz, *Poetics of Imperialism*. It should be emphasized that historians of the conquest have for the most part relied on European narratives without questioning the knowledge they contain, even though the problems of translation to which I refer are both implicitly and explicitly manifest in these narratives, which are, of course, ideologically driven. The text I use of Columbus's voyages is *The Four Voyages of Christopher Columbus*, ed. and trans. J. M. Cohen (New York: Penguin, 1969). The report of the

surviving Native translators can be found on page 151. I have also used the account of Columbus's four voyages by Hans Koning, *Columbus: His Enterprise* (New York: Monthly Review Press, 1976). Koning's volume is an on-point deconstruction of the Columbus myth, which masks the Indigenous genocide that Columbus and his brothers committed in the Americas. Columbus's logbooks do not survive, though two of his letters about the first and fourth voyages do. We have a redaction of his journal on the first voyage by Bartolomé de las Casas, a friend of the family. Accounts of the subsequent voyages are principally provided by Chanca and by Columbus's son, Hernando.

70. Columbus (ed. Cohen), *Four Voyages*, 190–91; Koning, *Columbus*, 82–89.
71. Columbus (ed. Cohen), *Four Voyages*, 186–87.
72. Koning, *Columbus*, 82–83.
73. Columbus (ed. Cohen), *Four Voyages*, 190.
74. Columbus (ed. Cohen), *Four Voyages*, 190.
75. Koning, *Columbus*, 87.
76. Gerald Vizenor, *The Heirs of Columbus* (Lebanon, N.H.: University Press of New England, 1991), 3.
77. Vizenor, *Heirs of Columbus*, 4. Samana Bay is in the Dominican Republic, named Hispaniola by Columbus. But there is no Samana Island.
78. Russell Thornton, *American Indian Holocaust and Survival: A Population History since 1492* (Norman: University of Oklahoma Press, 1987), 43–44.
79. Thornton, *American Indian Holocaust*, 78, 82, 100–102.
80. Thornton, *American Indian Holocaust*, 42.
81. Thornton, *American Indian Holocaust*, 32.
82. Thornton, *American Indian Holocaust*, 30.
83. Paul M. Robertson, "Wounded Knee Massacre," in *Encyclopedia of North American Indians*, ed. Frederick E. Hoxie (Boston: Houghton Mifflin, 1996), 694–97.
84. For an elaboration of the Canadian system of federal Indian law, see John Borrows, *Freedom and Indigenous Constitutionalism* (Toronto: University of Toronto Press, 2016).
85. Joseph M. Marshall, "Wounded Knee Takeover, 1973," in Hoxie, *Encyclopedia*, 697–99.
86. I recommend the film, available on video, *Kanehsatake: 270 Years of Resistance*, directed by Ala-nis Obomsawin (1993; National Film Board of Canada, 1994), available on YouTube at https://www.youtube.com/watch?v=7yP3srFvhKs (accessed April 11, 2023).
87. The Commission for Historical Clarification (CEH) report is available as "Guatemala: Memory of Silence—Report of the Commission for Historical Clarification, Conclusions, and Recommendations" at https://hrdag.org/wp-content/uploads/2013/01/CEHreport-english.pdf (accessed April 11, 2023). The quoted language is from the second paragraph of the prologue. Sections 13–14 implicate the United States. Sections 80–126 detail state violence against Indian communities. Section 122 reads, "In consequence, the CEH concludes that agents of the State of Guatemala, within the framework of counterinsur-

gency operations carried out between 1981 and 1983, committed acts of genocide against groups of Mayan people which lived in the four regions analysed."

88. I am using the undated translation of the *Constitution of the Plurinational State of Bolivia* by Luis Francisco Valle V.

89. Miguel Centellas, "Bolivia's New Multicultural Constitution: The 2009 Constitution in Historical and Comparative Perspective," in *Latin America's Multicultural Movements: The Struggle Between Communitarianism, Autonomy, and Human Rights*, ed. Todd A. Eisenstadt, Michael S. Danielson, Moisés Jaime Bailón Corres, and Carlos Sorroza Polo (New York: Oxford University Press, 2013), 88–110.

90. Valle, *Constitution of the Plurinational State of Bolivia*, article 289.

91. Eric Cheyfitz, "Native American Literature and the U.N. Declaration on the Rights of Indigenous Peoples," in *The Routledge Companion to Native American Literature*, ed. Deborah Lea Madison (New York: Routledge, 2015), 192–202. Article 46 (1) reads, "Nothing in this Declaration may be interpreted as implying for any State, people, group or person any right to engage in any activity or to perform any act contrary to the Charter of the United Nations or construed as authorizing or encouraging any action which would dismember or impair totally or in part, the territorial integrity or political unity of sovereign and independent States."

92. Centellas, "Bolivia's New Multicultural Constitution," 107.

93. Centellas, "Bolivia's New Multicultural Constitution," 90.

94. Glen Sean Coulthard, *Red Skin, White Masks: Rejecting the Colonial Politics of Recognition* (Minneapolis: University of Minnesota Press, 2014), 165.

95. Dina Gilio-Whitaker, *As Long as Grass Grows: The Indigenous Fight for Environmental Justice, from Colonization to Standing Rock* (Boston: Beacon Press, 2019), Kindle.

96. Estes, *Our History Is the Future*.

97. Estes, *Our History Is the Future*.

98. The video of LaDuke explaining the issues with Line 3 may be seen at https://www.culturalsurvival.org/news/anishinaabe-communities-fight-against-line-3-pipeline (accessed April 11, 2023).

99. Theia Chatelle, "The Story of Line 3," *CounterPunch*, July 8, 2022, https://www.counterpunch.org/2022/07/08/the-story-of-line-3/ (accessed April 11, 2023).

100. Simon J. Ortiz, *Fight Back: For the Sake of the People, for the Sake of the Land* (Albuquerque: Institute for Native American Development, Native American Studies, University of New Mexico, 1980); Leslie Marmon Silko, *Almanac of the Dead* (New York: Simon & Schuster, 1991).

101. Roxanne Dunbar-Ortiz, preface to Ortiz, *Fight Back*, n.p.

102. Ortiz, *Fight Back*, 68.

103. Mary F. Calvert and Andrew Romano, "Toxic Legacy of Uranium Mines on Navajo Nation Confronts Interior Nominee Deb Haaland," Yahoo News, February 23, 2021, https://news.yahoo.com/toxic-legacy-of-uranium-mines-in-navajo-nation-confronts-new-interior-secretary-deb-haaland-121534812.html (accessed April 11, 2023).

104. Ortiz, *Fight Back*, 58, 59–60.

105. *U.S. v. Sandoval*, 231 U.S. 28 (1913).
106. For a legal history of Pueblo Indian lands in the post-1492 period, see Cohen, *Felix Cohen's Handbook*, 383–400.
107. Ortiz, *Fight Back*, 71.
108. Ortiz, *Fight Back*, 57.
109. Ortiz, *Fight Back*, 55–56.
110. Silko, *Almanac of the Dead*, 759.
111. Silko, *Almanac of the Dead*, 519–20. For Marx's intellectual engagement with the Iroquois (Haudenosaunee), see Franklin Rosemont, *Karl Marx and the Iroquois* (Brooklyn, N.Y.: Red Balloon Collective, n.d.).
112. Silko, *Alamanc*, 713.
113. Silko, *Alamanc*, 716.
114. "Ghost Dance," in Hoxie, *Encyclopedia*, 223.
115. Silko, *Alamanc*, 725.
116. Silko, *Alamanc*, 713.
117. Silko, *Alamanc*, 714–15.
118. Silko, *Alamanc*, 724.
119. R. C. Gordon-McCutchan, *The Taos Indians and the Battle for Blue Lake* (Santa Fe: Red Crane Books, 1995), xvi.
120. *Johnson v. M'Intosh*, 21 U.S. 543 (1823) at 574. On March 30, 2023, the Vatican repudiated the medieval "doctrine of discovery," but this will have absolutely no effect on the historical federal seizure of Native land in the U.S.
121. "Breach of Close," *Black's Law Dictionary*, https://thelawdictionary.org/ (accessed April 12, 2023).
122. *Cherokee Nation v. Georgia*, 30 U.S. 1 (1831).
123. *Worcester v. Georgia*, 31 U.S. 515 (1832).
124. *Worcester*, 31 U.S. at 561; my emphasis.
125. *Worcester*, 31 U.S. at 557.
126. *Worcester*, 31 U.S. at 580.
127. A search both in Getches, *Cases and Materials*, and on the Westlaw website did not turn up any case entitled *Gila River Apache Tribe v. Arizona*. The case Weasel Tail has in mind would appear to be a water rights case involving the Gila River Indian Community, the San Carlos Apache Tribe, the United States, and private entities in Arizona, which goes back to 1925.
128. Of the cases that Weasel Tail lists in his poem, *Crow Dog* represented a temporary victory for Indian tribes to hold legal jurisdiction over all Indian-on-Indian crime. However, this was reversed by Congress in the Major Crimes Act of 1885, which was confirmed by the Supreme Court in *U.S. v. Kagama* in 1886. The act and the case severely limited tribal jurisdiction in Indian-on-Indian criminal matters, giving the federal government jurisdiction in major felonies. In *Williams*, the court, ruling on a civil suit involving a non-Indian doing business with Navajos on the Navajo reservation, upheld the jurisdiction of tribal courts in civil matters arising on reservations, involving suits brought by nonmembers against tribal members. While *Winters* can certainly be considered a formal victory for tribes in reserving water rights, Getches, in *Cases and Materials*, points out that historically, the doctrine has been more honored in the breach (799).

NOTES TO CHAPTER 1

The *Pyramid Lake Tribe* case is an example of this. The district court found in favor of the government's trust obligation to protect the tribe's reserved water rights. However, a subsequent suit brought to the Supreme Court found that a prior agreement superseded the district court's ruling. Getches, Wilkinson, and Williams, in *Cases and Materials,* 337–45.

129. Leslie Marmon Silko, *Yellow Woman and a Beauty of the Spirit: Essays on Native American Life Today* (New York: Simon & Schuster, 1996), 18, 19. Contra Silko, the Indian Claims Commission did award interest in the case of the Sioux claim for the wrongful taking of the Black Hills; Wilkins, *American Indian Sovereignty and the U.S. Supreme Court,* 224–25. Getches, Wilkinson, and Williams, in *Cases and Materials,* note that exceptions to the "no-interest" rule "require interest payments under some circumstances, such as when a Fifth Amendment taking is involved," which was the case in the Sioux claim (281).

130. Silko, *Yellow Woman,* 19, 20.

131. Silko, *Yellow Woman,* 20.

132. Cheyfitz, *Poetics of Imperialism.*

133. "Daniel Webster, Plymouth Oration," American Rhetoric Online Speech Bank, https://www.americanrhetoric.com/speeches/danielwebsterplymouthoration.htm (accessed April 12, 2023). I thank Arnold Krupat for calling the oration to my attention.

134. See Eric Cheyfitz, "Savage Law: The Plot against American Indians in *Johnson and Graham's Lesee v. M'Intosh* and *The Pioneers,*" in *Cultures of United States Imperialism,* ed. Amy Kaplan and Donald E. Pease (Durham, N.C.: Duke University Press, 1993), 109–28.

135. Ortiz, *Fight Back,* 35.

136. Trask, *From a Native Daughter,* 116.

137. Gary Witherspoon, *Navajo Kinship and Marriage* (Chicago: University of Chicago Press, 1975), 12, 21–22 (internal references omitted), 64.

138. Witherspoon, *Navajo Kinship,* 64.

139. Mark Rifkin, *When Did Indians Become Straight? Kinship, the History of Sexuality, and Native Sovereignty* (Oxford: Oxford University Press, 2011).

140. See Brian Joseph Gilley, *Becoming Two-Spirit: Gay Identity and Social Acceptance in Indian Country* (Lincoln: University of Nebraska Press, 2006). "Two-spirit" refers to Native persons who in present terminology are LGBTQ, though Gilley's book focuses on those biologically male who assumed traditional women's roles. Gilley notes, "'Two-Spirit' Men are well aware that at one time in the history of Native America, mostly before European contact, sexual and gender diversity was an everyday aspect of life among most indigenous people" (7). However, European colonization, following its rigid binary gender codes and religious mandates, suppressed two-spirit culture, with the resultant growth of homophobia in Native communities, which have significant Christian populations. For example, in 2005 the Navajo Nation council banned gay marriage over the veto of that bill by then-president Joe Shirley. Navajo has a long history of two-spirit culture predating the European invasion, embodied in the *nadleeh,* or two-spirit people, who play an important role in Diné (Navajo) origin narratives. Indeed, the central figure in Navajo philosophy is Asdzą́ą́ Nádleehé (Changing

Woman), which translates literally as "woman of indeterminate gender," thus suggesting that two-spirit culture is at the heart of Diné epistemology. In opposing the ban, gay rights groups at Navajo invoked the gender ambiguity of Changing Woman to argue that the banning of gay marriage and of any LGBTQ rights was contrary to Navajo tradition. Oklahoma Muscogee–Creek–Cherokee Craig Womack's novel *Drowning in Fire* narrates the two-spirit experience of Muscogee Josh Henneha from childhood (1964) to adulthood (1993), probing the history of the Muscogee nation and the changing attitudes to two-spirit people as Christianity subverts traditional Native practice.

141. Trask, *From a Native Daughter*, 117.
142. Trask, *From a Native Daughter*, 91.
143. Witherspoon, *Navajo Kinship*, 24.
144. William Bevis, "Native American Novels: Homing In," in *Recovering the Word: Essays on Native American Literature*, ed. Brian Swann and Arnold Krupat (Berkeley: University of California Press, 1987), 601.
145. Gregory Cajete, *Native Science: Natural Laws of Interdependence* (Santa Fe, N.M.: Clearlight, 2000), 152.
146. Witherspoon, *Navajo Kinship*, 16.
147. Witherspoon, *Navajo Kinship*, 21.
148. James Axtell, "The White Indians of Colonial America," in *The European and the Indian: Essays in the Ethnohistory of Colonial North America* (Oxford: Oxford University Press, 1981), 168–206.
149. Mary Jemison, *A Narrative of the Life of Mrs. Mary Jemison*, comp. and ed. James E. Seaver (1824; reprint, Syracuse, N.Y.: Syracuse University Press, 1990).
150. Kenneth Lincoln, *Native American Renaissance* (1983; reprint, Berkeley: University of California Press, 1985), 42, 44.
151. Lincoln, *Native American Renaissance*, 45.
152. Patrice H. Kunesh, "Banishment as Cultural Justice in Contemporary Tribal Legal Systems," *New Mexico Law Review* 37, no. 85 (2007): 88–89.
153. David E. Wilkins and Shelley Hulse Wilkins, *Dismembered: Native Disenrollment and the Battle for Human Rights* (Seattle: University of Washington Press, 2017), Kindle.
154. Wilkins and Wilkins, *Dismembered*.
155. Mike Baker, "A Tribe's Bitter Purge Brings an Unusual Request: Federal Intervention," *Seattle Times*, January 3, 2022, https://www.seattletimes.com/seattle-news/northwest/a-tribes-bitter-purge-brings-an-unusual-request-federal-intervention/ (accessed April 12, 2023).
156. Linda Hogan, *Power* (New York: Norton, 1998), 172.
157. Vine Deloria Jr. and Clifford M. Lytle, *American Indians, American Justice* (Austin: University of Texas Press, 1983), 111–13.
158. Circe Sturm, *Blood Politics: Race, Culture, and Identity in the Cherokee Nation of Oklahoma* (Berkeley: University of California Press, 2002), 32–33; internal reference omitted.
159. For an analysis of Hopi "fissioning," see Mischa Titiev, *Old Oraibi: A*

NOTES TO CHAPTER 1   209

Study of the Hopi Indians of Third Mesa (1944; reprint, Albuquerque: University of New Mexico Press, 1992), chaps. 5–6.

160. Arnold Krupat, *All That Remains: Varieties of Indigenous Expression* (Lincoln: University of Nebraska Press, 2009), 139. "Paul" refers to Paul Apak, who "wrote the screenplay in English and also in the Inuktitut syllabary" (137).

161. Krupat, *All That Remains*, 137.

162. I thank Shari Huhndorf for suggesting that I get in touch with the Alaska Native Language Center. There I contacted Professor Anna Berge, who put me in touch with Professor Dorais.

163. *Ex parte Crow Dog*, 109 U.S. 566 (1883); see Prucha, *Documents*, doc. 98.

164. Sidney L. Harring, *Crow Dog's Case: American Indian Sovereignty, Tribal Law, and United States Law in the Nineteenth Century* (Cambridge: Cambridge University Press, 1994), 1.

165. See Prucha, *Documents*, doc. 101.

166. *U.S. v. Kagama*, 118 U.S. 375 (1886). See Prucha, *Documents*, doc. 102.

167. Wilkins, *American Indian Sovereignty and the U.S. Supreme Court*, 10.

168. Pekka Hämäläinen, *The Commanche Empire* (New Haven, Conn.: Yale University Press, 2008), Kindle.

169. The English of the Jamestown Colony, for example, referred to Powhatan as a king. Cheyfitz, *Poetics of Imperialism*, 59.

170. Daniel K. Richter, *The Ordeal of the Longhouse: The Peoples of the Iroquois League in the Era of European Colonization* (Chapel Hill: University of North Carolina Press, 1992), 40–49.

171. See Franklin Folsom, *Indian Uprising on the Rio Grande: The Pueblo Revolt of 1680* (Albuquerque: University of New Mexico Press, 1973).

172. See Richard Middleton, *Pontiac's War: Its Causes, Course, and Consequences* (New York: Routledge, 2007).

173. See Colin G. Calloway, *The Shawnees and the War for America* (New York: Viking Penguin, 2007).

174. See Paul Chaat Smith and Robert Allen Warrior, *Like a Hurricane: The Indian Movement from Alcatraz to Wounded Knee* (New York: New Press, 1996).

175. *Worcester*, 31 U.S. 515 at 559–60.

176. *Cherokee Nation v. Georgia*, 30 U.S. 1 (1831) at 17.

177. Taiaiake Alfred, "Sovereignty," in *Sovereignty Matters: Locations of Contestation and Possibility in Indigenous Struggles for Self-Determination*, ed. Joanne Barker (Lincoln: University of Nebraska Press, 2005), 34.

178. Alfred, "Sovereignty," 42–43.

179. Quoted in Wilkins, *American Indian Sovereignty*, 20n9.

180. Vizenor, *Heirs of Columbus*, 7.

181. Alfred, "Sovereignty," 45.

182. Alfred, "Sovereignty," 45.

183. Alfred, "Sovereignty," 45.

184. Alfred, "Sovereignty," 46–47, 49.

185. Taiaiake Alfred, *Peace, Power, Righteousness: An Indigenous Manifesto* (Oxford: Oxford University Press, 1999), 25.

186. Alvaro Reyes and Mara Kaufman, "Sovereignty, Indigeneity, Territory: Zapatista Autonomy and the New Practices of Decolonization," in Cheyfitz, Duthu, and Huhndorf, "Sovereignty, Indigeneity, and the Law," 506.
187. Reyes and Kaufman, "Sovereignty, Indigeneity," 509.
188. Reyes and Kaufman, "Sovereignty, Indigeneity," 516.
189. Thomas Fatheuer, *Buen Vivir: A Brief Introduction to Latin America's New Concepts for the Good Life and the Rights of Nature*, trans. John Hayduska (Berlin: Heinrich Böll Stiftung, 2011), 17:16, 17:19.
190. Coulthard, *Red Skin, White Masks*, 15.
191. Coulthard, *Red Skin, White Masks*, 16–17; Coulthard's italics.
192. Antonio Gramsci, *The Antonio Gramsci Review: Selected Writings, 1916–1935*, ed. David Forgacs (New York: New York University Press, 2000), 306–7.

2. THE COLONIZATION OF NATIVE IDENTITY THROUGH BIOLOGIC

1. Francis Paul Prucha, *Documents of United States Indian Policy*, 3rd ed. (Lincoln: University of Nebraska Press, 2000), doc. 126; Francis Paul Prucha, *The Great Father: The United States Government and the American Indians* (Lincoln: University of Nebraska Press, 1984), 2:881–85.
2. The OED gives 1819 as the date of origin for the term "biology," used to refer to "the division of physical science which deals with organized beings or animals and plants, their morphology, physiology, origin, and distribution."
3. Theda Purdue, "Cherokee Planters: The Development of Plantation Slavery before Removal," in *The Cherokee Indian Nation: A Troubled History*, ed. Duane King (Knoxville: University of Tennessee Press, 1997), 115–16.
4. Richard V. Persico Jr., "Early Nineteenth-Century Cherokee Political Organization," in King, *Cherokee Indian Nation*, 93–95.
5. Persico, "Early Nineteenth-Century Cherokee Political Organization," 97–101, 105–6.
6. Wilma Mankiller and Michael Wallis, *Mankiller: A Chief and Her People* (New York: St. Martin's Press, 1993), 86.
7. This prohibition appears in §§ 3 and 4 of the Cherokee constitution. In 1866, the Cherokee Nation signed a treaty with the United States granting former slaves and their descendants (known as Cherokee Freedmen) Cherokee citizenship. "In the early 1980s, the Cherokee Nation administration amended citizenship rules to require direct descent from an ancestor listed on the 'Cherokee By Blood' section of the Dawes Rolls. The change stripped descendants of the Cherokee Freedmen of citizenship and voting rights unless they satisfied this new criterion." Years of internal conflict over the decision ensued, along with a federal court suit by the Cherokee Freedmen for reinstatement. In 2017, the District Court for the District of Columbia ruled in favor of the Freedmen, "granting the Freedmen descendants full rights to citizenship in the Cherokee Nation." The ruling was accepted by the Cherokee Nation. See "Cherokee Freedmen

Controversy," Wikipedia, https://en.wikipedia.org/wiki/Cherokee_freedmen_controversy (accessed April 21, 2023).
8. Elias Boudinot, *Cherokee Editor: The Writings of Elias Boudinot*, ed. Theda Purdue (Athens: University of Georgia Press, 1996), 4.
9. Purdue, "Cherokee Planters," 115.
10. Purdue, "Cherokee Planters," 117–18.
11. Purdue, "Cherokee Planters," 118; Mankiller and Wallis, *Mankiller*, 92.
12. Purdue, "Cherokee Planters," 118.
13. Purdue, "Cherokee Planters," 117.
14. Persico, "Early Nineteenth-Century Cherokee Political Organization," 107–8.
15. Leslie Marmon Silko, *Ceremony* (New York: Penguin, 1977), 125.
16. Purdue, "Cherokee Planters," 124–25, my emphasis. "Anarchy," in its popular meaning, is an unfortunate word choice to describe the democratic, consensus mode of decision making.
17. Persico, "Early Nineteenth-Century Cherokee Political Organization," 101.
18. Purdue in Boudinot (ed. Purdue), *Cherokee Editor*, 24.
19. *Opinions of the Attorney General of the United States* in 1856 at 746.
20. Mankiller and Wallis, *Mankiller*, 85–88.
21. Circe Sturm, *Blood Politics: Race, Culture, and Identity in the Cherokee Nation of Oklahoma* (Berkeley: University of California Press, 2002), 72; internal references omitted.
22. Mankiller and Wallis, *Mankiller*, 79.
23. Mankiller and Wallis, *Mankiller*, 85.
24. David E. Wilkins, *American Indian Sovereignty and the U.S. Supreme Court: The Masking of Justice* (Austin: University of Texas Press, 1997), 39.
25. 45 U.S. at 567. Ironically, as Wilkins points out, when the case did reach the Supreme Court, Rogers, unbeknownst to the court, had died by drowning during a prison break. Wilkins, *American Indian Sovereignty*, 40.
26. 45 U.S. at 568; my emphasis.
27. 45 U.S. at 568.
28. James Mooney, *Myths of the Cherokee* (1900; reprint, New York: Dover, 1995), 15.
29. 45 U.S. at 572–73.
30. Arnold Krupat, *Red Matters: Native American Studies* (Philadelphia: University of Pennsylvania Press, 2002), 78.
31. This apparently strange proviso may have been prompted by the anxiety expressed in the opinion that the Indian tribes will become refuge for adult white male criminals seeking to escape U.S. jurisdiction (45 U.S. at 573).
32. Peter Iverson, *Diné: A History of the Navajos* (Albuquerque: University of New Mexico Press, 2002), 245.
33. Prucha, *Documents*, doc. 126.
34. Prucha, *Documents*, doc. 104, §§ 6 and 5.

35. Felix Cohen, *Felix Cohen's Handbook of Federal Indian Law* (1942; reprint, Albuquerque: University of New Mexico Press, n.d.), 154.

36. David Getches, Charles F. Wilkinson, and Robert A. Williams Jr., *Cases and Materials on Federal Indian Law*, 4th ed. (St. Paul, Minn: West Group, 1998), 174; Cohen, *Felix Cohen's Handbook*, 167–69. For a discussion of competency commissions, see Janet A. McDonnell, *The Dispossession of the American Indian, 1887–1934* (Bloomington: Indiana University Press, 1991), chap. 7. Cohen, *Felix Cohen's Handbook*, has a section on "competency" (167–69).

37. *United States v. Shock*, 187 Fed. 862 (1911).

38. Cohen, *Felix Cohen's Handbook*, 169.

39. *Annual Report of the Commissioner of Indian Affairs* (1917), 169.

40. 65 Fed. Reg. at 20775. Before the publication of the *Columbia Guide* in 2006, I arrived at this information from a telephone conversation with Karen Ketcher, Branch of Tribal Operations, Eastern Oklahoma Region, Department of the Interior, Bureau of Indian Affairs, 101 North 5th Street, Muskogee, OK 74401.

41. 65 Fed. Reg. at 20776, 20778. "Base roll means the specified allotment, annuity, census, or other roll upon which membership in a federally recognized Indian tribe is based, as designated by a federal statute, by the Secretary, or by the tribe's written governing document, such as a constitution, enrollment ordinance, or resolution; or the Alaska Native Claims Settlement Act roll established pursuant to 43 U.S.C. 1604." 65 Fed. Reg. at 20781.

42. David H. Getches, Charles F. Wilkinson, and Robert A. Williams Jr., *Cases and Materials on Federal Indian Law*, 4th ed. (St. Paul, Minn.: West Group, 1998), 239n1.

43. *Morton v. Mancari*, 417 U.S. at 554.

44. *Morton v. Mancari*, 417 U.S. at 554. Title 25 of the Code of Federal Regulations, section 5.1 (25 CFR § 5.1) currently uses the criteria of 25 USC § 479, which do not require a minimum blood quantum of any kind if one is tribally enrolled or descended from a specific category of tribal member—though, once again, we ought to remember that tribal enrollment itself typically requires, among other criteria, a certain blood quantum. In the ACLU's handbook, by Stephen L. Pevar, *The Rights of Indians and Tribes*, 3rd ed. (Carbondale: Southern Illinois University Press, 2002), the author notes, "Many tribes require that a person have at least one-fourth tribal blood to be enrolled" (19).

45. Patricia Nelson Limerick, *The Legacy of Conquest: The Unbroken Past of the American West* (New York: Norton, 1987), 338.

46. Theodore W. Taylor, *The Bureau of Indian Affairs* (Boulder, Colo.: Westview, 1984), 79. The Census 2000 website notes that the form asks those who self-identify as Indians to also write in "your enrolled or principal tribe."

47. Pevar, *Rights of Indians and Tribes*, 19.

48. *U.S. v. Broncheau* (597 F. 2d 1260), at 1263; internal references omitted.

49. *Sixty-First Annual Report of the Commissioner of Indian Affairs* for 1892 at 31.

50. Cohen, *Felix Cohen's Handbook*, 2.

NOTES TO CHAPTER 2

51. BIA website at https://www.bia.gov/frequently-asked-questions (accessed April 22, 2023).

52. Nicole Chavez and Harmeet Kauer, "Why the Jump in the Native American Population May Be One of the Hardest to Explain," CNN, August 19, 2021, https://www.cnn.com/2021/08/19/us/census-native-americans-rise-population/index.html (accessed April 22, 2023).

53. Dedrick Asante-Muhammad, Esha Kamra, Connor Sanchez, Kathy Ramirez, and Rogelio Tec, "Racial Wealth Snapshot: Native Americans," National Community Reinvestment Coalition (NCRC), February 14, 2022, https://ncrc.org/racial-wealth-snapshot-native-americans/ (accessed April 22, 2023).

54. U.S. Department of the Interior, "Collection of Tribal Enrollment Count," https://www.bia.gov/service/american-rescue-plan-act/i-collection-tribal-enrollment-count (accessed April 22, 2023).

55. The NCRC report notes, "Based on the data from the 2018 U.S. Census cited by Poverty USA, Native Americans have the highest poverty rate among all minority groups. The national poverty rate for Native Americans was 25.4%, while Black or African American poverty rate was 20.8%. Among Hispanics, the national poverty rate was 17.6%. The White population had an 8.1% national poverty rate during the same period." Sociologist Beth Red Bird's 2020 report notes an even higher poverty rate: "Across the United States, 1 in 3 Native Americans are living in poverty, with a median income of $23,000 a year. These numbers from the American Community Survey highlight the stark income inequality the nation's first peoples face." Northwestern Institute for Policy Research, "What Drives Native American Poverty?," February 24, 2020, https://www.ipr.northwestern.edu/news/2020/redbird-what-drives-native-american-poverty.html (accessed April 22, 2023).

56. Quoted in Emily Benedek, *The Wind Won't Know Me: A History of the Navajo–Hopi Land Dispute* (New York: Knopf, 1992), 151.

57. See Eric Cheyfitz, "The (Post)colonial Predicament of Native American Studies," *Interventions* 4, no. 3 (2000): 405–27.

58. Louise Erdrich, *The Night Watchman* (New York: Harper Collins, 2020), 98. It is worth juxtaposing to Thomas's notion that Indians have been "conquered" this passage by Taiaiake Alfred: "There are inherent constraints to the exercise of indigenous governmental authority built into the notion of indigenous sovereignty, and these constraints derive from the myth of conquest that is the foundation of mainstream perspectives on indigenous–white relations in North America." Taiaiake Alfred, "Sovereignty," in *Sovereignty Matters: Locations of Contestation and Possibility in Indigenous Struggles for Self-Determination*, ed. Joanne Barker (Lincoln: University of Nebraska Press, 2005), 44.

59. Erdrich, *Night Watchman*, 407.

60. Charles R. Larson, *American Indian Fiction* (Albuquerque: University of New Mexico Press, 1978), 2.

61. Larson, *American Indian Fiction*, 4.

62. Larson, *American Indian Fiction*, 2, 4.

63. Larson, *American Indian Fiction*, 115–16.

64. Larson, *American Indian Fiction*, 5.
65. Larson, *American Indian Fiction*, 180.
66. Larson, *American Indian Fiction*, 6–8.
67. Gerald Vizenor, *Bearheart: The Heirship Chronicles* (Minneapolis: University of Minnesota Press, 1978), 14.
68. Louis Owens, *Other Destinies: Understanding the American Indian Novel* (Norman: University of Oklahoma Press, 1992), 3.
69. Owens, *Other Destinies*, 5.
70. "Louis Owens," Wikipedia, https://en.wikipedia.org/wiki/Louis_Owens (accessed April 22, 2023).
71. Owens, *Other Destinies*, 4.
72. Owens, *Other Destinies*, 30.
73. Owens, *Other Destinies*, 40
74. Thomas King, *Green Grass, Running Water* (1993; reprint, New York: Bantam, 1994), 317.
75. Owens, *Other Destinies*, 26
76. Owens, *Other Destinies*, 27
77. Silko, *Ceremony*, 33.
78. The Laguna constitution, with membership requirements, as ratified in 1958, is available at https://thorpe.law.ou.edu/IRA/1958nmpuebcon.html (accessed April 22, 2023). Although Tayo was born in a fictional time that lies outside the purview of the Laguna constitution (the novel is set immediately after World War II, presumably placing Tayo's birth date somewhere in the late 1920s), he would appear to be a half-blood Indian with an enrolled mother, which would afford him membership in the tribe if the constitution were applicable.
79. Alfonso Ortiz, ed., *Handbook of North American Indians* (Washington, D.C.: Smithsonian Institution Press, 1979), 9:443.
80. Silko, *Ceremony*, 30.
81. Silko, *Ceremony*, 68.
82. Silko, *Ceremony*, 63.
83. Leslie Marmon Silko, *Yellow Woman and a Beauty of the Spirit: Essays on Native American Life Today* (New York: Simon & Schuster, 1996), 102–3, 104.
84. Owens, *Other Destinies*, 167–91.
85. Vizenor, *Bearheart*, 12.
86. Vizenor, *Bearheart*, 195, 189.
87. Vizenor, *Bearhear*, 195, emphasis added.
88. Vizenor, *Bearheart*, 194.
89. Vizenor *Bearheart*, 194.
90. Vizenor, *Bearheart*, 195.
91. Gerald Vizenor, *Manifest Manners: Narrative on Postindian Survivance* (Lincoln: University of Nebraska Press, 1994), 11.
92. Alfred, "Sovereignty," 44.
93. Vizenor, *Manifest Manners*, 2.

3. COLLABORATIVE IDENTITIES

1. Louis Owens, *Other Destinies: Understanding the American Indian Novel* (Norman: University of Oklahoma Press, 1992), 20.
2. Owens, *Other Destinies*, 45.
3. See Beth Piatote, *Domestic Subjects: Gender, Citizenship, and Law in Native American Literature* (New Haven, Conn.: Yale University Press, 2013). Although not focusing on allotment specifically, Arnold Krupat reads *Cogewea* within the historical context of race theory in the early twentieth century; see Arnold Krupat, *Red Matters: Native American Studies* (Philadelphia: University of Pennsylvania Press, 2002), chap. 4.
4. Black Elk, *Black Elk Speaks: The Complete Edition*, ed. John G. Neihardt (1932; reprint, Lincoln: University of Nebraska Press, 2014), annotated by Raymond J. DeMallie.
5. Black Elk, *Black Elk Speaks: Being the Life Story of a Holy Man of the Oglala Sioux*, ed. John G. Neihardt (1932; reprint, Lincoln: University of Nebraska Press, 1988).
6. Black Elk, *The Sixth Grandfather: Black Elk's Teachings Given to John G. Neihardt*, ed. Raymond J. DeMallie (Lincoln: University of Nebraska Press, 1984), 52. Ellipses and brackets are DeMaillie's.
7. U.S. Department of the Interior, "The Indian Arts and Crafts Act of 1990," https://www.doi.gov/iacb/act (accessed April 29, 2023). See Ward Churchill, *Indians Are Us? Culture and Genocide in Native North America* (Monroe, Maine: Common Courage Press, 1994), 89–113.
8. Black Elk (ed. DeMallie), *Sixth Grandfather*, 51.
9. David H. Brumble III, *American Indian Autobiography* (1988; reprint, Berkeley: University of California Press, 1990), 21 (internal references omitted).
10. Black Elk, *Black Elk Speaks* (introduction by Vine Deloria Jr., 1979), xiv. This introduction is printed in the 1988 Bison Book edition and as the foreword in the Bison Books twenty-first-century edition (xvi–vii) of *Black Elk Speaks* (Lincoln: University of Nebraska Press, 1988).
11. Black Elk, preface to the 1961 edition, in *Black Elk Speaks: The Complete Edition* (annotated DeMallie ed.), xxii.
12. Black Elk (ed. DeMallie), *Sixth Grandfather*, 26.
13. Black Elk, *Black Elk Speaks: The Complete Edition* (annotated DeMallie ed.), xxi.
14. Black Elk (ed. DeMallie), *Sixth Grandfather*, 27.
15. Hertha Dawn Wong, *Sending My Heart Back across the Years: Tradition and Innovation in Native American Autobiography* (Oxford: Oxford University Press, 1992), 122.
16. DeMallie, introduction to Black Elk (ed. DeMallie), *Sixth Grandfather*, xxiv.
17. Black Elk (ed. DeMallie), *Sixth Grandfather*, 32.
18. Black Elk (ed. DeMallie), *Sixth Grandfather*, 9, 11.
19. Black Elk, *Black Elk Speaks: The Complete Edition* (annotated DeMallie ed.), xxiii.

20. Black Elk (ed. DeMallie), *Sixth Grandfather*, 9.
21. Black Elk (ed. DeMallie), *Sixth Grandfather*, 52.
22. William Powers, "When Black Elk Speaks, Everybody Listens," *Social Text* 24 (1990): 49. Powers is quoting *Sixth Grandfather*, 47; he omits "very" and adds the italics and "(Petri)."
23. Black Elk (ed. DeMallie), *Sixth Grandfather*, 54.
24. DeMallie, introduction to Black Elk (ed. DeMallie), *Sixth Grandfather*, xxii.
25. Black Elk (ed. DeMallie), *Sixth Grandfather*, xxiii–xxiv.
26. Wong, *Sending My Heart Back*, 122, 12.
27. Wong, *Sending My Heart Back*, 119.
28. Black Elk (ed. DeMallie), *Sixth Grandfather*, 3.
29. Black Elk (ed. DeMallie), *Sixth Grandfather*, 7.
30. Powers, "When Black Elk Speaks," 45.
31. Black Elk (ed. DeMallie), *Sixth Grandfather*, 12.
32. Black Elk (ed. DeMallie), *Sixth Grandfather*, 12.
33. "Ghost Dance," in *Encyclopedia of North American Indians*, ed. Frederick E. Hoxie (Boston: Houghton Mifflin, 1996), 223.
34. The first stage consisted of open armed warfare. Subsequent stages include forced assimilation (allotment and the boarding school period); mass sterilization of Indian women without consent; forced adoptions to non-Natives (ended nominally in 1978 with the Indian Child Welfare Act); poverty, including poor health care (as witnessed by the disproportionate Covid-19 deaths in Native America); the federal and capitalist subversion of Native economies grounded in subsistence initiatives dependent on a fossil fuel–free environment, as well as dereliction of federal duty in pursuing the rape and murder of Indian women. These are just the prime instances I focus on in this book, all engaging in ongoing Native genocide.
35. Black Elk (ed. DeMallie), *Sixth Grandfather*, 13.
36. Black Elk (ed. DeMallie), *Sixth Grandfather*, 14.
37. Black Elk (ed. DeMallie), *Sixth Grandfather*, 14.
38. Powers, "When Black Elk Speaks," 47.
39. Black Elk (ed. DeMallie), *Sixth Grandfather*, 14. In a marginal note to me, Darlene Evans notes, "His wife and children being Catholic would have been a strong incentive for him to convert without the conflict with the priest."
40. Black Elk (ed. DeMallie), *Sixth Grandfather*, 15n17.
41. Black Elk (ed. DeMallie), *Sixth Grandfather*, 15.
42. Black Elk (ed. DeMallie), *Sixth Grandfather*, 15.
43. Black Elk (ed. DeMallie), *Sixth Grandfather*, 36–37, 34.
44. Black Elk (ed. DeMallie), *Sixth Grandfather*, 38, 36–37.
45. Black Elk (ed. DeMallie), *Sixth Grandfather*, 63, 64.
46. Black Elk (ed. DeMallie), *Sixth Grandfather*, 66.
47. Black Elk (ed. DeMallie), *Sixth Grandfather*, 59–60.
48. Black Elk (ed. DeMallie), *Sixth Grandfather*, 16.
49. Black Elk (ed. DeMallie), *Sixth Grandfather*, 16, my emphasis.

NOTES TO CHAPTER 3

50. Black Elk (ed. DeMallie), *Sixth Grandfather*, 25.
51. Black Elk (ed. DeMallie), *Sixth Grandfather*, 66.
52. Julian Rice, *Black Elk's Story: Distinguishing Its Lakota Purpose* (Albuquerque: University of New Mexico Press, 1991).
53. Rice, *Black Elk's Story*, x. Neihardt returned to Pine Ridge in 1944 to gather information for a cultural history of the Oglala. He interviewed Black Elk once again. Black Elk (ed. DeMallie), *Sixth Grandfather*, 68–69.
54. Black Elk (ed. DeMallie), *Sixth Grandfather*, 62.
55. See Wong, *Sending My Heart Back*, 120, and Black Elk (ed. DeMallie), *Sixth Grandfather*, 62–63.
56. Brumble, *American Indian Autobiography*, 10.
57. Brumble, *American Indian Autobiography*, 11.
58. DeMallie, *Sixth Grandfather*, 7–9.
59. DeMallie, *Sixth Grandfather*, 56, 62.
60. Vine Deloria Jr., foreword to Black Elk, *Black Elk Speaks: The Complete Edition* (annotated DeMallie ed.), xiv–xv.
61. Powers, "When Black Elk Speaks," 54.
62. Black Hawk, *Black Hawk: An Autobiography*, ed. Donald Jackson (1955; reprint, Champaign: University of Illinois Press, Prairie State Books edition, 1990).
63. Gerald Vizenor, *The People Named the Chippewa* (Minneapolis: University of Minnesota Press, 1984), 107. Bracketed ellipses in quotation are mine.
64. Susan Walsh, "'With Them Was My Home': Native American Autobiography and *A Narrative of the Life of Mrs. Mary Jemison*," *American Literature* 64 (1992): 51.
65. James E. Seaver, introduction to Mary Jemison, *A Narrative of the Life of Mrs. Mary Jemison*, comp. and ed. Seaver (1824; reprint, Syracuse, N.Y.: Syracuse University Press, 1990), xx, xxvii.
66. Black Hawk (ed. Jackson), *Black Hawk*, 35.
67. Black Hawk (ed. Jackson), *Black Hawk*, 37, 36.
68. Black Hawk (ed. Jackson), *Black Hawk*, 38–39.
69. Black Hawk (ed. Jackson), *Black Hawk*, 26.
70. Francis Paul Prucha, *Documents of United States Indian Policy*, 3rd ed. (Lincoln: University of Nebraska Press, 2000), doc. 42.
71. Black Hawk (ed. Jackson), *Black Hawk*, 25, my emphasis.
72. *Johnson v. M'Intosh*, 21 U.S. 543 (1823) at 590.
73. Vine Deloria Jr., *Behind the Trail of Broken Treaties: An Indian Declaration of Independence* (Austin: University of Texas Press, 1974), 158.
74. Maureen Konkle, *Writing Indian Nations: Native Intellectuals and the Politics of Historiography, 1827–1863* (Chapel Hill: University of North Carolina Press, 2004), 41.
75. Konkle, *Writing Indian Nations*, 162.
76. Walsh, "With Them Was My Home," 49.
77. Black Elk, *Black Elk Speaks: The Complete Edition* (annotated DeMallie ed.), 3.

78. See Eric Cheyfitz, "Framing Ward Churchill: The Political Construction of Research Misconduct," in *Works and Days: Academic Freedom and Intellectual Activism in the Post-9/11 University*, ed. Edward J. Carvalho and David B. Downing (London: Palgrave Macmillan, 2011), 51–52, 53–54.
79. Black Hawk (ed. Jackson), *Black Hawk*, 88–89.
80. Black Hawk (ed. Jackson), *Black Hawk*, 138.
81. Black Hawk (ed. Jackson), *Black Hawk*, 53–54.
82. Black Hawk (ed. Jackson), *Black Hawk*, 159.
83. Black Hawk (ed. Jackson), *Black Hawk*, 104.
84. Black Hawk (ed. Jackson), *Black Hawk*, 114–15.
85. Black Hawk (ed. Jackson), *Black Hawk*, 101.
86. Black Hawk (ed. Jackson), *Black Hawk*, 63–64, 86–87.
87. Walt Kelly, creator of the comic strip *Pogo*; see https://library.osu.edu/site/40stories/2020/01/05/we-have-met-the-enemy/ (accessed April 29, 2023).
88. A useful introduction to the comparison of Indigenous literatures in a global context can be found in Scott Richard Lyons, ed., *The World, the Text, and the Indian: Global Dimensions of Native American Literature* (Albany: State University of New York Press, 2017).
89. Keith H. Basso, *Portraits of "The Whiteman": Linguistic Play and Cultural Symbols among the Western Apache* (Cambridge: Cambridge University Press, 1979).
90. Frantz Fanon, *Black Skin, White Masks*, trans. Charles Lam Markmann (1952; reprint, New York: Grove, 1967), 30–35.
91. Jack Campisi, "Pequot," in Hoxie, *Encyclopedia*, 476.
92. For a discussion of Apess's Methodism in relation to Native communalism, see Karim M. Tiro, "Denominated 'SAVAGE': Methodism, Writing, and Identity in the Works of William Apess, a Pequot," *American Quarterly* 48 (1996): 653–79.
93. Mourning Dove (Hum-Ishu-Ma), *Cogewea, the Half-Blood: A Depiction of the Great Montana Cattle Range* (1927; Lincoln: University of Nebraska Press, 1981).
94. W. S. Penn, *All My Sins Are Relatives* (Lincoln: University of Nebraska Press, 1995), 129.
95. Penn, *All My Sins*, 128.
96. Penn, *All My Sins*, 130.
97. Penn, *All My Sins*, 131.
98. Penn, *All My Sins*, 135.
99. Penn, *All My Sins*, 135, 124.
100. Michael Wilson, "Writing a Friendship Dance: Orality in Mourning Dove's *Cogewea*," *American Indian Culture and Research Journal* 20, no. 1 (1996): 31.
101. Wilson, "Writing a Friendship Dance," 33.
102. Wilson, "Writing a Friendship Dance," 28–29.
103. Fisher, introduction to Mourning Dove, *Cogewea*, xv. Further references to the primary text are cited parenthetically in text.

104. Fisher, introduction to Mourning Dove, *Cogewea*, xxv.
105. Jay Miller (Lenape), "Mourning Dove [Christine Quintakset]," in Hoxie, *Encyclopedia*, 401.
106. Jay Miller, introduction to Mourning Dove, *Mourning Dove: A Salishan Autobiography*, ed. Jay Miller (Lincoln: University of Nebraska Press, 1990), xvi.
107. Lucullus Virgil McWhorter, introduction to Mourning Dove, *Cogewea*, 9.
108. McWhorter, introduction to Mourning Dove, *Cogewea*, 9.
109. Frederick E. Hoxie, *A Final Promise: The Campaign to Assimilate the Indians, 1880–1920* (Cambridge: Cambridge University Press, 1989), 157.
110. Miller, introduction to Mourning Dove, *Mourning Dove*, xvi.
111. Miller, introduction to Mourning Dove, *Mourning Dove*, xvii.
112. Fisher, introduction to *Cogewea*, xiv.
113. Miller in Hoxie, *Encyclopedia*, 401.
114. Miller, introduction to Mourning Dove, *Mourning Dove*, xiii.
115. Hoxie, *Final Promise*, 181.
116. Miller, introduction to Mourning Dove, *Mourning Dove*, xiii.
117. Miller, introduction to Mourning Dove, *Mourning Dove*, xiii.
118. Though an exact date for the action of *Cogewea* is not given, it clearly takes place during allotment and after 1905, when the Flathead reservation was opened to settlement. Because competency standards varied with different Department of the Interior administrations and the novel does not spell them out, it is unclear exactly what standards might be at play in Cogewea's attaining competency. I think it is safe to say, however, that whatever the standards (from education to evidence of self-sufficiency), blood quantum always played some part in the decision about competency, and that the more white blood a person had, all other criteria being equal, the more competent the individual was assumed to be.
119. The Burke Act, among its other provisions, gave the secretary of the Interior the power to transfer title of trust allotments in fee to allottees who were judged competent to handle their own affairs. See Prucha, *Documents*, doc. 127.
120. The Osage murders form the plot of the Chickasaw writer Linda Hogan's novel *Mean Spirit* (1990) and most recently of Osage novelist Charles H. Red Corn's *A Pipe for February* (2002). The date of the Osage murders in the early 1920s and the date of the publication of *Cogewea* suggest that the novel may well have been worked on after 1916, which is projected to be the time it was written. Buttressing this suggestion is also the date 1921, when Mourning Dove was judged competent to receive her allotment in fee. For an historical account of the murders, see Donald L. Fixico, *The Invasion of Indian Country in the Twentieth Century: American Capitalism and Tribal Natural Resources* (Boulder: University Press of Colorado, 2012), 27–53.
121. Wilson, "Writing a Friendship Dance," 29–30; Krupat, *Red Matters*, 85–86.
122. Hoxie, *Encyclopedia*, 607.
123. Hoxie, *Encyclopedia*, 607.
124. For a discussion of racism and federal Indian law, see Robert A. Williams

Jr., *Like a Loaded Weapon: The Rehnquist Court, Indian Rights, and the Legal History of Racism in America* (Minneapolis: University of Minnesota Press, 2005).

125. Patricia Nelson Limerick, *The Legacy of Conquest: The Unbroken Past of the American West* (New York: Norton, 1987), 337–38.

126. Subcomandante Insurgente Marcos, *Beyond Resistance Everything: An Interview with Subcomandante Insurgente Marcos*, ed. El Columbo Intergalactico (Durham, N.C.: PaperBoatPress, 2007), 30.

4. SETTLER COLONIALISM AND THE TYRANNY OF BORDERS

1. Patrick Wolfe, "Settler Colonialism and the Elimination of the Native," *Journal of Genocide Research* 8, no. 4 (2006): 387–409.

2. See Mark LeVine and Eric Cheyfitz, "Israel, Palestine, and the Poetics of Genocide," *Jadaliyya*, May 2, 2017, https://www.jadaliyya.com/Details/34248 (accessed May 4, 2023); translated to Arabic and published in *Al Mustaqbalal Arabi*, no. 473.

3. Wolfe, "Settler Colonialism," 388.

4. Russell Thornton, *American Indian Holocaust and Survival: A Population History since 1492* (Norman: University of Oklahoma Press, 1987), 43.

5. See Kevin Bruyneel, *The Third Space of Sovereignty: The Postcolonial Politics of U.S.–Indigenous Relations* (Minneapolis: University of Minnesota Press, 2007). In particular, see Bruyneel's discussion of Tuscarora leader Clinton Rickard's opposition to the ICA as an attack on Indian sovereignty (112–21).

6. "A study by the U.S. General Accounting Office [found] that 4 of the 12 Indian Health Service regions sterilized 3,406 American Indian women without their permission between 1973–1976. [. . .] Two years earlier, an independent study by Dr. Connie Pinkerton-Uri, Choctaw/Cherokee, found that one in four American Indian women had been sterilized without her consent. Pinkerton-Uri's research indicated that the Indian Health Service had 'singled out full-blooded Indian women for sterilization procedures.'" "1976: Government Admits Unauthorized Sterilization of Indian Women," *Native Voices* timeline, https://www.nlm.nih.gov/nativevoices/timeline/543.html (accessed May 4, 2023).

7. A challenge to the Indian Child Welfare Act in *Haaland v. Brackeen* was heard by the Supreme Court, which upheld the Act by a 7–2 decision in June 2023.

8. See Eric Cheyfitz and Shari Huhndorf, "Genocide by Other Means: U.S. Federal Indian Law and Violence against Native Women in Louise Erdrich's *The Round House*," in *New Directions in Law And Literature*, ed. Elizabeth S. Anker and Bernadette Meyler (Oxford: Oxford University Press, 2017), 264–78.

9. See Indian Health Service, "Coronavirus (Covid-19)," https://www.ihs.gov/coronavirus/ (accessed May 4, 2023).

10. Wolfe, "Settler Colonialism," 388; italics mine.

11. Louise Erdrich, *The Round House* (New York: Harper Perennial, 2013). Further references to the primary text are cited parenthetically in text.

12. The Trade and Intercourse Act of June 30, 1834, § 25, reads, "That so

much of the laws of the United States as provides for the punishment of crimes committed within any place within the sole and exclusive jurisdiction of the United States, shall be in force in the Indian country. *Provided,* The same shall not extend to crimes committed by one Indian against the person or property of another Indian." Francis Paul Prucha, *Documents of United States Indian Policy,* 3rd ed. (Lincoln: University of Nebraska Press, 2000), doc. 48. The exemption for Indian-on-Indian crime was revoked for major felonies in the Major Crimes Act of 1885 (doc. 101).

13. See Cheyfitz and Huhndorf, "Genocide by Other Means."

14. On November 15, 2021, President Biden signed the Executive Order on Improving Public Safety and Criminal Justice for Native Americans and Addressing the Crisis of Missing or Murdered Indigenous People. It remains to be seen if the rhetoric will be translated into reality.

15. For an example of traditional tribal law adapted to contemporary tribal courts, see Raymond D. Austin, *Navajo Courts and Navajo Common Law: A Tradition of Tribal Self-Governance* (Minneapolis: University of Minnesota Press, 2009).

16. David E. Wilkins, *American Indian Sovereignty and the U.S. Supreme Court: The Masking of Justice* (Austin: University of Texas Press, 1997), 10.

17. Eric Cheyfitz, *The Disinformation Age: The Collapse of Liberal Democracy in the United States* (2017; reprint, Durham, N.C.: PaperBoat Press 2019). In the final chapter of the book, "Thinking from a Different Place: What Is a Just Society? A Brief Manifesto," I write, by way of conclusion, "Finally, then, let me offer what is perhaps a provocation: the dominant Western story of 'America'—the master narrative of equal opportunity and justice based in free enterprise—has reached its limit and exhausted itself, an exhaustion marked by the increasing distance of its narrative from reality. Ideology has become pathology, that is, Disinformation. This story has always confused capitalism with democracy, when in fact the two systems are fundamentally at odds. In this story, we, the people, say we care for each other, the model is one of Christian Charity; but the gesture is one of pseudo-kinship. For history tells us we do not care for each other (a relatively few of us eat while many of us starve). We, the people, live today in a one-party state, an oligarchy (we do not stand side by side), where what we call 'democracy' or 'individualism' has become an alibi for various forms of exploitation, which do not fit under the heading of democracy but under the heading of empire. So here at this juncture of history, we are in desperate need of another story, one that answers the question, what is a just society?, one of extended kinship, of the kind that has been told in Native American societies for thousands of years" (324).

18. Bruyneel, *Third Space,* 10.
19. Bruyneel, *Third Space,* 21.
20. Bruyneel, *Third Space,* 21.
21. Bruyneel, *Third Space,* 217–18.
22. Bruyneel, *Third Space,* 218.
23. Bruyneel, *Third Space,* 219.

24. *United States v. Lara* (124 S. Ct. 1628, 2004) at 1642.
25. *U.S. v. Lara* at 1648.
26. *U.S. v. Lara* at 1648.
27. Bruyneel, *Third Space*, 221–22.
28. Bruyneel, *Third Space*, 224.
29. Taiaiake Alfred, *Peace, Power, Righteousness: An Indigenous Manifesto* (Oxford: Oxford University Press, 1999), 56.
30. Alfred, *Peace, Power, Righteousness*, 56.
31. Bruyneel, *Third Space*, 223.
32. *Worcester*, 31 U.S. 515 (1832) at 519.
33. In opposition to the colonial politics of recognition, Coulthard posits "an alternative politics of recognition, one that is less oriented around attaining legal and political recognition by the state, and more about Indigenous peoples empowering themselves through cultural practices of individual and collective self-fashioning that seek to *prefigure* radical alternatives to the structural and subjective dimensions of colonial power. [. . .] I call this a *resurgent politics of recognition.*" Glen Sean Coulthard, *Red Skin, White Masks: Rejecting the Colonial Politics of Recognition* (Minneapolis: University of Minnesota Press, 2014), 18.
34. Taiaiake Alfred, "Sovereignty," in *Sovereignty Matters: Locations of Contestation and Possibility in Indigenous Struggles for Self-Determination*, ed. Joanne Barker (Lincoln: University of Nebraska Press, 2005), 38.
35. Alfred, "Sovereignty," 42.
36. Gerald Vizenor, *The Heirs of Columbus* (Lebanon, N.H.: University Press of New England, 1991), 7.
37. N. Scott Momaday, *House Made of Dawn* (1968; reprint, New York: Perennial Classics, 1999), 90.
38. Momaday, *House Made of Dawn*, 90.
39. James Welch, *Winter in the Blood* (New York: Penguin, 1974), 2.
40. Vizenor, *Manifest Manners*, vi.
41. See Helen B. West, "Starvation Winter of the Blackfeet," *Montana, the Magazine of Western History*, winter 1958, 2–19
42. Welch, *Winter in the Blood*, 154.
43. Welch, *Winter in the Blood*, 158.
44. Welch, *Winter in the Blood*, 159.
45. See Cheyfitz, *Disinformation Age*, 10–16.
46. Robert A. Williams Jr. in David H. Charles, F. Wilkinson, and Robert A. Williams Jr., *Cases and Materials on Federal Indian Law*, 4th ed. (St. Paul, Minn.: West Group, 1998), 71.
47. Layli Long Soldier, *Whereas* (Minneapolis, Minn.: Graywolf, 2017), Kindle.
48. Long Soldier, *Whereas*.
49. Long Soldier, *Whereas*.
50. Leslie Marmon Silko, *Ceremony* (New York: Penguin, 1977), 132. Subsequent references are noted in the body of the text.

5. TRICKSTER LOGIC

1. Eric Wolf, *Europe and the People without History* (Berkeley: University of California Press, 1982), 95, 97. For a study that addresses issues of rank and how it is balanced in one such kinship society, see Alfonso Ortiz, *The Tewa World: Space, Time, Being, and Becoming in a Pueblo Society* (Chicago: University of Chicago Press, 1969). Ortiz points to a conception of rank that is never fixed in particular individuals or groups but circulates throughout the social network over time. The most exclusive category, for example, "the Made people," strives to be inclusive: "The Made people and their assistants comprise a very sizeable percentage of the population. This was more true in the past. [. . .] Until about the turn of the century, nearly every Tewa adult belonged to a group of Made People" (82).

2. Gerald Vizenor, *The People Named the Chippewa* (Minneapolis: University of Minnesota Press, 1984), 3–4.

3. Basil Johnston, *The Manitous: The Supernatural World of The Ojibway* (New York: Harper Perennial, 1995), 90.

4. Paul Radin, comp., *The Trickster: A Study in American Indian Mythology* (London: Routledge and Kegan Paul, 1956), 124. References to the Winnebago trickster cycle in Radin are cited parenthetically in text as the textual divisions imposed on the narrative, not to page numbers. Radin explains that Blowsnake received the narratives in 1912 from "an old Winnebago Indian living near the village of Winnebago, Nebraska. It was written down in the Winnebago syllabary. [. . .] Who this individual was I do not know. There were a number of reasons, into which I cannot enter here, why it was inadvisable for me to ask, the most important being that the myth was a sacred one and that I was a stranger and a white man. [. . .] The identity of the narrator is, however, not really of great importance. What is important is whether it was obtained under the proper conditions and whether Sam Blowsnake wrote it down as it was told to him. By proper conditions I mean that adequate offerings of tobacco were presented to the narrator and gifts commensurate with the traditionally accepted value of the myth given to him. This I know was done" (Radin, *Trickster*, 111–12). Radin also assures the reader that "Sam Blowsnake recorded it as he heard it" (112) and that Baptiste and Lamere, "both of whom knew English very well, particularly the former," "made" "the initial translation" and that "it was then revised by [Radin him]self," who "could read the syllabary with some ease and knew Winnebago well" (112). What Radin does not tell the reader is whether or not the Winnebago elder, whose story it was, was informed by Blowsnake of its intended incorporation into Western print culture.

5. Arnold Krupat, *All That Remains: Varieties of Indigenous Expression* (Lincoln: University of Nebraska Press, 2009), 2–3, 4–5.

6. Krupat, *All That Remains*, 23.

7. Quoted in Michael A. Elliott, "Coyote Comes to the *Norton*: Indigenous Oral Narrative and American Literary History," *American Literature* 75 (2003): 744n7.

8. Krupat, *All That Remains*, 20, 23.
9. Gary Witherspoon, *Navajo Kinship and Marriage* (Chicago: University of Chicago Press, 1975), 28, 42.
10. I thank my brother, Kirk Cheyfitz, for passing this story on to me via a tape of a public performance of Johnny Moses, in Detroit, Michigan. In my transcription of the Crow story, I have only supplied the English-language version. Moses's approach is to give the Native-language version for a sentence or two, followed immediately by the English version. A performance of this story by Moses can be found at on YouTube at https://www.youtube.com/watch?v=gp_Uixq7OYg (accessed May 6, 2023).
11. Darlene Evans contributed this insight.
12. Greg Sarris, *Keeping Slug Woman Alive: A Holistic Approach to American Indian Texts* (Berkeley: University of California Press, 1993), 46.
13. Sarris, *Keeping Slug Woman Alive*, 39.
14. Sarris, *Keeping Slug Woman Alive*, 38.
15. Krupat, *All That Remains*, 13.
16. Krupat, *All That Remains*, 13; my emphasis.
17. Krupat, *All That Remains*, 14.
18. Gerald Vizenor, *Dead Voices* (Norman: University of Oklahoma Press, 1992), 5, 6, 18.
19. Krupat notes, "Just as there is no people without history, so, too, is there no people without writing—by which I mean material or tangible means of information storage, or in I. J. Gelb's phrase, 'A system of human intercommunication by means of conventional visible marks.'" Arnold Krupat, *Red Matters: Native American Studies* (Philadelphia: University of Pennsylvania Press, 2002), 66. I concur, which is why I have emphasized "alphabetic" in distinguishing oral from written cultures. In alphabetic cultures, writing subsumes speech; in oral cultures, the reverse is true. When I refer to writing, then, the reader should understand alphabetic writing. From time to time, to emphasize this understanding, I will use the phrase "alphabetic writing." For a generative study of Indigenous writing, see Birgit Brander Rasmussen, *Queequeg's Coffin: Indigenous Literacies and Early American Literature* (Durham, N.C.: Duke University Press, 2012).
20. Kenneth Lincoln, *Native American Renaissance* (1983; reprint, Berkeley: University of California Press, 1985), 52.
21. Lincoln, *Native American Renaissance*, 52.
22. Lincoln, *Native American Renaissance*, 59.
23. Lincoln, *Native American Renaissance*, 45.
24. Lewis Hanke, *Aristotle and the American Indians* (London: Hollis & Carter, 1959), 16.
25. Linda Legarde Grover, *The Dance Boots* (Athens: University of Georgia Press, 2010), Kindle.
26. Diane Glancy, *Fort Marion Prisoners and the Trauma of Native Education* (Lincoln: University of Nebraska Press, 2014), Kindle.
27. Glancy, *Fort Marion Prisoners*.

28. Glancy, *Fort Marion Prisoners*.
29. Glancy, *Fort Marion Prisoners*.
30. Katherine Smith's comment about being imprisoned by Western law is taken from a videotape that I made with my wife, Darlene Evans, in 1998. We have the permission of the author, now deceased, to use this tape and the letter cited below.
31. Diane Glancy, *Trigger Dance Boulder* (Boulder, Colo.: Fiction Collective Two, 1990), 22.
32. In 1830, Congress passed the Indian Removal Act, which gave the president the authority to negotiate treaties with Indian tribes that would legalize their removal from Native lands to lands west of the Mississippi. Needless to say, Indian communities signed these treaties under duress. The Removal Act is the foundation for the infamous Trail of Tears, on which the so-called Five Civilized Tribes were forced to march to Oklahoma territory throughout the 1830s. The Cherokees were the last to undergo this march. Elias Boudinot, who initially opposed removal, became an advocate because he thought resistance to U.S. force was futile and removal was the best chance the Cherokees had for survival as a nation. Though the overwhelming majority of the tribe, through its elected president, John Ross, opposed removal, Boudinot and a group of dissident Cherokee leaders agreed to sign a treaty with the United States, which they did at the Cherokee capital of New Echota in 1835. Shortly after their arrival in Oklahoma, several of the leaders of this group, including Boudinot, were assassinated for having violated a provision of the Cherokee constitution that forbade the sale of land to outsiders without the express permission of the tribe. Diane Glancy has written two innovative historical novels about the Trail of Tears and its aftermath, *Pushing the Bear: A Novel of the Trail of Tears* (1996) and *Pushing the Bear: After the Trail of Tears* (2009).
33. Plato, *The Phaedrus*, trans. R. Hackforth in *The Collected Dialogues of Plato*, ed. Edith Hamilton and Huntington Cairns (Princeton, N.J.: Princeton University Press, 1961), 274c-276 (pp. 520-21).
34. See Carol Hampton, "Native American Church," in *Encyclopedia of North American Indians*, ed. Frederick E. Hoxie (Boston: Houghton Mifflin, 1996), 418-20.
35. N. Scott Momaday, *House Made of Dawn* (1968; reprint, New York: Perennial Classics, 1999), 84-85.
36. Momaday, *House Made of Dawn*, 85.
37. Momaday, *House Made of Dawn*, 52-53.
38. Leslie Marmon Silko, *Yellow Woman and a Beauty of the Spirit: Essays on Native American Life Today* (New York: Simon & Schuster, 1996), 20.
39. Silko, *Yellow Woman*, 52.
40. Silko, *Yellow Woman*, 21.
41. Darlene Evans made me aware of this paradox.
42. Leslie Marmon Silko, *Ceremony* (New York: Penguin, 1977), 125-26.
43. Lincoln, *Native American Renaissance*, 237.
44. Silko, *Yellow Woman*, 14-15.

45. G. M. Mullett, *Legends of the Hopi Indians: Spider Woman Stories* (Tucson: University of Arizona Press, 1979), 7–43.

6. BEARHEART

1. Gerald Vizenor, *Bearheart: The Heirship Chronicles* (Minneapolis: University of Minnesota Press, 1978), 102, 97. Further references to the primary text are cited parenthetically in text.

2. Alan Velie, "The Trickster Novel," in *Narrative Chance: Postmodern Discourse on Native American Literatures*, ed. Gerald Vizenor (Norman: University of Oklahoma Press, 1993), 131. Vizenor's essay "Trickster Discourse" appears in the same volume (187–211).

3. "When an Indian allottee died, the interest in the allotment was divided among his or her heirs but the land itself was not divided. This situation resulted in numerous individuals owning an interest in the same parcel of land, and that interest continued to divide—potentially exponentially—across generations. This is known as *fractionation*. The situation also fractionated the ability to use or derive income from the land among many owners, and owners often sought to sell their interests." "Tribal Land and Ownership Statuses: Overview and Selected Issues for Congress, Updated July 21, 2021."

4. For an account of AIM including this takeover, see Paul Chaat Smith and Robert Allen Warrior, *Like a Hurricane: The Indian Movement from Alcatraz to Wounded Knee* (New York: New Press, 1996).

5. See Vizenor, *Bearheart*, 30, for the passage in context. Throughout *Bearheart*, the author uses ellipses, perhaps to suggest parts of the narrative that are omitted for reasons that are not forthcoming. On the one hand, the ellipses suggest conscious omission; on the other, they suggest that which cannot be articulated.

6. See David L. Shaw, "Online Petition Seeks Removal of Halftown as Cayuga Nation Representative," *Finger Lakes Times*, October 5, 2021.

7. Gerald Vizenor, *The Heirs of Columbus* (Lebanon, N.H.: University Press of New England, 1991), 7.

8. Kevin Bruyneel, *The Third Space of Sovereignty: The Postcolonial Politics of U.S.–Indigenous Relations* (Minneapolis: University of Minnesota Press, 2007), 98.

9. Basil Johnston, *The Manitous: The Supernatural World of The Ojibway* (New York: Harper Perennial, 1995), xviii.

10. In light of this passage, Darlene Evans suggests that we might think of Andrew Jackson as no more than an organ of federal Indian law.

11. Paul Pasquaretta, "Sacred Chance: Gambling and the Contemporary Native American Indian Novel," *MELUS* 21, no. 2 (1996): 21, 22–23.

12. Pasquaretta, "Sacred Chance," 22.

13. Pasquaretta, "Sacred Chance," 23.

14. Patricia Monture-Angus, *Journeying Forward: Dreaming First Nations Independence* (Halifax, Canada: Fernwood, 1999), 9.

15. See Eric Cheyfitz, "Thinking from a Different Place: What Is a Just Soci-

ety? A Brief Manifesto," in *The Disinformation Age: The Collapse of Liberal Democracy in the United States* (2017; reprint, Durham, N.C.: PaperBoatPress, 2019).

16. Pasquaretta, "Sacred Chance," 28.

17. Claude Lévi-Strauss, *Tristes Tropiques* (1955), trans. John and Doreen Weightman in 1973 (New York: Penguin, 2012), Kindle.

18. Alfred, "Sovereignty," 44.

19. Gerald Vizenor, "Aesthetics of Survivance: Literary Theory and Practice," in *Survivance: Narratives of Native Presence*, ed. Gerald Vizenor (Lincoln: University of Nebraska Press, 2008), Kindle.

20. Robert Cover makes a similar point, noting that word and act are one in legal interpretation, producing violence, whereas in literary production, "it will not do to insist on the violence of strong poetry, and strong poets. Even the violence of weak judges is utterly real." Robert Cover, "Violence and the Word" (1986), in *Narrative, Violence, and the Law: The Essays of Robert Cover*, ed. Martha Minow, Michael Ryan, and Austin Sarat (Ann Arbor: University of Michigan Press, 1995), 213.

21. See Keith H. Basso, *Wisdom Sits in Places: Landscape and Language among the Western Apache* (Albuquerque: University of New Mexico Press, 1996).

22. The quote from *Survivance* and the paragraph of commentary that follows was originally published in Eric Cheyfitz and Shari Huhndorf, "Genocide by Other Means: U.S. Federal Indian Law and Violence against Native Women in Louise Erdrich's *The Round House*," in *New Directions on Law and Literature*, ed. Elizabeth S. Anker and Bernadette Meyler (Oxford: Oxford University Press, 2017), 264–66.

INDEX

Alaska Native Claims Settlement Act, 2, 7
Alfred, Taiaiake: *Peace, Power, Righteousness*, 60–62, 149–51; *Sovereignty*, 58–60, 196
allotment, 9–10, 13–14, 65, 75, 97, 125–26; and citizenship, 22; termination of, 19, 21. *See also* Dawes Act
Almanac of the Dead (Silko), 35, 38–41, 44, 156
American Indian Autobiography (Brumble), 100
American Indian Holocaust and Survival (Thornton), 28–29
American Indian Literature. *See* Native American literature
American Indian Movement, 30, 178, 182
American Indian Sovereignty and the U.S. Supreme Court (Wilkins), 17, 56, 72, 144
Apess, William, 121–22, 170, 173; *Eulogy on King Phillip*, 122, 170; *Indian Nullification of the Unconstitutional Laws of Massachusetts*, 122, 170; *A Son of the Forest*, 122
As Long as Grass Grows (Gilio-Whitaker), 33–34
autobiography, 50, 105, 112–13, 117; as-told-to, 97–98, 110, 117; self-written, 110, 117. *See also Black Elk Speaks*; *Black Hawk*; *Mourning Dove*; Native American–European literary collaboration; *Son of the Forest, A*

Basso, Keith: *Portraits of the Whiteman*, 120–21
Bearheart (Vizenor), 93–94, 152, 175–98. *See also* cedar nation; trickster
Black Elk Speaks (Neihardt), 86, 98–105, 107–20; and Lakota religious ceremonies, 106–8. *See also* Brumble, David, III; Deloria, Vine, Jr.
Black Hawk (Black Hawk), 113–20
Black Hawk: *Black Hawk*, 113–20. *See also Johnson v. M'Intosh*
blood quantum, 65–66, 83–85, 94, 125–26, 212, 219; and biologic of Indian identity, 66, 76, 78, 80–81, 117, 134–35; and Cherokee nation, 70–73; and enrollment, 91–93, 95, 97; and mixed-blood, 66, 71–72, 89–94, 123–24, 129–33. *See also* Certificate of Degree of Indian or Alaska Native Blood; *U.S. v. Rogers*
Bolivia: constitution, 31–32; Indigenous communities, 2, 30; Evo Morales, 30–31
borders, 137, 144–45, 150–53, 157–59, 178, 188, 191; and resistance to, 152–53, 181–82. *See also Bearheart*
Brumble, David, III: *American Indian Autobiography*, 100; and *Black Elk Speaks*, 100
Bruyneel, Kevin: *The Third Space of Sovereignty*, 139, 145–47, 149, 184
Buen Vivir (Fatheuer), 62, 135
Buffalo Bill, 102, 105, 110
Bureau of Indian Affairs, 8, 12, 21, 24–26, 86, 126–27, 177–78; and definition of Indian, 76–80, 82–84, 93–94, 133–34. *See also* Certificate of Degree of Indian or Alaska Native Blood; federal Indian law; Native identity
Burke Act, 66, 75, 127, 219n119

Canada, 33–34, 161, 168; and United States, 2, 7, 47, 59, 62, 138, 184
capitalism, 186, 193–94; against global, 135; and democracy, 221n17; and Native subsistence, 17–18; and neoliberalism, 62; and property, 45, 120, 190–91; resistance to, 34–35, 38, 174. See also *Buen Vivir*
Cases and Materials on Federal Indian Law (Getches, Wilkinson, Williams), 19, 44, 75, 78, 206–7nn128–29
Catholicism, 101, 103, 105–9. See also Christianity
cedar nation, 94, 181–85, 193, 195. See also *Bearheart*
Centellas, Miguel, 31–32
Ceremony (Silko), 13, 68, 89, 91–93, 152, 172–73, 189
Certificate of Degree of Indian or Alaska Native Blood, 76–79, 81
Cherokee Nation, 43, 47, 66, 70–73, 75, 144, 165, 210n7; and Cherokee Constitution, 67–69, 210n7; and John Ross, 70, 72, 225n32; and slavery, 66–70. See also *Cherokee Nation v. Georgia*; Trail of Tears
Cherokee Nation v. Georgia, 5, 43, 58, 89, 116, 142, 147
Christianity, 92, 105, 171. See also Catholicism
citizenship. See Indian Citizenship Act; U.S. citizenship
Churchill, Ward, 118
Claims Resolution Act, 11
Cobell case, 9–13, 80
Cogewea, the Half Blood (Mourning Dove), 1, 86, 97, 100, 122–35, 215n3, 219n118. See also McWhorter, Lucullus Virgil
Cohen, Felix: *Felix Cohen's Handbook of Federal Indian Law*, 80, 144, 151
colonialism, 1, 3, 35, 79, 86, 171; and anticolonial resistance, 31, 42–44, 63, 121–22, 148, 180, 183–84, 193;
European, 71, 88, 167; and federal Indian law, 7–8, 42, 147, 150, 152, 166, 190, 198; in Hawaii, 200n2; and Indian self-determination, 78; postcolonial system, 59, 84, 88, 139, 145, 147, 151. See also settler colonialism
Columbus, Christopher, 26–28, 73–74, 95, 128–29, 167, 203
Cook-Lynn, Elizabeth, 2, 44
Coulthard, Glenn, 2, 33, 151; *Red Skin, White Masks*, 62–63, 151, 222n33
Coyote Stories (Mourning Dove), 123

Dakota Access Pipeline: protests against, 22, 33–35, 181
Dance Boots, The (Legarde), 168
Dauenhauer, Nora Marks, 2, 17
Dawes Act, 13, 65, 75, 78, 80, 83, 105; and allotment, 126; and Burke Act, 75; and Cobell case, 9; and forced assimilation, 95, 138; and Indian Reorganization Act, 9
Deloria, Vine, Jr., 52–53, 59, 116; and *Black Elk Speaks*, 98, 100, 111–12
DeMallie, Raymond J.: and *Black Elk Speaks*, 98–104, 106; and religion, 107–9, 111
Department of the Interior, 8, 26, 36, 98, 219
disenrollment, 51–52, 79, 95, 97
Dismembered (Wilkins and Wilkins), 51–52
dispossession, 20–21, 114, 119, 142, 168, 170, 176
Documents of United States Indian Policy (Prucha), 8–9, 65–66, 75, 114, 200n6, 219n119, 221–22n12
Dwellings (Hogan), 15, 46

Erdrich, Louise, 139, 144, 151; *Love Medicine*, 189; *The Night Watchman*, 18, 21, 84; *The Round House*, 139, 141, 146, 152
Estes, Nick: *Our History Is the Future*, 22, 34

INDEX

Eulogy on King Phillip (Apess), 122, 170
Europeans, 4, 26, 39, 67, 75, 119, 142, 186
Ex parte Crow Dog, 41, 44, 55–56, 181, 206n128

Fatheuer, Thomas: *Buen Vivir*, 62, 135
federal government, 8, 75, 84, 87, 113, 176, 183; and boarding schools, 176; and forced assimilation, 95; and Indian identity, 79, 84, 85, 87, 113, 134; and legal jurisdiction in Indian Country, 138, 141, 148, 180–81, 206n128; and monetary settlements, 17; and relationship with Native Americans, 2, 8, 57, 116; and treaties, 182. See also Dakota Access Pipeline; federal Indian law; Indian land
federal Indian law: and biologic, 72, 80, 93–94, 133–34; and borders, 152, 154–55, 175; and Indian land, 7, 14, 21, 37, 39–40, 44, 46; and justice, 50, 55, 119; and Native identity, 18, 66, 87–88, 95, 98–99, 117, 132, 135; and Native literature, 1–3, 6, 35, 44, 66, 89, 116, 121, 124, 198; and property law, 190; and sovereignty, 62, 145–51, 183–84; and Supreme Court cases, 43, 58, 115, 116, 142, 144, 154; and treaties, 3, 5, 57–58, 111; and U.S. colonialism, 11, 23, 26, 37, 42, 166. See also *Felix Cohen's Handbook of Federal Indian Law*; *Indian Nullification of the Unconstitutional Laws of Massachusetts*; settler colonialism
Felix Cohen's Handbook of Federal Indian Law (Cohen), 80, 144, 151
Fight Back (Ortiz), 35–38, 46, 156
Fort Marion Prisoners and the Trauma of Native Education (Glancy), 168–69, 177

General Allotment Act, 9, 125. See also Dawes Act
genocide, 4, 28, 141, 151, 154–55, 181, 216; of the Blackfeet, 153; cultural, 138; and forced assimilation, 95; Indigenous, 30, 182, 204n69, 205n87; and settler colonialism, 137–39; U.S. Indian policy, 11; and Wounded Knee massacre, 29, 106. See also *American Indian Holocaust and Survival*; Indian Removal Act; Trail of Tears
Getches, David: *Cases and Materials on Federal Indian Law*, 4th ed., 19, 44, 75, 78, 206–7nn128–29
Gila River Apache Tribe v. Arizona, 41, 44
Gilio-Whitaker, Dina: *As Long as Grass Grows*, 33–34
Glancy, Diana, 170; *Fort Marion Prisoners and the Trauma of Native Education*, 168–69, 177; *Pushing the Bear*, 8
Gover, Kevin, 8, 10, 25–26
Great Father, The (Prucha), 14, 22, 55–56, 65–66

Heirs of Columbus (Vizenor), 28, 59, 181–82
Hogan, Linda, 1, 16; *Dwellings*, 15, 46; *Power*, 52, 54; *Solar Storms*, 1, 15
House Made of Dawn (Momaday), 1, 19, 152–53, 170
human rights, 30, 32–33, 122

Indian Arts and Crafts Act, 98–99
Indian Background of American Theatricals, The (Rourke), 3, 5
Indian boarding schools, 95, 102, 137–38, 166, 168–69, 176–77
Indian Child Welfare Act, 138, 216n34
Indian Citizenship Act, 22–24, 95, 138–39, 184
Indian Civil Rights Act, 22–23, 51
Indian Country, 2, 8, 13–14; and

Cherokee, 66, 73; and colonialism, 26, 71, 78, 118; and federal Indian law, 7; and poverty, 24–25, 83, 139; and tribal government, 22; and U.S. legal jurisdiction, 55–56, 138, 140–41. *See also* reservation
Indian land: Cherokee, 66, 69; dispossession of, 36, 168; and federal Indian law, 7, 42, 116, 190; financial compensation for, 42; government trusteeship of, 7–10, 75, 142; Indian claims to, 26, 44; and kinship, 16–17, 39, 65, 119–20, 170–72; and Native American literature, 21, 59; Native relationship with, 12, 14–20, 23, 36, 45–48, 50, 69, 177, 167, 184; and Navajo–Hopi dispute, 26, 169, 181; as property, 13–17, 19, 21, 45–46, 56–57, 60, 68–69, 112, 119, 167, 190–91; rights, 30, 33; settler claims to, 37, 137–39; and sovereignty, 22, 33; and speculation, 120; theft of by U.S. government, 12, 14, 40–43, 82, 118, 127–28, 138, 142, 154, 156–57, 169; and treaties, 4, 118. *See also* allotment; Dawes Act; reservation; termination
Indian nations, 3, 7–9, 44, 58, 148, 150. *See also* Cherokee Nation; Navajo Nation
Indian Nullification of the Unconstitutional Laws of Massachusetts (Apess), 122, 170
Indian Removal Act (IRA), 114, 187, 225n32. *See also* Trail of Tears
Indian Reorganization Act, 9, 51, 93, 168
Indian Self-Determination and Education Assistance Act, 13
Indian Treaty as Literature, The (Wroth), 3–5
Indian tribes: Anishinaabe, 34, 140, 152, 161, 168, 179, 189–90, 197; Apache, 38, 41, 120–21; Arapaho, 36; Cheyenne, 36, 161; Chickasaw, 138, 188; Choctaw, 88, 138; Colville, 125–26; Flathead, 129, 219n118; Fox, 115, 118, 140· Hopi, 22, 36, 53, 169, 173; Iroquois, 3–5, 47, 57, 117; Laguna Pueblo, 36, 38, 44, 91; Menominee, 18; Muscogee, 138, 188; Navajo, 26, 37, 47–49, 75, 162, 169; Oglala Lakota, 12, 29, 34, 87, 103–11, 161, 203n58; Oklahoma Cherokee, 21, 79; Osage, 128, 219n120; Pequot, 122; Plains, 86, 105, 111, 153, 168–69, 177; Salishan, 125; Sauk, 115, 118; Seminole, 138, 188; Sioux, 17, 34, 42, 47, 56, 103, 107, 161; Spokane, 36. *See also* Cherokee Nation; Indian nations; Navajo Nation

Johnson v. M'Intosh, 42, 115–16, 142, 154, 190
Johnston, Basil: *The Manitous,* 160, 186
justice, 43, 141, 171; agonistic, 55–56; and injustice of U.S. legal system, 44, 141; Native system of, 50–55, 60; restorative, 11, 55, 194; social, 30, 119, 149, 176; and treaties, 5; U.S. system of, 140–41, 151, 194–95, 197

Keeping Slug Woman Alive (Sarris), 164–65
kinship: and animals, 177, 186; and capitalism, 175, 192–93; communities, 49, 52–53, 57, 75, 159; economies, 45; and families, 47–48; groups, 107, 109, 134, 163, 167; and identity, 66, 93; Indigenous, 31, 38, 60, 62, 134; and land, 16–17, 39, 65, 120, 172; and literary communities, 86–87, 110–11; and Native relations, 17, 34, 46, 49–50, 178; and Native storytelling, 171–73; Navajo system of, 47–48, 75; responsibilities, 32, 150–51, 161–62; and Western property, 109, 112.

See also system of justice: Native system of
Krupat, Arnold, 172, 215n3; *All That Remains*, 54, 160–61, 165; *Red Matters*, 17, 224n19
Kunuk, Zacharias, 2, 54

Larson, Charles, 85–88
Legarde, Linda: *The Dance Boots*, 168
Lévi-Strauss, Claude: *Tristes Tropiques*, 195–96
Lincoln, Kenneth, 50; *Native American Renaissance*, 166–67, 173
literature, 44, 96; American, 84; and federal Indian law, 2, 3, 40, 42, 44, 66, 111, 116, 124; Indigenous, 28; of resistance, 1, 34–35, 45, 57, 121, 152, 170, 184; Western, 111, 197–98. *See also* Native American–European literary collaboration; Native American literature; oral narratives; storytelling. *See also* autobiography: as-told-to; autobiography: self-written
Lone Wolf v. Hitchcock, 41, 44, 142, 144
Long Soldier, Layli: *Whereas*, 154–55
Love Medicine (Erdrich), 189
Lyng v. Norwest Indian Cemetery Protective Association, 15

Major Crimes Act, 56, 141, 150, 153, 206n128, 221n12
Manifest Manners (Vizenor), 95–96, 153
Manitous, The (Johnston), 160, 186
Mankiller, Wilma, 67, 71–72
Marshall Trilogy, 42–44, 58, 142. *See also Cherokee Nation v. Georgia*; *Johnson v. M'Intosh*; *Worcester v. Georgia*
McWhorter, Lucullus Virgil, 86, 97, 122–26
missionaries, 105, 107, 109, 180
Momaday, N. Scott, 19, 85; *House Made of Dawn*, 1, 19, 152–53, 170

Morton v. Mancari, 78, 133–34, 212n44
Moses, Johnny, 163, 224n10
Mourning Dove (Quintasket, Christine): *Cogewea, the Half Blood*, 1, 86, 97, 100, 122–35, 215n3, 219n118; *Coyote Stories*, 123; *Mourning Dove: A Salishan Autobiography*, 125
Mourning Dove (Mourning Dove), 125

Narrative of the Life of Mrs. Mary Jemison, A (Seaver), 50, 98, 113, 117
National Community Reinvestment Coalition, 25, 82
National Congress of American Indians, 19
Native American–European literary collaboration, 3, 86, 97, 110, 112, 122, 160. *See also* autobiography: as-told-to; *Black Elk Speaks*; *Cogewea, the Half Blood*; *Narrative of the Life of Mrs. Mary Jemison, A*
Native American literature, 1–6, 8, 14, 21, 35, 111–12, 130, 173; and federal Indian law, 44, 66; and colonialism, 57. *See also* autobiography: as-told-to; autobiography: self-written; Native American–European literary collaboration; Native American writers; oral narratives
Native American Renaissance (Lincoln), 166–67, 173
Native American resistance: anticapitalist, 38; armed, 119; to assimilation, 138, 177; to institution of property, 45, 57, 68–69, 110, 167; to genocide, 4, 30, 105–6, 154; and community, 112, 146; to environmental destruction, 17, 34; to imperialism, 14, 17, 37, 42, 57, 63, 112, 118, 121, 167; and literature, 1, 35, 152, 167, 170–71; to loss of identity, 112, 115–16; pan-Indian, 19, 38; to pipelines, 22, 33,

35, 181; to settler colonialism, 56, 180, 183–84; Sauk, 118; Sioux, 56; against Spanish, 27–29, 35; strategies of, 166; Tlingit, 17–18; to tribal leadership, 21–22, 181, 202n58; trickster, 183, 193–94; to Western law, 152, 195. *See also* Dakota Access Pipeline; Pueblo Revolt; *Third Space of Sovereignty, The*

Native Americans, 7, 18, 57, 119, 154, 169; Alaska Natives, 7, 46, 47, 76, 81; and Congressional apology, 154; and land, 15–16, 46, 119; Native Hawaiians, 7, 46, 47; and nature, 49; and non-Natives, 9, 84, 129, 167, 169, 216; and population, 82; and poverty, 25, 82, 213n55; and resistance to imperialism, 84, 167; and violence against, 140. *See also* Native American literature

Native American writers, 85–88, 97, 99

Native identity: and American Indians, 81, 87–88, 95, 97, 99, 123, 127, 192; and biologic, 65–66, 69, 76, 80, 83, 94, 130, 133–35; and Black Elk, 98, 101, 107–9, 111–12; Cherokee, 68–74, 118; and colonial politics, 124; and culture, 108, 132, 189; and federal government, 85, 134; Indigenous, 134–35; and identity politics, 63, 76, 95, 97, 104, 109, 111, 117, 124; Laguna, 93; and land, 18–20, 23, 65, 128, 12; and legal identity, 51, 80, 98–99, 107, 135; and literature, 88, 93–94, 97, 99–101, 110, 123, 127; and political identity, 184; Sioux identity, 17; tribal identity, 52, 65, 81; and Western notions of, 49, 72, 132. *See also* blood quantum

Navajo Kinship and Marriage (Witherspoon), 47, 49

Navajo Nation, 21, 36, 38, 207n140

Neihardt, John G.: *Black Elk Speaks,* 86, 98–105, 115; and kinship with Black Hawk, 107–11, 135

Night Watchman, The (Erdrich), 18, 21, 84

Oklahoma v. Castro-Huerta, 144

Oliphant v. Suquamish, 142–43

oral narratives, 4–6, 50, 123–24, 159, 164–67, 170–75, 184; and American studies, 84; and Pueblo Revolt, 38; and translation into writing, 104–5, 110–12, 120–22, 124, 167, 172; trickster, 159, 164–65, 174–75, 195–96. *See also* autobiography: as-told-to; Native American literature; storytelling

Orange, Tommy: *There There,* 1, 5, 20–21, 112

Organized Village of Kake v. Egan, 41, 44

Ortiz, Simon: *Fight Back,* 35–38, 46, 156

Other Destinies (Owens), 88–90, 92–93, 97, 122

Our History is the Future (Estes), 22, 34

Owens, Louis: *Other Destinies,* 88–90, 92–93, 97, 122

Peace, Power, Righteousness (Alfred), 60–62, 149–51

Penn, William, 122–24, 126

Portraits of the Whiteman (Basso), 120–21

poverty, 9, 24–25, 83, 138, 191, 213n55, 216n34; and Sioux communities, 17; and termination, 18

Power (Hogan), 52, 54

Powers, William, 103–6, 109, 112

Prucha, Francis Paul: *Documents of United States Indian Policy,* 3rd ed., 8–9, 65–66, 75, 114, 200n6, 219n119, 221–22n12; *The Great Father,* 14, 22, 55–56, 65–66

Pueblo Lands Act, 37

Pueblo Revolt, 35, 38, 57

Purdue, Theda, 66–70
Pushing the Bear (Glancy), 8
Pyramid Lake Paiute Tribe v. Morton, 41, 44

Radin, Paul: *Trickster*, 160, 162, 173, 223n4
Red Skin, White Masks (Coulthard), 62–63, 151, 222n33
reservation, 12, 88, 134, 176, 178–79, 193, 195; and allotment, 9–10; and census, 82–83; Colville, 125–27; and federal Indian law, 21; and federal jurisdiction, 153, 181, 193; Flathead, 125, 219n118; government, 71, 93–94, 180–83, 193; Great Sioux, 55, 105; and Indian Citizenship Act, 22–23; and Indian Civil Rights Act, 22; Laguna, 157; Navajo, 36, 21, 206n128; Pine Ridge, 12, 22, 30, 101, 105, 108, 203n58; and poverty, 2, 24–25; and religion, 106, 108; Standing Rock Sioux, 22, 33; and termination, 19–20; Turtle Mountain Chippewa, 18
Round House, The (Erdrich), 139, 141, 146, 152
Rourke, Constance: *Indian Background of American Theatricals*, 3, 5

Sacred White Turkey, The (Washburn), 12, 21–22, 127
Santa Clara Pueblo v. Marinez, 23
Sarris, Greg: *Keeping Slug Woman Alive*, 164–65
Seaver, James E.: *A Narrative of the Life of Mrs. Mary Jemison*, 50, 98, 113, 117
self-determination, 13, 24–26, 78, 184
settler colonialism: and elimination of the Native, 135, 137–39, 177, 192; and federal Indian law, 140, 144–47, 150, 152, 176, 188; land claims, 37; and Native sovereignty, 147–49; resistance to, 56, 183–84;

and tribal governments, 62, 180; and violence, 153
Settler Colonialism and the Elimination of the Native (Wolfe), 137–39, 147
Silko, Leslie Marmon, 132, 171–72; *Almanac of the Dead*, 35, 38–41, 44, 156; *Ceremony*, 13, 68, 89, 91–93, 152, 172–73, 189; *Yellow Woman and a Beauty of the Spirit*, 44, 92
Solar Storms (Hogan), 1, 15
Son of the Forest, A (Apess), 122
sovereignty, 35, 43, 58–61, 96, 148, 150–51, 181; and domestic dependent nations, 5; federal, 153, 181; and federal Indian law, 62, 147, 195; Indigenous, 2, 31, 46, 58, 147–49, 184, 213; and land, 14, 22, 33; of the nation-state, 32; tribal, 5, 19, 23, 35, 43–44, 57–61, 83–84, 116, 143–48; Western, 149–52, 184. *See also* Alfred, Taiaiake; cedar nation; human rights; *Third Space of Sovereignty, The*
Sovereignty (Alfred), 58–60, 196
storytelling, 39, 110, 122–23, 165–66, 170–72, 196
survivance, 153, 168, 177, 197. *See also* Survivance
Survivance (Vizenor), 196

Tee-Hit-Ton Indians v. United States, 142, 144
termination, 13–14, 18–21, 84–85, 138, 152
There There (Orange), 1, 5, 20–21, 112
Third Space of Sovereignty, The (Bruyneel), 139, 145–49, 184
Thornton, Russell: *American Indian Holocaust and Survival*, 28–29
Trade and Intercourse Acts, 55, 72–73, 141, 220
Trail of Tears, 8, 138, 187, 225
Trask, Haunani-Kay, 2, 14, 46, 48, 119, 200n2
tribes, 8, 24, 47, 74, 102; as dependent

nations, 5, 21, 31; and disenrollment, 50–52; and enrollment, 75–77, 79–83, 95, 134; federally recognized, 199n1; and land claims, 44; and religion, 105; and self-determination, 13, 24; and sovereignty, 23, 43, 55, 147–48; and termination, 18–19, 95, 138; and treaties, 57. *See also* genocide; identity; Indian Citizenship Act; Indian tribes; tribal council
tribal council, 21–22, 36, 87, 93; *See also* reservation: government
tribal law, 44, 55, 140–41
trickster: figure, 28, 89, 120, 152, 159–63, 165, 173; logic, 159, 165; narrative, 89, 121, 160–65, 172–74. See also *Bearheart*
Trickster, The (Radin), 160, 162, 173, 223n4
Tristes Tropiques (Lévi-Strauss), 195–96

United States v. Lara, 147
United States v. Shock, 75
U.S. citizenship: and Cherokee Freedman, 210n7; of Indians, 23–24, 75, 137, 184. *See also* Burke Act; Dawes Act; Indian Citizenship Act
U.S. v. Broncheau, 80
U.S. v. Kagama, 56
U.S. v. Rogers, 72, 76, 80, 87, 97, 133
U.S. v. Sandoval, 37
U.S. v. Wheeler, 147

Vizenor, Gerald: *Bearheart*, 93–94, 152, 159, 175; *Dead Voices*, 166; *Heirs of Columbus*, 28, 59, 181–82; *Manifest Manners*, 95–96, 153; *Survivance*, 196. *See also* trickster

war, 19, 52, 56, 57, 115, 191; anticolonial, 42, 44, 193; anti-Indigenous, 30; and atomic explosion, 39; captives, 67; cedar, 180–82, 194; colonial, 29, 117; French and Indian, 3, 117, 134; intertribal, 105; as holocaust, 28–29; Mexican, 36; post–World War II, 13, 20, 30, 84, 152; and treaties, 3, 57; World War II, 90–91, 155, 157, 172
Washburn, Frances: *The Sacred White Turkey*, 12, 21–22, 127
Welch, James: *Winter in the Blood*, 152
Western law, 11, 15, 37, 150, 152, 169, 194, 197
Whereas (Long Soldier), 154–55
Wilkins, David E., 201n24; *American Indian Sovereignty and the U.S. Supreme Court*, 17, 56, 72, 144; *Dismembered*, 51–52
Wilkins, Shelly Hulse: *Dismembered*, 51–52
Wilkinson, Charles F.: *Cases and Materials on Federal Indian Law*, 4th ed., 19, 44, 75, 78, 206–7nn128–29
Williams, Robert A.: *Cases and Materials on Federal Indian Law*, 4th ed., 19, 44, 75, 78, 206–7nn128–29
Williams v. Lee, 41, 44
Wilson, Michael, 123–24
Winter in the Blood (Welch), 152
Winters v. United States, 41, 44
Winton v. Amos, 23
Witherspoon, Gary: *Navajo Kinship and Marriage*, 47, 49
Wolfe, Patrick: *Settler Colonialism and the Elimination of the Native*, 137–39, 147
Worcester v. Georgia, 41, 43, 58, 89, 142, 144, 150
Wounded Knee: massacre, 29, 40, 95, 106; Second, 30, 181–82, 203n58
Wroth, Lawrence C.: *The Indian Treaty as Literature*, 3–5

Yellow Woman and a Beauty of the Spirit (Silko), 44, 92

(*continued from page ii*)

Indigenous Americas
Robert Warrior, Series Editor

Leanne Betasamosake Simpson, *Noopiming: The Cure for White Ladies*
Paul Chaat Smith, *Everything You Know about Indians Is Wrong*
Lisa Tatonetti, *The Queerness of Native American Literatures*
Lisa Tatonetti, *Written by the Body: Gender Expansiveness and Indigenous Non-Cis Masculinities*
Gerald Vizenor, *Bear Island: The War at Sugar Point*
Robert Warrior, *The People and the Word: Reading Native Nonfiction*
Robert A. Williams Jr., *Like a Loaded Weapon: The Rehnquist Court, Indian Rights, and the Legal History of Racism in America*

Eric Cheyfitz is Ernest I. White Professor of American Studies and Humane Letters at Cornell University, where he is on the faculty of the American Indian and Indigenous Studies Program. He is author of *The Poetics of Imperialism: Translation and Colonization from "The Tempest" to "Tarzan"* and *The Disinformation Age: The Collapse of Liberal Democracy in the United States,* and coeditor of "Sovereignty, Indigeneity, and the Law," a special issue of *South Atlantic Quarterly.*